Accelerating Software Quality:
Machine Learning and Artificial Intelligence in the Age of DevOps

INTRODUCTION

As I set out to create this book following my previous two, the market is now in a much more advanced state — both from a DevOps value realization perspective as well as the technological evolution.[1,2]

The book, "Accelerating Software Quality: Machine Learning and Artificial Intelligence in the Age of DevOps" is a complete asset for software developers, testers, and managers that are on their journey to a more mature DevOps workflow with better automation and data-driven decision making.

DevOps is a mature process across the entire market. However, with existing Non-AI/ML technologies and models, it comes short in expediting release cycle, identifying productivity gaps and addressing them.

This book, which was created by myself with the help of DevOps and test automation leaders, covers the basics of AI and ML in software development and testing, the implications of AI and ML on existing apps, processes, and tools, practical tips in applying commercial and open source AI/ML tools within existing tool chains, chatbot testing, visual-based testing using AI, automated security scanning for vulnerabilities, automated code reviews, API testing and management using AI/ML, reducing effort and time

D1132541

1 Continuous Testing for DevOps Professionals
   https://www.amazon.com/Continuous-Testing-DevOps-Professionals-Practical-ebook/dp/B07H8PH7VB/ref=sr_1_2
2 The Digital Quality Handbook
   https://www.amazon.com/Digital-Quality-Handbook-Achieving-Continuous/dp/0692885994/ref=sr_1_1

through test impact analysis (TIA), robotic process automation (RPA), AIOps[3] for smarter code deployments and production defects prevention, and many more topics.

When properly leveraging such tools, DevOps teams can benefit from greater code quality and functional and non functional test automation coverage. This increases release cycle velocity, reduces noise and software waste, and enhances app quality.

The book is divided into three main sections:

- **Section 1** covers the fundamentals of AI and ML in software development and testing. It includes introductions, definitions, the basics for testing AI-based applications, classifications of AI/ML, defects that are tied to AI/ML, and more.

- **Section 2** focuses on practical advice and recommendations for using AI/ML-based solutions within software development activities. This section includes topics like visual AI test automation, AI in test management, testing conversational AI applications, RPA benefits, API testing, and much more.

- **Section 3** covers the more advanced and future-focused angles of AI and ML with projections and unique use cases. Among the topics in this section are AI and ML in logs observability, the benefits of AIOps for the entire DevOps teams, how to maintain AI/ML test automation, test impact analysis with AI, and more.

The book is packed with proven best practices, real life examples, and many other open source and commercial solution recommendations that are set to shape the future of DevOps together with ML/AI.[4]

---

3 *AIOps Definition https://searchitoperations.techtarget.com/definition/AIOps*
4 *Forrester Research on Autonomous Testing Maturity Model*
   https://go.forrester.com/blogs/autonomous-testing-is-like-autonomous-driving-the-ai-needs-human-assistance/

The Book Was Created in Collaboration With the Following Industry Experts:

Tzvika Shahaf, Yoram Mizrachi, Jennifer Bonine, Tariq King, Jason Arbon, Justin Reock, Chuck Gehman, Shani Shoham, Nico Krüger, Ahmed Datoo, Florian Treml, Christoph Börner, Thomas Haver, Claude Bolduc, Konstantin Popov, Andrew Bedford, Jonathon Wright, Roy Nuriel, Charlie Klein, Raj Subrameyer, and Eran Sher

---

The Book Was Created in Partnership With:

Edited by
KRISTINA ERICKSEN[5]

Designed by
CHRISTOPHER KIRSH[6]

Special thanks to **Erin Hofstrom**[7] and **Colleen Kulhanek**[8]
for helping manage and drive this project.

5   Kristina Ericksen https://www.linkedin.com/in/klericksen/
6   Christopher Kirsh https://www.linkedin.com/in/christopher-kirsh-8695198/
7   Erin Hofstrom https://www.linkedin.com/in/erin-hofstrom-mba-46932613/
8   Colleen Kulhanek https://www.linkedin.com/in/colleenkulhanek/

In Memory Of
CHARLES (CHUCK) GEHMAN

Our hearts are broken at the loss of such a devoted and passionate Perforcian, Charles (Chuck) Gehman. Chuck was such a wonderful person who loved to share his always interesting life stories. He was a dedicated father and husband who knew family was his first priority. He loved his family and was so proud to talk about them. Chuck's depth of knowledge and experience across multiple technologies made him invaluable to our company, our partners, and the industry. For those less technical, Chuck was a great teacher and exercised patience and kindness, ensuring that our teams were equipped for success. I wish he were here to see the final publication of this book — he was so excited to be a part of this great project.

Table of Contents

SECTION ONE

INTRODUCTION TO AI/ML IN SOFTWARE TESTING TOOLS
AND WHY IT'S NEEDED

Chapter 1:
Intro to AI and Machine Learning in Testing

As I'm writing this book, the software testing market and its practitioners are experiencing a huge barricade in evolving their test automation coverage, velocity, and stability. When referring to testing, it's important to be on the same page with what it covers — including activities, challenges, and owners of these activities.

Before I explore the different activities and use cases that can benefit from AI and ML capabilities, let's look back at the evolution of testing practices over the past decades.[1]

EVOLUTION OF TESTING

MANUAL TESTING	BULKY AUTOMATION TOOLS	MORE ROBUST AUTOMATION TOOLS + OPEN SOURCE FRAMEWORKS	MORE ABOUT SCALE	AUTONOMOUS TESING, MACHINE LEARNING AND AI

1980 - 1990 Waterfall Methodology	1990 - 2000 Experimentation with different Development Approaches	2000 - 2010 Agile Approaches, faster release cycles	2010 - 2018 DevOps, Continous Testing, CI/CD	The Future Collaborative, Smart Testing

Fig. 1: Evolution of testing (Source: CloudQA[2])

It is interesting to see the evolution of software testing since it is what really shaped and contributed to today's tool growth. The software industry grew from traditional waterfall models to basic Agile practices and advanced Agile and DevOps. Today's reality aims for mature CI/CD pipelines.

---

1 Evolution of Testing Overview https://cloudqa.io/ai-in-testing-the-third-wave-of-automation/
2 Evolution of Testing, Cloud QA https://becominghuman.ai/ai-in-testing-the-third-wave-of-automation-cfdd43f55d9c

As the future in this image suggests, the market is in a junction of evolving the automated pipeline. To do so, it needs a much smarter set of tools and capabilities.

Mature DevOps teams produce large sets of data in each activity in the pipeline. Specifically, testing teams create large amounts of monitoring, code coverage and quality, and usage data, among other types.

The cloud is one tool that helps sustain the environments and storage. However, AI and ML algorithms are growing into becoming the real source of truth within the above-mentioned activities.

If I were to list the top reasons why AI and ML are important in software testing, I would focus on the following:

TEST AUTOMATION PAINS

- **Test engineering skillset = flakiness**
- **Test automation maintenance/coverage**
- **Slow feedback and test visibility**
- **Software release velocity**

Test Creation Skillset = Flakiness

Even after so many years of test evolution, test automation coverage across the market is less than 50%.[3] In most cases, test engineering lacks the skills to properly create test code that is stable, does not produce false negatives, and uses proper object locators. Most advanced test automation frameworks are code based and require good coding skillsets to create tests that can run at scale, continuously, and across platforms. The reality shows that it is quite difficult.

Test Automation Maintenance and Coverage

Test automation within Agile and DevOps runs upon each code commit. However, with each software iteration new code and functionalities are introduced, hence,

---

3 *Perfecto by Perforce State of Test Automation Survey https://www.perfecto.io/resources/state-test-automation*

the tests ought to keep up as well. Otherwise, the noise these tests generate hides real defects. Test maintenance is among the other big challenges organizations are facing regardless of the testing type — functional, unit, non-functional, etc. In addition, test coverage and the inability to test everything that is required causes test coverage limitation.

Slow Feedback and Test Visibility

Agile and DevOps rely on fast feedback upon each code change. The more time it takes developers to figure out what happened after they committed the changes, the later defects are detected, and the more the projects are at risk. Being able to understand root cause of failures — and act upon them quickly — is another driver for smarter testing solutions.

Here is a visual summary of the key pain points that block test automation maturity in DevOps. The interesting part in this visual is the link between some of these pain points. For example, when test and dev are separate this not just causes lack of test creation synchronization, but it also creates escaped defects to production, manual testing backlog, and more.

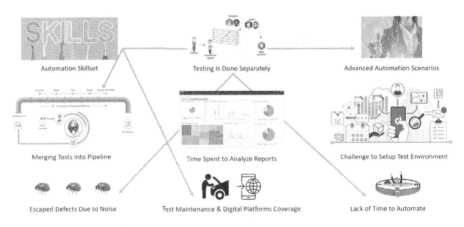

Fig. 2: Key Pitfalls in Test Automation Maturity

Software Release Velocity

Organizations are always looking to optimize their pipeline and deliver new value to clients faster. They seek to release on demand, upon code commit through continuous deployment capabilities. However, very few large organizations can release code to production on demand today. To release code faster, test automation must be stable, run across platforms, and provide concrete feedback. And this requires smarter solutions.

Terms like self-healing and autonomous testing come into play around expediting software releases through smarter automaton. Since each technological challenge has a dedicated solution, here are some of the common ML categories embraced today by tool vendors or as proprietary implementations by internal IT organizations.[4]

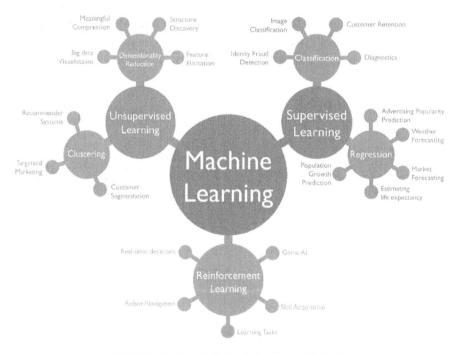

Fig. 3: Machine Learning Categorization (Source: Medium)

4   Types of Machine Learning Categories
    https://towardsdatascience.com/what-are-the-types-of-machine-learning-e2b9e5d1756f

Supervised Learning

- Description: Learn a function based on tagged inputs.

- Algorithm example: Linear regression.

- Real life examples: Face recognition, email scanning for spam.

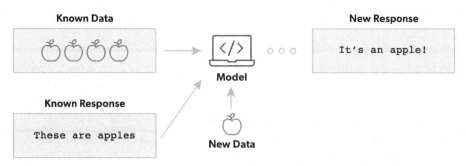

Fig. 4: Supervised Learning Example

Unsupervised Learning

- Description: Learn classifications and patterns in untagged data.

- Algorithm example: K-means clustering.

- Real life examples: Buying habits, recommendation system (videos, ads, etc.).

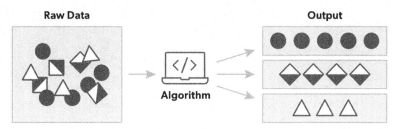

Fig. 5: Unsupervised Learning Example

Reinforcement Learning

- Description: Learn by trial and error in a scenario that generates reward feedback.

- Real life example: Video games with rewards based on successful actions.

Deep Learning

- Description: A specific take on the use of neural networks.

An additional great resource that I can across as I was authoring this book was the set of lectures and blogs from Matthew Reinbold.[5]

In the below visual, we see a training process of a machine that can identify a chihuahua dog from a large set of inputs. Training this model took the developers over 300,000 images.

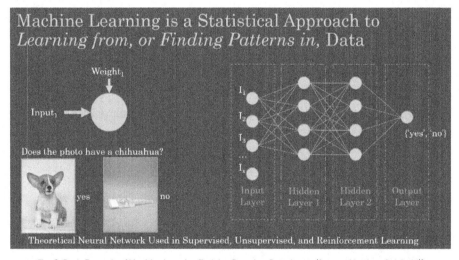

Fig. 6: Basic Example of Machine Learning Training Based on Data Inputs (Source: Matthew Reinbold)[6]

From an engineering perspective, practitioners typically are not aware of which ML category is behind the tool or framework that they use, even though it's important for them to understand the power of such tools so they can match the tool (algorithms) to their specific problems.

5 Matthew Reinbold Website https://matthewreinbold.com
6 Matthew Reinbold AI and APIs Session https://www.youtube.com/watch?v=DAm6o9LULts&feature=youtu.be

To provide better guidance on which categories might be useful to specific use cases, here are the top challenges in the testing domain that ML and AI are addressing. Keep in mind that in most cases, an organization will need more than one ML/AI solution to solve all of its challenges.

I would also like to quote an insightful article written by Ran Bechor guiding early adopters of AI and ML on how to get started based on cost, data quality, process fit, use cases, pains, and available solutions.[7]

"There is no doubt that AI and ML have become the most powerful and dominant force in technology over the past decade, it'll be interesting to see how far can AI go and if Artificial General Intelligence (AGI) and Explainable Artificial Intelligence (XAI) will be a part of our everyday life.

For now, if what you need already exists and you can take advantage of it then jump right in, if not, then you should probably wait for it. Because no matter which industry you work in, AI is heading your way."

Software Testing: Use Cases for Using ML/AI Solutions

Test automation enables continuous testing. That's a fact already stated in my previous books. Test automation creation, however, is only one use case for ML/AI. To succeed in test automation continuously, organizations should look at various use cases, especially in the digital landscape of mobile and web apps.

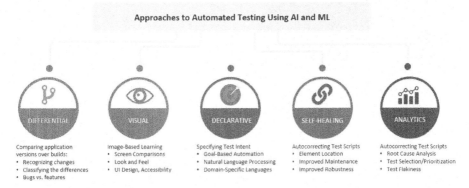

Fig. 7: Machine Learning Approaches for Automated Testing (Tariq King)

---

7 *AI Is Not Overrated, But Often Overused* https://www.linkedin.com/pulse/ai-overrated-often-overused-ran-bechor/

As categorized in the previous visual, there are five different use cases that teams can mature when embracing AI and ML.

1. Differential

In Agile and DevOps practices, teams are either pushing new software builds to production daily or weekly. To manage the entire build data, realize the changes, determine if a roadmap is on track, and realize software waste throughout the build process, ML algorithms can be applied and used.

This **differential**[8] use case has real-life examples in the field where ML algorithms are used to identify bugs in mobile app code. Facebook's project Infer[9] is a great static code analysis solution for Java, C, C#, and Objective C that can detect exceptions, memory leaks, unavailable APIs, and more using its built-in ML algorithms.[10]

In addition, developers today boost their app development productivity through a set of ML kits for web services, including mobile and web apps. Google ML kit is a great example of an SDK that developers can use to easily build advanced features into their mobile apps like face recognition, natural language processing for supporting multi-language apps, and more.[11]

Fig. 8: Facebook Project Infer

8   Machine Learning for Detecting Code Bugs
     https://towardsdatascience.com/machine-learning-for-detecting-code-bugs-a79f37f144b7
9   Facebook GitHub Repository for Project Infer https://github.com/facebook/infer
10 Project Infer https://fbinfer.com/
11 Google ML Kit https://developers.google.com/ml-kit/

Lastly, an additional differential use cases that leverages ML is the review of automated code. Later in this book you'll find a dedicated chapter on how it's done.

2. Visual

Especially in digital apps like web and mobile, the end user experience is key for success. The problem with these platforms is the fragmentation of the digital domain. There are endless permutations across mobile OSes and devices, as well as desktop browsers and OS versions.

This is where ML algorithms like neural networks can support test automation by automatically spotting differences between an expected image that is "approved" in a baseline of visuals versus other different tested screens.

In the following screenshot taken from Applitools, an AI-based visual testing solution, there is an example of a test with an unresolved status. This is due to detected mismatches compared to the previously saved baseline.[12] Such changes can be waived and approved by the user once, and in the next run, they will be ignored automatically. If there is a bug, the tool will automatically raise it. For those that are interested in giving this tool a try, please refer to this repository as reference.[13]

Fig. 9: Applitools Visual AI Dashboard

12 Applitools Visual Testing https://applitools.com/
13 Applitools and Perfecto Integration GitHub Repository

3. Declarative

An additional use case for test automation is based on test intent and intent classification.[14] In this category or use case, we see tools that embrace NLP (natural language processing), ALP (adaptive language processing), and goal-based automation.[15]

If you're familiar with behavior-driven development (BDD), think about an automated test that generates test scenario files into actionable test cases. As opposed to BDD and Gherkin where a test engineer would need to develop custom functions in Java or other languages to be used and supported by the scenario files, here with ALP/NLP, the ML engine "reads" the scenarios written in plain English, and contextually converts them into tests.

In the below screenshot from Functionize, you can see a complete test scenario that leverages web specific commands like open URL, click, verify, and more while a test engineer only specifies the business flows.[16]

In such case, a user will follow exploratory or other structured test cases and include them in the solution in the logical flow. The engine will then "read" the flow and perform the steps on the target website (relevant to the below example).

SampleTestCasePipeDrive

Step	Test Data	Expected Results
Open URL www.pipedrive.com		
Click Login		
Enter Email	brad@functionize.com	
Enter Password	Temp1234	
Verify Pipe Logo		
Click Contacts		
Click People		
Click Add person		
Enter Name	John Doe	
Enter Lead	Hot Lead	
Enter Phone	303 555-5555	
Select Phone Type	Mobile	
Enter email	Random email address	
Enter Job Title	Director of QA	
Enter Organization Department	Information Technology	
Select Decision Maker	Yes	
Select Influencer	Yes	
Select Lead Status	New	
Click Save		
Verify Contact Created		John Doe exists in Name Column

Fig. 10: Natural Language Processing Test Creation (Source: Functionize)

14 *Intro to ML with Intent Classification*
   https://towardsdatascience.com/a-brief-introduction-to-intent-classification-96fda6b1f557
15 *Wikipedia's Definition of NLP https://en.wikipedia.org/wiki/Natural_language_processing*
16 *Functionize ALP™ Demo - https://www.functionize.com/blog/alp-teaching-a-computer-to-understand-test-plans/*

Fig. 11: Execution Example of an NLP-Based Test Script (Source: Functionize)

Underneath NLP/ALP and intent classification methods, there is a trained engine that can convert intents based on the relevant category. To make such a model work, the vendors that utilize such algorithms need to prepare the data and methods in advance so they can be used in the proper "intents." For example, to create a test that opens a web browser with a specific URL, there needs to be a built-in option like in the above screenshot called "Open URL," and so forth.[17]

Another advanced use case for NLP is the one that Wit.ai uses.[18] Similarly to the above example, Wit.ai resides between the user and the app and accepts commands, then translates them into intents and actions.

In the below example, when a user engages with an app through voice or bot and asks to set the temperature in the bedroom to 70 degrees, the intent will be classified by the NLP engine (heating control), the location will be set, and the temperature will be set. Such capability can be executed either through a mobile app, a chatbot, or a wearable or other hardware device that support this capability. As in the first test automation example above, the intent is driven through a command that the user specifies, and the ML/AI algorithm knows when to do next.

---

17 Intent Classification https://towardsdatascience.com/a-brief-introduction-to-intent-classification-96fda6b1f557
18 Wit.ai NLP Resource https://wit.ai/

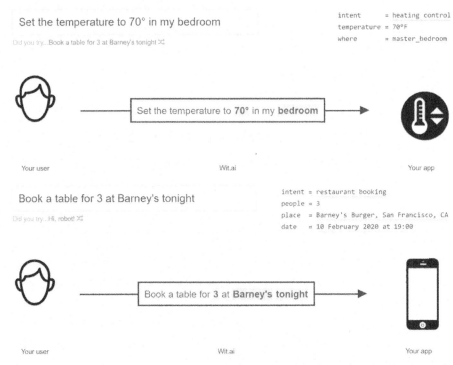

Fig. 12: NLP Processing and Classification Example (Source: Wit.ai)

As opposed to other record and playback ML tools, or the other use cases that are mentioned in this chapter, this specific use case is mostly for non-coding manual/ business testers. This allows them to automate some of their tedious test cases and contribute to overall test coverage.

4. Self-Healing Use Cases

As introduced briefly in the book introduction, "self-healing" is an advanced ML capability that can fix code or support test code, like object locators in runtime, through supervised algorithms and big data analysis.

While this use case also appeals to business testers and non-coders, this is also a very useful solution for developers that do not have the time to deal with test creation, execution, and maintenance. Hence, such a capability can boost their productivity through a one and done test authoring (recording/playback).

Most self-healing tools are built via a test recorder and playback mechanism. The main difference between these tools and old generation recorders is the dynamic adaptivity and maintenance of these tools. Old non-ML tools recording UI scenarios and more were generating static tests. As soon as anything changed in the test, app, business flows, object, or anything else, the test broke without manual intervention.

In modern ML test recording solutions, the algorithm scans the app pages in run-time, and the element locators or specific steps adhere to the current state of the app. In the majority of cases, this is done without the user even being aware to the changes made by the tool. In more advanced implications on the test, there will be a trigger to the test owner to act upon the changes.

Fig. 13: Automated Self-Healing Illustration (Source: Perfecto)

5. Test Reporting and Analytics Use Cases

Lastly, to summarize the top ways ML/AI can support advanced test automation creation, let's focus on the final stage of test automation — the reporting itself.

The test report is where teams realize value from their investment and put in place corrective actions so the feedback is timely, the risks of releasing new software to production are mitigated, and the overall cost of testing is maintained. The areas in which AI and ML are contributing to smarter reporting are in error classification and automatic root cause analysis for failures. Both use cases contribute to noise reduction in the pipeline and higher-quality test suites.

Key contributors to test automation flakiness and noise that test engineers and developers face include:

- Scripts and test automation framework issues.
- Backend issues.
- Issues with orchestration and execution at scale.
- Lab-related issues.

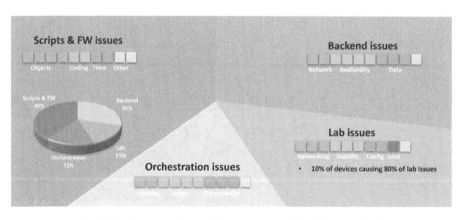

Fig. 14: Main Root Cause Reasons for Test Automation Failures (Source: Perfecto)

Automating the classification of issues based on the above categories is a great step toward cleaning up the test suites from flakiness. Some of the above issues can be eliminated through self-healing/codeless tools that reduce most element locator issues and minor test code maintenance. Other issues with the lab can be solved through machine learning that can identify lab availability issues, platform disconnections (image below), and more.

Fig. 15: Use of Machine Learning in Test Reporting for Error Classification (Source: Perfecto)

Lastly, if you're building ML algorithms on top of your mobile app, it is recommended that you look into the three leading ML SDKs:

1. **ML Kit** — Google's machine learning package for Android and iOS mobile apps that supports capabilities like text and face recognition, image labeling, landmark recognition, and more.[19]

2. **OpenCV** — An open source library for ML-based application development that supports capabilities like camera movement recognition, face recognition, building 3D models, and other computer vision abilities.[20]

3. **TensorFlow**[21] — Also developed by Google, this package supports pre-built ML algorithms, computer vision (CV) capabilities, natural language processing (NLP) capabilities, and more. Try the built-in neural network example for classifying clothing types.[22]

---

19 *MLKit APIs Documentation https://developers.google.com/ml-kit*
20 *OpenCV GitHub Repository https://github.com/opencv/opencv*
21 *TensorFlow Home Page https://www.tensorflow.org/*
22 *TensorFlow Neural Net Classification Example https://www.tensorflow.org/tutorials/keras/classification*

DEVELOPMENT AND TESTING USE CASE USING AI/ML

Amazon Web Services took AI and ML to a new level by enabling mobile and web app developers to inject AI capabilities into progressive web apps to build better user engagement and automation.

AWS offers a large set of services for natural language processes, chatbot creation, and other data processing activities. They use Amplify among other solutions to build, develop, and deploy rich applications like those referenced in the below visual.[23]

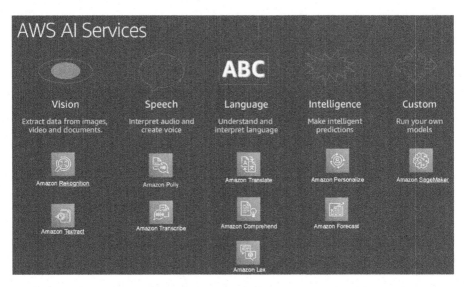

Fig. 16: Amazon Re:Invent 2019 Session on AI Within Mobile Apps (Source: AWS)

Borrowing from the session example, here are chatbot creation snippets for an on-line pizza ordering flow, all using Amplify.[24]

```
Welcome to the Amazon Lex chatbot wizard
You will be asked a series of questions to help determine how to best construct your chatbot.

   Provide a friendly resource name that will be used to label this category in the project: AndyPizzaOrder
   Would you like to start with a sample chatbot, import a chatbot, or start from scratch? Start from scratch
   Enter a name for your bot: AndyPizzaOrder
   Choose an output voice: Female
   After how long should the session timeout (in minutes)? 30
   Please indicate if your use of this bot is subject to the Children's Online Privacy Protection Act (COPPA).
   Learn more: https://www.ftc.gov/tips-advice/business-center/guidance/complying-coppa-frequently-asked-questions No
```

Fig. 17: Chatbots Creation Flow With AWS Amplify (Source: AWS Amplify Documentation)

23 AWS Amplify Documentation https://aws.amazon.com/amplify/framework/
24 Full Guide for Building AWS-Based Chatbots https://mob302.learn-the-cloud.com/add_ai/add_chat_service/

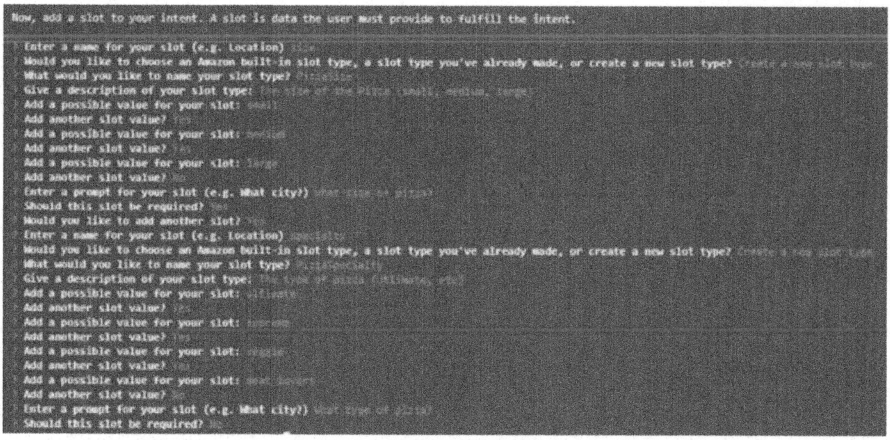

Fig. 18: Chatbot Creation Flow With AWS Amplify (Source: AWS Amplify Documentation)

The above two snippets are being fed to the chatbot within the app and can be easily created through the AWS services and Amplify. The solution also supports a JSON file as an input source for the chatbot information with a command "Amplify push" at the end of editing to upload and provision the file to the server.

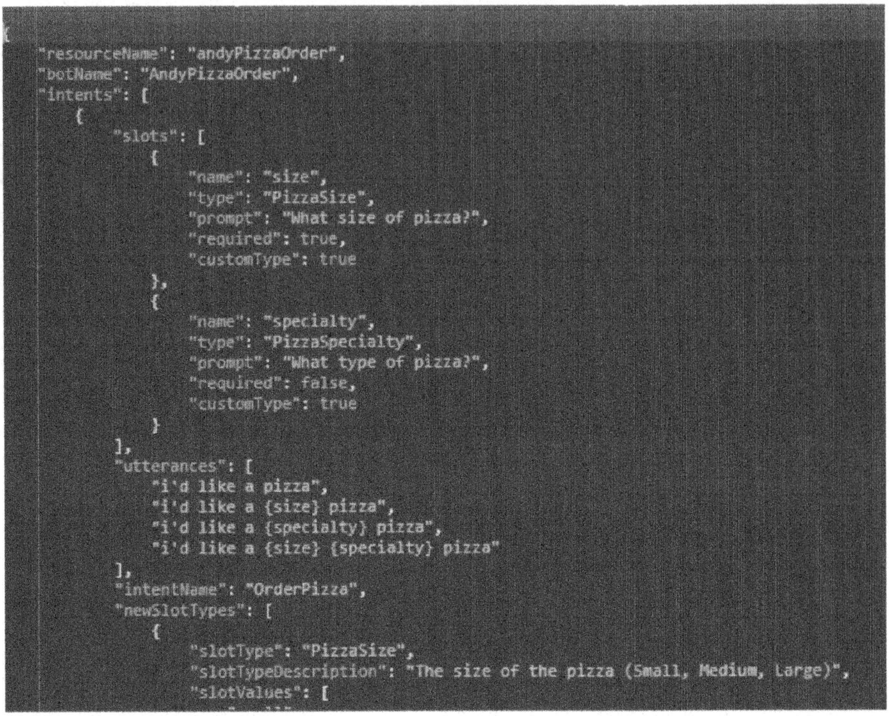

```
{
  "resourceName": "andyPizzaOrder",
  "botName": "AndyPizzaOrder",
  "intents": [
    {
      "slots": [
        {
          "name": "size",
          "type": "PizzaSize",
          "prompt": "What size of pizza?",
          "required": true,
          "customType": true
        },
        {
          "name": "specialty",
          "type": "PizzaSpecialty",
          "prompt": "What type of pizza?",
          "required": false,
          "customType": true
        }
      ],
      "utterances": [
        "i'd like a pizza",
        "i'd like a {size} pizza",
        "i'd like a {specialty} pizza",
        "i'd like a {size} {specialty} pizza"
      ],
      "intentName": "OrderPizza",
      "newSlotTypes": [
        {
          "slotType": "PizzaSize",
          "slotTypeDescription": "The size of the pizza (Small, Medium, Large)",
          "slotValues": [
```

Fig. 19: Chatbots Creation Flow With AWS Amplify (Source: AWS Amplify Documentation)

```
hoog:~/environment/andy-pizza-shop (master) $ amplify push

Current Environment: dev

| Category     | Resource name          | Operation | Provider plugin   |
| ------------ | ---------------------- | --------- | ----------------- |
| Interactions | andyPizzaOrder         | Create    | awscloudformation |
| Auth         | andypizzashopeefc3f03  | Update    | awscloudformation |
| Api          | andypizzashop          | No Change | awscloudformation |
Are you sure you want to continue? (Y/n)
```

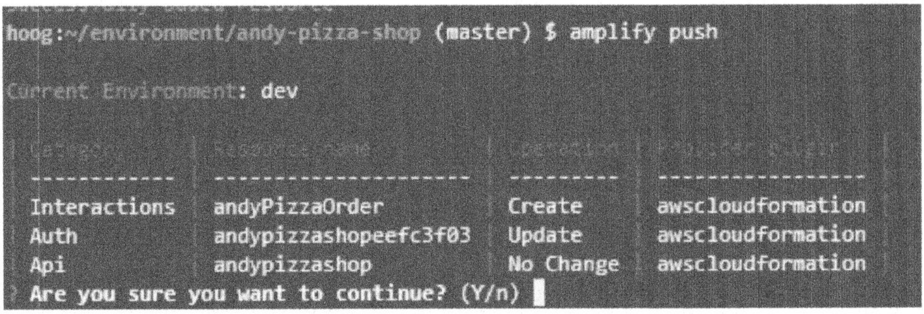

Fig. 20: Chatbots Creation Flow With AWS Amplify (Source: AWS Amplify Documentation)

Obviously, the same service or solution can and should be the foundation for creating similar JSON files for testing the website chatbot application with different languages, answers, and other user inputs to asses things like how the website and bot would respond to a wrong answer, spelling mistakes, illegal characters, and more (AI apps tested by AI ●).

The final website including the chatbots screenshot is below as a reference.

Welcome, edge21! Home Menu Account
Recommended for you!
Choco Cake
Chocolate mixed in with chocolate, and cake, and topped with chocoloate
Add this to Order
Your Current Cart
Item Name
Options
Price
Checkout
Place an Order
Type a message
Send

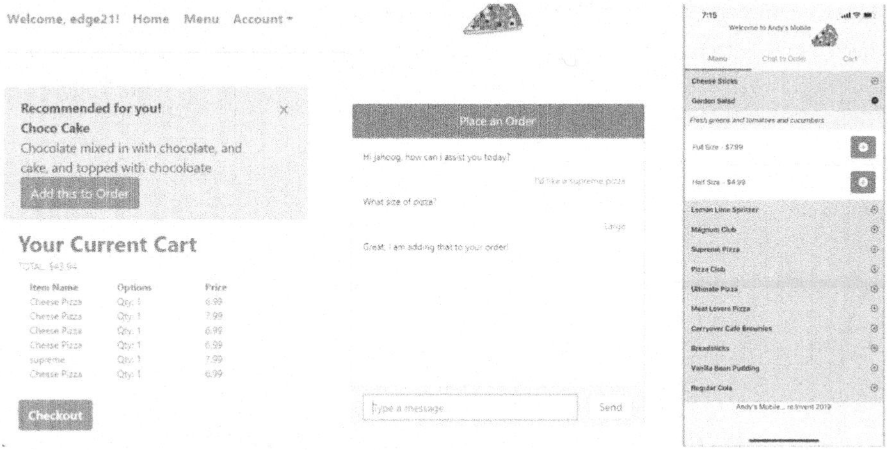

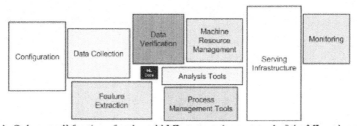

Fig. 21: Online Pizza Ordering Form With Built-in Chatbot Created With AWS Amplify (Source: AWS)

While there are a lot of benefits in AI and ML across various use cases and segments, it is important to note that AI and ML are in most cases only cover a subset of the applications code and business logic, hence it is important to keep an holistic development and testing strategy. Google has very much highlighted this point in one of its paper referenced below.

Hidden Technical Debt in Machine Learning Systems
Google, 2015
Configuration
Data Collection
Data Verification
Machine Resource Management
Serving Infrastructure
Monitoring
Analysis Tools
Feature Extraction
Process Management Tools
Figure 1: Only a small fraction of real-world ML systems is composed of the ML code, as shown by the small black box in the middle. The required surrounding infrastructure is vast and complex.
https://papers.nips.cc/paper/5656-hidden-technical-debt-in-machine-learning-systems.pdf

Fig. 22: Online Pizza Ordering Form with Built-in Chatbot Created with AWS Amplify (Source: Google)

Now that most of the use cases around testing (functional and non-functional are equally eligible to leverage AI/ML algorithms) are defined, the following chapters will dive deeper into real life examples, practices, how this all fits into DevOps and more.

Chapter 2:
How Do AI and ML Testing Tools Fit and Scale in the DevOps Pipeline?

After we've defined some key use cases for using AI and ML methods to improve overall test automation stability and reliability, let's map and integrate new types of testing within the DevOps pipeline. We need to define this because new types of tests often originate from external tool stacks and different personas.

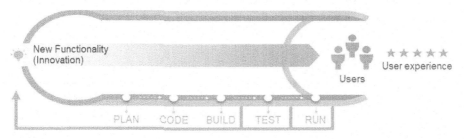

Fig. 23: DevOps Pipeline Illustration (Source: Perfecto)

A typical DevOps pipeline looks like the image above. New requirements, story points, and functionalities are introduced. They then undergo development, building, integration, testing, and deployment. Hopefully, at the end, there are happy customers and a 5-star experience.

More specifically, as seen in the below illustration, the process is being divided into phases by personas. The developer codes based on the product requirements. They perform unit testing against their web and/or mobile apps from their local machine. Once the unit tests pass, they will perform a software build and perform some build acceptance testing upon a commit to the main branch.

Once integrated to the main repository, the entire build is tested more thoroughly through cloud solutions, scalable environments, and more. In this stage, a lot of end-to-end testing, regression testing, new functionality testing, and non functional testing — including security, acceptance, performance, accessibility, and more — are performed until quality level is met. After that, software is deployed to the production environment.

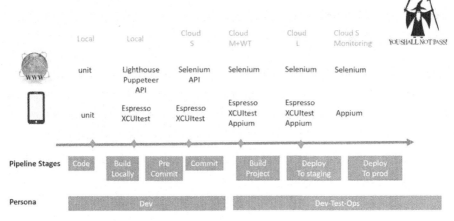

Fig. 24: DevOps Pipeline by Stages Across Phases (Source: Perfecto)

The above process is fine and should not change dramatically by introducing AI and ML tools into various phases of the pipeline. The complexity, as well as the need, in this case is to incorporate and integrate AI and ML tools and techniques into the working processes above. In addition, ML and AI can enable continuous learning and improvements based on gathered data, defect analysis, code analysis, and more.

Before outlining recommendations for AI and ML tools to use alongside non-AI/ML tools, here are some of the main differences between code-based tools (testing only) and codeless (ML-based) tools. The comparison is done from end to end, meaning, from creation through execution, integration, and analysis.

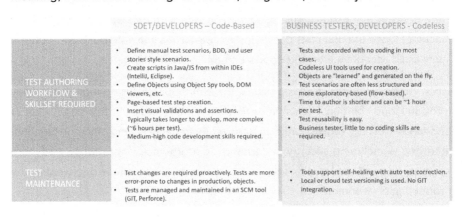

	SDET/DEVELOPERS – Code-Based	BUSINESS TESTERS, DEVELOPERS- Codeless
TEST EXECUTION	• Configured environment using tools like TestNG Data Provider. • Execution done locally, via CI, cloud-based.	• Execution management is built into the codeless tools. • Execution done locally, via CI, cloud-based.
TOOLS MATURITY	• Highly mature, includes samples, best practices, documentation. • Integrations exist for ALM tools, defect management, etc.	• Emerging technology, less mature, no well-defined guidelines and practices (guide to shift from standard to ML). • Web is more mature than mobile codeless, basic integrations only.
TESTING & APP TYPES SUPPORTED	• Functional, API, load, etc. • Mobile native (Appium) and desktop web (Selenium).	• Mostly functional (E2E) and basic API. • Most support for web, mobile is lagging behind.

Fig. 25: Key Differences in Code-Based Testing and Codeless Testing Approaches (Source: Perfecto)

As outlined in the above tables, there are few material differences between the two approaches. While they complement each other from a test coverage percentage perspective, each requires a different methodology and cross-team discipline. The main consideration is the process, specifically around the following key questions.

How Are New Test Scripts Created Using Both Codeless and Coded Approaches?

As identified above, codeless mostly uses record and playback, while coded is being done in an IDE like IntelliJ or Eclipse. The art in combining both methods involves communication between two different types of personas. Communication prevents duplication of test scenarios. It also ensures that there's a full sync around test coverage, as well as alignment regarding test execution schedules and other project risks.

How Does One Maintain the Two Sets of Test Automation Suites?

Maintaining code should be done as a developer maintains his production code. However, for codeless, maintenance is done through a mix of touch-free self-healing capabilities and overriding pre-recorded scenarios manually.

How Can Management Get Full Visibility Into Quality and Test Results Per Execution?

This is another tricky part since the two approaches report the results into two different dashboards. Leaders should insist on a single pane of glass that captures both results regardless of their origin. While test automation reports prior to codeless originated through API tools, unit testing, CI, and more, and management was able to view it all, codeless should be just one additional origin into the entire pipeline.

Fig. 26: Combination of Code and Codeless Test Automation (Source: Perfecto)

How Do I Fit ML and Codeless Testing Within the Other Tools in My Stack?

To try answering this question, here is a basic summary table that lists the leading test automation frameworks, divided into various considerations:

- Skills.
- Coverage areas.
- Supported platforms.
- Supported testing types.
- Maturity.

The most important column in this table is the persona matching under the required skillset. It's clear that we want both approaches complementing each other as figure 26 suggests. However, there are personas behind these tools that should drive and own the quality objectives for each. Let's take an example from the table below. Developers that mostly tackle the unit testing challenge will continue to focus on more advanced frameworks that require minimal setup and maintenance like Cypress.io, Puppeteer for web, Flutter, or Espresso/XCUITest for mobile.

On the other hand, test automation engineers that own end-to-end test automation will work mostly with Selenium for web and Appium for mobile to get greater coverage of tests and platforms.

So, where does this leave codeless and BDD (behavior driven development)? For BDD, business testers will own the gherkin test scenario creation, while depending on test automation developers or application developers to implement the custom functions (Java, Python, other). For codeless, business testers can own the entire lifecycle of test creation, execution, maintenance, and reporting since these tools don't require coding skills.

Test Framework	Supported Dev Languages	Supported Platforms	Supported Test Frameworks	Setup and Execution	Integrations	Breadth of Testing Options	Maturity, Documentation, Support	Required Skillset	Cloud and Execution at Scale
Selenium/Appium WebDriver	Java, C#, Java Script, Python, Ruby, Objective-C	Chrome, Safari, Firefox, Edge, IE/iOS/Android	Mocha JS, Jest, other super set on top of Selenium (Protractor, WebDriverIO, etc.)	Download relevant driver, set up a grid, network and location impacts execution speed	Plenty of integrations (CI, CD, reporting, visual testing, cloud vendors)	End-to-end, security, unit,	Robust community, multiple bindings, best practices	Coding skills required (SDET Oriented)	Perfecto fully supports Selenium and its WebDriver configurations. Local execution requires setting up a Selenium grid
XCUI Test/Espresso/ Headless/Cypress	Objective C/Java/Java Script	Chrome, Electron	NA	Embedded into IDEs, headless bundles a browser in the FW	CI/CD	UI/Unit	Good documentation and code samples	Dev Oriented	Built-in Chrome/Firefox browsers in headless, Perfecto Cloud supports scaling Espresso/XCUITest
Codeless	Irrelevant, based on record and playback	All	Proprietary UI with underlying Selenium WebDriver APIs	Mostly SaaS/browser plugin installation	Limited	Functional /UI	Growing, limited	No coding skills required (Business Tester Oriented)	Perfecto supports codeless in the cloud
BDD	Java, Ruby, JS, Kotlin	All	Junit, Selenium, Appium	Open source, Maven/Gradle /TestNG	Plenty + APIs (e.g. Rest Assured)	Functional	Robust community, docs, adoption	Step-definition development in code is required/scenarios are no-code (Mix of Business Tester and SDETs)	Perfecto Quantum is a web/mobile BDD framework

Fig. 27: Mapping Sample Test Automation Frameworks to Personas, Objectives, and Skillsets (Source: Perfecto)

Note that the pipeline can accommodate more than a single test automation framework and can benefit even more personas contributing to the overall quality based on their skillsets, capabilities, and objectives.

In addition to software testing opportunities for AI and ML to help optimize an ongoing pipeline, there is additional software waste — known as 'TIMWOOD' — that can be enhanced when applying AI models.[25]

Think about eliminating the transfer of sign-offs and approvals between phases. This can be done with AI algorithms that automatically scan a release based on lists of data points and approve the transition to the next phase. Defects and rework

25 Tackle Software Wastes in DevOps - https://enterprisersproject.com/article/2019/10/how-scale-devops-time-wasters

activity created by regression issues (covered as "d" in the above acronym) can be eliminated with automated regression suites that are automatically changed and updated based on historical issues.

BOTTOM LINE

Taking all of this into a strategic consolidation of AI, ML, and traditional tools, DevOps teams must work based on actionable and up-to-date data. Such data should cover events and relevant content across all phases of the DevOps pipeline, including production data. Being able to tune software iterations based on real-time production insights automatically is a DevOps dream.

Think about a pipeline that gets production inputs on a real-time defect, or a new release on a specific platform that is buggy and can loop all relevant services into a quick response. In these cases, remediation is a massive productivity and velocity boost.

AI and ML are able to look into historical data analysis, software anomalies, performance analysis, correlation of issues to code and product areas, and much more. Such data can be passed automatically to the right systems and personas for re-assessment, automation of new tasks, and resolution.

An automated end-to-end process for the AI/ML pipeline can accelerate development and drive reproducibility, consistency, and efficiency across AI/ML projects. Since AI and ML models take time to be built into consistent and predictable tools, consider matching such models in the "right" places, and that will be best used over long periods of time as opposed to applying these to one-time model use cases.

As noted in the Continuous Testing for DevOps Professionals book, DevOps is all about bringing together business, development, testing, release, and operational expertise to deliver a valuable solution to customers. Ensure that AI/ML is represented on feature teams and is included throughout the design, development, testing, and operational sessions.

Chapter 3:
Advancing the State
of the Art in AI for Testing

Jason Arbon, CEO, test.ai

Jason Arbon is a test nerd and currently the CEO of test.ai, where his mission is to auto-mate the testing of the world's apps with AI. He has been the director of product and engineering at uTest/Applause.com. Jason previously held engineering leadership roles at Google (Chrome/Search) and Microsoft (WindowsCE, SQL Server, BizTalk, Bing). He also co-authored How Google Tests Software and App Quality: Secrets for Agile App Teams. In his spare time, Jason likes to read up on Artificial General Intelligence and consciousness and is working on a new personalized search engine.

Tariq King, Chief Scientist, test.ai

Tariq King enjoys working on challenging testing problems and is currently the Chief Scientist at test.ai. He started his career in academia as a tenure-track professor and later transitioned into the software industry. Tariq previously held positions as a test architect, manager, director, and head of quality and performance engineering. He has published over 40 articles in peer-reviewed software testing books, journals, conferences, and workshops. He is a member of the ACM and IEEE Computer Society and serves as a board member for several international software engineering and testing conferences.

INTRODUCTION

The software testing community has readily embraced AI and ML technologies, with many researchers and industry practitioners recognizing its potential to trans-form test automation as we know it.[26] During the last decade, we ushered in a new wave of AI-based test automation tools. However, most of the focus has been on functional test automation with some performance benchmarking.[27] It makes sense that identifying and interacting with UI elements would be a natural place for us to start with this technology. After all, this is where conventional test automation tech-niques also began. Unfortunately, such techniques did not go much further, and as a result there are still several gaps between human and machine-driven testing.

Developing AI bots that automatically explore an application and generate func-tional tests is a notable achievement — one that is quite remarkable. The ability to access free, open source tools, prototypes, and models that enable us to integrate

---

26 *AI-Driven Testing: A New Era of Test Automation, Tariq King https://tinyurl.com/king-ai-driven-testing*
27 *Functional Test Automation With AI, Jason Arbon, Continuous Testing for DevOps Professionals.*

AI into our testing projects should make us proud as a community.[28,29] However, these should be viewed as the first steps that inspire us to do even more with this technology.

In this chapter, we explore some of the latest advances in AI for software testing. Our goal is to bring you to the bleeding edge of where AI and ML technologies are being applied to difficult software testing problems in the real world today. AI is no longer just doing functional testing, it's testing user interface designs, video stream quality, gameplay, and more.

AI FOR UI DESIGN TESTING

A quick internet search over the last few decades will produce a set of blog posts, articles, and presentations that describe why automated testing will never replace manual testing. One of the popular points for this argument is that it is not possible to automate tests that require human judgement, typically in the form of qualitative assessments.

A qualitative assessment is one that is based on users' experiences, perceptions, opinions, or feelings. User interface (UI) design attributes such as usability, accessibility, and trustworthiness all fall into this category that has been labeled as extremely difficult, if not impossible, to automate.

It is important to recognize that just because the performance of a given task has historically required human presence, it does not mean that the task cannot or will not be automated. Once upon a time, it was thought that tasks such as voice recognition, image recognition, driving, and musical composition were too difficult for computers to tackle.

However, the automation of these tasks has been made possible through AI and machine learning. In some cases, AI is outperforming human experts in tasks such as medical diagnosis, legal document analysis, and aerial combat tactics, among others. It should therefore not come as a surprise that the power of AI is being harnessed for automating aspects of UI design testing that have traditionally relied on the expertise of human testers.

---

28 Test.ai Classifier Server and Appium Plugin https://github.com/testdotai/appium-classifier-plugin
29 Autonomous Generation and Exploration in Test https://github.com/tariqking/AGENT

TESTING MOBILE UI TRUSTWORTHINESS

AI can beat humans in the games of chess, Jeopardy!, and Go. An important lesson that we've learned over the last couple of years is that AI systems can also beat human testers at their own game — software testing. The truth is that even human testers get confused about qualitative assessments on software quality. However, as testers we have to be able to answer questions such as, *How easy is this app to use? Does the user interface look good? Is this screen trustworthy?*

While co-presenting a full-day tutorial on the topic of AI and machine learning for testers, we had the opportunity to engage the audience in playing an intriguing software testing game of humans versus AI.[30]

Who Were the Players?

We had 70 testers in the room. But these testers are no ordinary testers. These were professional, technical testers, who work in roles where their company has chosen to send them to an international testing conference for a week of training. These testers were also confident enough in themselves to brave a full day learning about AI and machine learning algorithms. The room was full of great testers. Their opponent was a neural network. The AI was trained in on data related to the same question we were about to ask them.

What Was the Challenge?

Let's pretend you were in that room with us and see if the AI can beat you too. We asked the audience a qualitative testing question: If you were looking at images of login screens, how would you tell if the app is trustworthy or not? In other words, how would you rate the app's trustworthiness based on how the login screen looks?

Think about it for a moment...

Take your time and look at some of the example login screens in Figure 28.

30 Tariq King and Jason Arbon, AI and ML Skills for the Testing World, STARWEST 2018
https://www.slideshare.net/tariqking1/ai-and-ml-skills-for-the-testing-world-tutorial

Fig. 28: Samples of the least trusted apps vs. the most trusted apps in a mobile app store.

What Do You Think?

The 70 testers in the room took their time to think about it too. There were no quick answers. To make folks feel better about drawing a blank, we mentioned that originally, we had no idea either and encouraged folks to keep thinking. A woman in the front row, whose son works on AI at Google, ventured to guess and said "foreign languages."

If the login page was in the U.S. app store, but it had non-English words in it, it could be viewed as less trustworthy to a user because they wouldn't know what the app was telling them. This was a great start, but only after 3 minutes of 70 human minds thinking in parallel.

After a few more moments, a second hand went up, and this gentleman suggested that if the login had a well-trusted and recognized brand name or logo, the login page would be more trustworthy. If the login page showed the Google or Microsoft logo, then it would probably be more trustworthy than the average app. If the login page had a logo the user had never seen or heard of before, it would be seen as less trustworthy.

At this point, we burned perhaps 5 minutes of human computing time across 70 testers, which is about 6 hours of top human testing brain power trying to answer this question. And yet, we only had 2 ideas on how to measure trustworthiness. We also didn't have a method of scoring exactly how trustworthy or untrustworthy a login screen may be — just some ideas on what might influence that qualitative judgment of quality.

How Did the AI Perform in the Challenge?

Previously, at test.ai headquarters, we had a few non-technical humans look at a large number of login screens and rate the trustworthiness of the pages from 1 to 10. We then trained a neural network on that data. To understand the AI's answer to this question of the trustworthiness of a login screen, we peeked inside the neural network weights and found the AI's answer:

- **Foreign characters** — If the screen has foreign words or characters, it is less trustworthy.

- **Brand recognition** — If the screen has a popular brand image, it is more trustworthy.

- **Number of elements** — If the screen has a high number of elements, it is less trustworthy.

The machine beat the humans! Not only did the AI discover an additional aspect of the application that correlates to trustworthiness, but the AI also gave a precise score of how trustworthy or untrustworthy a login screen is on a scale of 1 to 10.

Interestingly, the trained AI was "smarter" than any single human that labeled the data. The neural network effectively learned the collective intelligence of all humans that provided the training data. No single human figured out more than one aspect of trustworthiness, where the AI discovered three aspects.

There are additional benefits to leveraging AI for this problem. For example, the AI reflects how real users view trustworthiness. On the other hand, human testers try to emulate that assessment indirectly with empathy but are not the actual target user. How much better is it to have the oracle be real-world users versus a tester trying to reverse engineer and guess at end-user qualitative assessments of quality? The AI is also less expensive, reusable across app teams, and faster than the humans.

This was a day that AI beat 70 humans at what is commonly viewed as one of the tougher problems in testing — qualitative assessment. However, there are other ways in which AI is being used to address the area of UI design test automation.

Representing good and bad design practices as a set of testable guidelines allows our view of the UI design testing problem to shift from a subjective, qualitative assessment into a more objective, quantitative, formal evaluation using AI.

In the next two subsections, we'll cover how AI is being applied to testing various UI design guidelines for mobile and web testing.

TESTING MOBILE HUMAN INTERFACE GUIDELINES

There is a painful corner of mobile app testing: Human Interface Guidelines (HIGs). HIGs define how applications should look and behave on mobile. This helps make sure that mobile apps are well designed and deliver a consistent user experience. However, these guidelines come at the cost of unpredictable release schedules.

For example, both Android and iOS have HIGs. But Google Play has simple test bots while iOS has human reviewers to check for HIG compliance. When a developer pushes a new version of their application to the Google Play Store, they are supposed to understand and comply with the Android HIGs.[31] However, the store only does simple automated checks that the mobile app is stable and virus free. On iOS, the same care is expected of developers to adhere to the iOS HIGs,[32] but with humans who actually verify compliance before the application is released. In other words, on one side there is little to no automated testing for HIG compliance, and on the other side there are human reviewers in the loop.

A major challenge on the manual side is that when human reviewers reject an app for HIG violations, it can take a day or so to find out about these violations. This leaves the app developers and designers scrambling to redesign and reimplement the UI to comply, resubmit the application for review, and wait to find out if the new version of the app is compliant.

Furthermore, app teams generally want to keep feature parity between both the Android and iOS versions of their app. This means that although the app team may be finished with their Android build, they may still have to wait for an indefinite period of time until they know their iOS build is good before they can release the Android app. Not only does this create some sprint complexity, but it puts additional

---

31 Design for Android https://developer.android.com/design
32 iOS Design. https://developer.apple.com/design/human-interface-guidelines/ios/overview/themes/

pressure on companies to complete features far in advance of pre-scheduled marketing announcements.

Although HIGs can cause project management and testing headaches for app teams, they are written with good intentions to protect the user experience. Some examples of HIGS include:

- **When Possible, Present Choices** — Make data entry as efficient as possible. Consider using a picker or table instead of a text field, for example, because it's easier to choose from a list of predefined options than to type a response.

- **Enable the Clear Button** — Most search bars include a Clear button that erases the contents of the field.

Fig. 29: A HIG violation in a mobile app (Source: Tariq King and Jason Arbon).

Figure 29 shows an an example of a search box that does not have a Clear button. This HIG violation was found in a major app by AI bots. So how can AI help with all of the challenges associated with HIGs? Bots are trained to automatically walk through an application and catch many of the common HIG violations.

Today we can validate and catch about 30 of the most common issues and we're adding more every sprint. AI is a great way to catch these issues as the bots have been trained to see the screen in a way that is similar to the customer's and reviewer's minds. They don't look at code or have app-specific checks but are instead trained to look at the application UI by recognizing toolbars, shopping carts, and login buttons. Much like human HIG testers, AI testing bots:

- Explore the application as a real user or review would.

- Visually examine the elements and groups of elements on the screen.

- Check all these visual elements against an AI trained on example HIG violations.

- Flag any issues that are found for human review.

Bots find HIG violations in many of the top applications in production today. Importantly, they find these issues almost instantly, and in a repeatable manner that avoids the error of human memory and interpretation. With AI enabling the automatic validation of HIGs, there really is little reason for humans to look for the issues that machines can now identify. App teams can rest knowing that their release schedules do not have to be unnecessarily impacted. We hope that someday soon HIG testing bots will be embedded in IDEs, developer tools, build systems, and app store platforms to automatically perform these checks on each new build.

TESTING WEB CONTENT ACCESSIBILITY GUIDELINES

In an effort to promote universal access to web technologies, the World Wide Web Consortium (W3C) developed a set of Web Content Accessibility Guidelines (WCAG). These guidelines provide criteria to make software accessible to people with physical, visual, cognitive, and learning disabilities. Not only do web development companies have a moral obligation to construct applications that provide universal access, but in most countries they also have a legal obligation. Although several tools support static WCAG web page analysis, present tools lack the automation required to automatically evaluate an entire application for accessibility. Furthermore, current automation techniques are capable of discovering less than 30% of WCAG Level A and Level AA conformance issues.

AI is proving to be an effective way to extend the capabilities of current accessibility testing tools. Agent A11Y extends an open source, AI-based bot platform with accessibility testing capabilities.[33] The bots, also referred to as agents, are trained to explore a website and evaluate its compliance with WCAG.[34] As the bots explore the site, they conduct static accessibility checks and execute supported dynamic

33 Keith Briggs, Dionny Santiago, David Adamo, Philip Daye, and Tariq M. King. Semi-Autonomous, Site-Wide A11Y Testing Using An Intelligent Agent. PNSQC 2019. https://tinyurl.com/agent-a11y
34 Web Content Accessibility Guidelines. https://www.w3.org/WAI/standards-guidelines/wcag/

accessibility checks as relevant testing patterns are recognized. An accessibility report of the results is then consolidated for the user. The approach leverages machine learning (ML) for recognizing and interacting with web pages and elements, understanding and filling out forms, and identifying and clustering accessibility issues. Figure 30 provides an architectural model showing the major components of Agent A11Y.

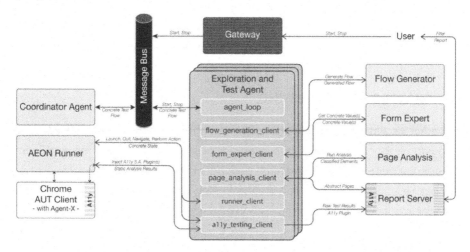

Fig. 30: Agent A11Y performs static and dynamic accessibility testing on web applications (Source: http://uploads. pnsqc.org/2019/papers/Briggs-Semi-autonomus-Sitewide-A11Y-Testing-Using-an-Intelligent-Agent-.pdf).

The workflow of the AI-based accessibility testing approach, as corresponds to the architecture, is described as follows:

1. A Coordinator Agent (top left) initiates accessibility testing through a Message Queue.

2. Exploration and Test Agents (center) leverage the Flow Generator (upper right) to select paths through the application with the goal of visiting as many distinct pages as possible.

3. During exploration, agents use ML algorithms in the Page Analysis component (mid right) to identify pages, controls, and other elements on the web UI.

4. When a web form needs to be filled, agents consult a natural language processing (NLP) engine in the Form Expert component (mid right) to generate test data.

5. Tests are executed using AEON, an open source Selenium-based framework that is capable of integrating with accessibility tools such as aXe.

6. A Report Server (bottom right) utilizes an unsupervised ML algorithm to cluster similar results together to produce a traceable accessibility report for the user.

Although there is still much work to be done in automated accessibility testing with AI, the implementation and application of Agent A11Y to a real-world system provides yet another example of how AI is breaking down the barriers of traditional test automation approaches.

AI FOR VIDEO STREAM TESTING

Whether it's watching a movie on Netflix, getting live match updates on NBA.com, logging on to a Zoom meeting for work, or playing games via Microsoft xCloud, people are becoming more and more dependent on video streaming technologies for business and entertainment. Video streaming is now a core experience in many familiar applications and next-generation gaming systems.

Traditional Approaches to Video Stream Testing

Testing the quality of streaming videos is a difficult but important testing problem. Best practices for testing video quality today involve asking humans to watch videos and rate them using a mean opinion score (MOS). The MOS is a value in the range of 1 to 5, where 1 is the lowest perceived quality and 5 is the highest perceived quality.

Not only is this manual approach an expensive and slow way to test video streaming quality, but it also doesn't scale. When network engineers at streaming companies make changes to networks, tweak their decoders, or switch to new devices or carriers, they often can't do a full manual pass at testing the new or modified configurations. The traffic on the network, the variety of devices, and even the types of videos make it difficult to measure the user experience.

The state-of-the-art test automation for video quality consists of code that combs through every frame of a video during playback under various network, device, and encoder conditions, and tries to detect known types of failure modes through the image pixel patterns. This approach can fall short in several ways and its full impact on the end user is difficult to quantify.

The failure modes of video streaming range from simple blank screens to horizontal and vertical lines, to freezing frames, low frame rates, and more. But knowing how all these functional issues detract from the user playback experience measured by humans can be difficult. What if the issues happen during the credits versus the core of an action sequence? What if multiple failure modes occur at the same time? Automation today can find some of the issues, but it is difficult to map these failure modes back to the ultimate oracle — the end-user experience.

Subjective measures of quality are made even more difficult because videos can be riddled with issues that go unnoticed because they are in noisy or less relevant areas of the screen. For example, Figure 31 shows a variety of scenes in a movie with people dancing. During a given stream, these videos may have issues in the sky, buildings, or even people in the background.

However, because the human eye is likely focused on the areas of the video where the subjects are dancing in the foreground, the background issues may not be noticed at all and the video segment is given a perfect 10 out of 10 MOS. To be great at subjective quality, test automation would have to understand all of this, and score it!

Fig. 31: Human focus areas in movie scenes with dancing people.

TRAINING AI BOTS TO TEST VIDEO STREAM QUALITY

How can we get test automation to replicate this subjective human score? The good news is that AI is here to help. Leveraging machine learning, we can train bots to test for video stream quality as follows:

1. Gather or generate many video clips and their associated human MOS values.

2. Train neural networks to classify video clips into categories as each has its own special quality attributes, e.g., cartoon, romantic comedy, action, etc.

3. Perform scene analysis by training neural networks to recognize which objects in the video streams are interesting.

4. Train neural networks to identify common streaming failure modes, especially those within the bounds of interesting objects.

5. Train neural networks to map all of the above network outputs to the corresponding human MOS values.

By creating a set of internal video benchmarks and working with crowd-sourced human judges, engineers at test.ai were able to use the aforementioned approach to implement a MOS predictor for video stream quality.

Initially the results from training were promising with a 65% correlation between the AI predicted scores and the human MOS values. Correlations of 70% or higher are considered strong. However, after adding video categorization and scene analysis, we saw the correlation rise to 78% and 89% respectively.

Being perfectionist data nerds, we worked further still to verify the stability of our multi-deep network cascade and training pipelines for the AI streaming quality bots on larger, independent, academic sets of videos with MOS scores such as those from the University of Texas at Austin Laboratory for Image and Video Engineering.[35]

The bots held up and even performed better on some categories such as Asian Fusion with a correlation of 93%. In testing, even the worst-performing categories such as CGI videos still had correlations of 75%, resulting in AI that is definitely useful in real-world testing. The bots also perform less predictably for cartoon videos. We suspect that this type of video may require additional specialized training and features. Interestingly, the less "human" and real world the video, the worse the human-emulating bots are at determining video quality.

Applying AI to the problem of video streaming quality is generating great steps forward compared to traditional manual or automated testing approaches. With AI providing an automated way to replicate human MOS judgment scores, engineers building, designing, testing, and monitoring video quality can now get near real-time measurements of true video quality scores — not just detected failure modes.

---

35 *Image and Video Quality Assessment at LIVE, The University of Texas at Austin*
   https://live.ece.utexas.edu/research/Quality/index.htm

Although there is more work to be done, the progress so far in this area is note-worthy. It also serves as a good example of how analyzing the data characteristics and gathering a large corpus of real-world data can be combined with creative AI modeling, training, and architecture to solve hard testing problems.

AI FOR GAME TESTING

Video games are perhaps the toughest pieces of software to test. Many games have an infinite number of states, incredibly custom interaction models, and frequent releases to a finicky audience. A human tester or bot can click about 10 steps deep into an average application, and at each step have perhaps 10 different options of what to click.

Games, however, are even more complex. For example, at any given moment in a massively multiplayer online role-playing game, a player can choose from numer-ous options when acting in an open environment where it is possible to interact with hundreds or thousands of other human and non-human players also playing the game. Creating an automated test script using traditional technologies to sequence every tap or swipe, step, scroll, or swinging of the axe has infinite complexity.

However, in the past year, AI has evolved to address many of these testing prob-lems. Let's explore the pain points of game testing and how AI is helping.

Testing Gameplay

Writing automation to test gameplay is extremely challenging in practice. Any ap-proach that hardcodes assumptions will constantly break as the underlying game engine and its elements are usually in flux. The content, characters, items, maps, and storylines of games are continually evolving. Some games even let the user change these elements in real time as they play.

It is worth mentioning that software development toolkits for games are generally packaged with a low-level internal test scripting language. Such scripting languag-es enable developers to write unit tests for verifying core game logic and that layer of the application tends to be quite stable.

However, these scripting languages generally do not drive the user interface and runtime rendering. As a result, automated tests developed at this level cannot catch the issues that real-world players encounter during gameplay. Furthermore, even if they could, the most important bugs found during gameplay are often related to rendering, not game logic.

In the last few years, there has been some interesting progress on testing game engines with AI such as the experiences shared by King.com, the developers of Candy Crush.[36] The current state of the art focuses on developing tools and strategies that are custom crafted to individual games with relatively straightforward user interfaces. However, many games have highly complex user interfaces that need to be tested before they can be released to players. And many gaming companies need a robust, general purpose solution to test automation.

Fig. 32: AI bots using reinforcement learning to execute gameplay tests.

Advances in AI are bringing us closer to the automation of gameplay testing. In our recent work, human testers can describe test steps as goals for an AI bot, and then, through the process of reinforcement learning, the AI is left to play the game until it achieves the goal. In other words, the bot interprets the goals of a high-level test case, and then autonomously executes the gameplay steps necessary to conduct the test.

Figure 32 shows an AI-driven test where the bot "spawns a player" and "attacks a minion." Using this approach, steps are specified in an abstract language that

36 How King Uses AI to Test Candy Crush Saga, Alexander Andelkovic
https://www.infoq.com/articles/candy-crush-QA-AI-saga/

describes test intent, thereby allowing the definition of steps such as "open trea-sure chest," "score a kill," "equip the axe," "build a ramp," or "exit the spaceship."

The AI can learn how to accomplish these tasks and verify that they are not only possible but working as intended, all without human intervention. Even when the gameplay changes, the AI-based testing approach can autonomously relearn how to accomplish the same tasks in the new environment.

TESTING IN-GAME STORES

As shown in Figure 33, many leading games have an in-game store where players can purchase items for their character, e.g., weapons, clothing. This is a direct avenue for game developers to make their money, and so this functionality needs to be tested.

These stores are often difficult to automate with traditional test automation meth-ods. The items in the store's user interface are often animated, constantly changing position from build to build, and they appear in custom orders as the player can pick any given item at any time. For example, a game may render an axe with varying vi-sual effects at runtime, which may prevent traditional image-seeking or pixel-scan-ning automation techniques from finding the axe. However, AI-based solutions can be utilized to overcome these challenges.

Fig. 33: AI bots validating in-game store features by selecting and purchasing an axe
(Source: https://medium.com/@jarbon/ai-for-testing-games-c5bd90c3153).

Much like a human, AI-based testing tools scan the screen looking for something that appears to be an axe. But wait — that axe might be slowly rotating, glowing, or have a feather attached to the end of it for artistic effect. AI is great at this fuzzy matching for something that looks like a two-dimensional (2D) axe despite the rendering variations. Even better for the AI approach, items like axes in games are rendered from small 3D models of an axe. Loading up that model and generating thousands of different 2D perspectives of the axe makes for perfect training data for the AI.

The AI will recognize that axe on the screen, just like a human who has seen many different axes, from almost any angle or under any dynamic lighting effect. AI therefore makes it possible to identify dynamically rendered items in video games — something which foils standard testing approaches.

IS THE GAME FUN?

We will likely still have to wait a few years for AI testing bots to be smart enough to tell us if the game is fun to play or if it will be a success. That will still probably be a human assessment for a while.

However, from some of the previous sections in this chapter, we've learned that with the right approach to data analysis and collection, it is possible to train AI to simulate human judgement and intuition. In the meantime, AI-based testing approaches are rapidly enabling test automation where it was once impossible for games.

IT'S NOT ALL FUN AND GAMES!

The aforementioned technologies, techniques, and scenarios aren't just fanciful ideas — they are already running and deployed in production today. AI is helping some of the top game development companies via gameplay verification, error recognition, and reuse.

Bots are trained to do application testing, and while the AI plays the game, the bots have additional classifiers watching the screen ready to detect any problems in the video quality, text wrapping, and other rendering issues.

Most interestingly, since the AI sees and plays the game like a human player, the same tests can be leveraged across multiple devices and platforms. So, although at first this may seem like fun and games, after putting it altogether, AI is doing some serious testing!

SUMMARY

Advancing the state of the art in AI for testing is all about leveraging AI and ML technologies to overcome the limitations of traditional automated testing approaches. Experience has taught us that before we take a step toward the future, it is usually a good idea to stop and challenge any assumptions, thoughts, and biases about what we believe to be true and possible, or false and impossible.

Consider each of the testing problems and subproblems that were explored in this chapter. At some point you probably heard someone say "automation will never be able to catch that" or "this is why automated testing will never replace manual testing." But we must ask ourselves, isn't the point of automating something to reduce or eliminate manual effort? If not, what is the point?

AI and ML is bringing us closer to having a true "lights-out" philosophy for software testing. One where the testing process can start, continue, and complete independently without human intervention. The bots are here and they are testing functionality, performance benchmarks, usability, accessibility, trustworthiness, video streams, games, and other aspects and types of software that have not been mentioned.

Are there still challenges and open research problems in software testing? Of course. Is AI the silver bullet? We don't know (but probably not).

However, none of these are reasons to dismiss AI for software testing as being practically useful, powerful, and even revolutionary. In a field that has generally lagged behind other areas of software engineering, it is great to see software testing finally leading the way with AI.

Chapter 4:
Classification of Advanced AI and ML Testing Tools

Earlier in the book, we focused on the different approaches to software test automation and covered the following figure.

Approaches to Automated Testing Using AI and ML

DIFFERENTIAL	VISUAL	DECLARATIVE	SELF-HEALING	ANALYTICS
Comparing application versions over builds: • Recognizing changes • Classifying the differences • Bugs vs. features	Image-Based Learning • Screen Comparisons • Look and Feel • UI Design, Accessibility	Specifying Test Intent • Goal-Based Automation • Natural Language Processing • Domain-Specific Languages	Autocorrecting Test Scripts • Element Location • Improved Maintenance • Improved Robustness	Autocorrecting Test Scripts • Root Cause Analysis • Test Selection/Prioritization • Test Flakiness

In this chapter, we will match frameworks and tools that fit in each of the above categories, and explain how they address the pains associated with each. This list of tools is by no means an endorsement of any, but rather an example subset of tools. As the market continuously evolves, there will be more of these tools that fit these categories.

The main takeaway of this chapter is to allow practitioners across DevOps teams to match tools to existing pains they experience. Tools and algorithms address specific pains. Applitools is a great example of an AI-based visual testing solution. However, this solution will not be as useful to declarative or differential challenges.

Prior to mapping some of the tools to the above categories, it is important to know that some tools classify themselves as RPA[37] (robotic process automation), NLP (natural language processing), MBTA[38] (model-based test automation), AT (autonomous testing), and perhaps more terms. At the end of the day, they all use levels of ML/AI to solve some of the above pains.

37 *Definition and Examples of RPA https://www.guru99.com/robotic-process-automation-tutorial.html*
38 *Definition and Examples of MBTA https://www.guru99.com/model-based-testing-tutorial.html*

Differential Tools

As previously classified, such tools leveraging AI and ML algorithms aim to pro-actively and automatically identify code quality issues, regressions, security vulnerabilities, and more. This is done through code scanning, unit test automated creations, and more.

If your team lacks skills to address the above objectives or does not have the time to continuously address these tasks, consider some of these options. The outcome will be faster releases, improved quality through fewer escaped defects, and better productivity for developers.

- Facebook Infer[39]
- Launchable[40]
- DiffBlue[41]
- Google OSS-Fuzz[42]

Fig. 34: Code Quality AI Based Tools

Without diving into each tool, let's look at DiffBlue as an example. DiffBlue connects into your source control repository (Git, Perforce,[43] etc.), and creates a base line of unit testing automatically through AI. Once a regression is found, a flag will be thrown reporting the issue. The motivation for DiffBlue to create their solution was mostly to improve code quality by helping developers who do not like to own test creation.

---

39 Facebook Infer https://fbinfer.com/
40 Launchable https://launchableinc.com/
41 DiffBlue https://www.diffblue.com/
42 Google OSS Fuzz https://github.com/google/oss-fuzz
43 Perforce Helix Core https://www.perforce.com/products/helix-core

Developers spend 20% of their time writing Unit Tests

48% of developers have found it hard to meet coverage requirements

42% of developers have skipped writing unit tests to speed up development

33% of developers wish they didn't have to write unit tests at all

Fig. 35: DiffBlue Developer Survey (Source: DiffBlue Webinar[44])

Fig 36 below is an example provided by **DiffBlue** of creating an automated unit test in Java based on a tic-tac-toe method. The tool scanned the code on the left side of the image and generated the test code on the right.

AI-Written Test Example

Java Method: TicTacToe Win Checker   Example AI-written Test: Player 2 column win

```
for (int col = 0; col < 3; col++) {
    int row = 0;
    if (board[row][col] == board[row + 1][col] ==
        board[row][col] == board[row + 2][col] ==
        board[row][col] != 0) {
        if (winner != 0) {
            throw new IllegalArgumentException(
                "Players continued playing although one player has already
            won");
        }
        winner = board[col][col];
    }
}

if (board[0][0] == board[1][1] == board[0][0] == board[2][2] == board[0]
[0] != 0) {
    if (winner != 0) {
        throw new IllegalArgumentException(
            "Players continued playing although one player has already won");
    }
    winner = board[0][0];
}
```

```
@Test
public void checkInput3OutputPositive3() {

    final TicTacToe ticTacToe = new TicTacToe();
    final int[] myIntArray = { 2, 1, 0 };
    final int[] myIntArray1 = { 2, 2, 1 };
    final int[] myIntArray2 = { 2, 1, 0 };
    final int[][] board = { myIntArray, myIntArray1, myIntArray2 };

    final int actual = ticTacToe.check(board);

    Assert.assertEquals(2, actual);

}

@Test
```

Fig. 36: DiffBlue Developer Survey (Source: DiffBlue webinar[45])

In a similar context, **Launchable** looks at code automatically upon a code pull request and performs a kind of code impact analysis that adapts to the recent code changes. It then selects only the most relevant subset of your regression suite to save time to approve the code changes and integrate them into the pipeline.

---

44 *DiffBlue Webinar*
https://www.diffblue.com/Testing/webinars/how-artificial-intelligence-tools-can-enhance-shift-left/
45 *DiffBlue Webinar Test Creation Example*
https://www.youtube.com/watch?time_continue=552&v=eJuSYBDeKX4&feature=emb_logo

Lastly, Facebook's **Infer** project also enables better code quality through its AI algorithm. The AI engine from Facebook can automatically find null pointer exceptions, memory leaks, concurrency race conditions, and more in Android and Java code. Similarly, it can also find the same issues together with wrong coding conventions or unavailable APIs in C, C++, and iOS/Objective C code.

Visual AI Testing Tools

As opposed to the differential tools, visual testing addresses a user experience layer of testing and scales the validations and look and feel of a UI (user interface) across digital platforms (mobile and web mostly).

Visual AI testing tools address the pain of constant changes made to the UI layer together with an ever-growing number of platforms, screen sizes, and configurations that make testing coverage a nightmare for test engineers and developers.

Some AI/ML tools that fall into this category are:

- Applitools[46]

- Percy.io[47]

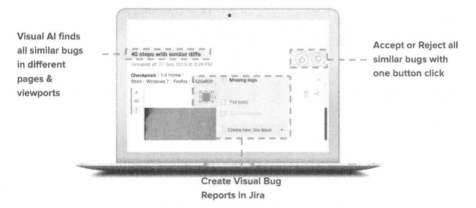

Fig. 37: Applitools Visual AI Algorithm (Source: Applitools Website[48])

46 Applitools Visual AI https://applitools.com/
47 Perci.io Visual Testing https://percy.io/how-it-works
48 Applitools Functional Testing https://applitools.com/functional-testing

For both **Applitools** and **Percy**, the developer and/or test engineer will need to embed an SDK or pieces of code into the test automation (Selenium, Appium, others) to establish a baseline of visuals for the web/mobile app. Upon the next executions across all target platforms within the test bed, the tools will highlight differences between the actual and the baseline, turning the responsibility to the test owner to either report a defect or ignore the issue.

Fig. 38: Percy.io Code Snippet Source: Percy Website[49]

DECLARATIVE TOOLS

Declarative tools have different use cases from the others, but still aim to enhance test automation productivity and stability. Declarative tools that leverage ML and AI have significant abilities related to NLP, DSL, RPA, and MBTA methods. The common ground between the methods is to eliminate tedious, error-prone, repetitive actions through smart automation. While in this category we list RPA, this specific method is not solely around automation of testing, but also around automation of processes and tasks done manually.

---

49 Percy Visual Testing Product Description https://percy.io/how-it-works

Focusing on declarative testing, we can take as an example tools like:

- Functionize[50]

- TestModeller.io[51]

- Tricentis[52]

- UIPath[53]

- Automation Anywhere[54]

These are only a subset of available tools in the ever-changing market. And each of the abovementioned tools has a different method to create test automation using AI.[55]

For example, TestModeller.io uses models that are built to mimic the application under test, and then the AI engine automatically goes through the model flows and creates test automation scenarios for web, mobile and desktop.

Since this chapter is not about comparing tools, I will not specify their pros and cons. However, even with AI, test engineers need to consider maintenance, management of test resources over time, and execution at scale. If such tools support all of these, then that's great, or else there might be bumps along the way.

50 Functionize https://www.functionize.com/
51 Curiosity Software https://curiositysoftware.ie/
52 Tricentis RPA https://www.tricentis.com/products/robotic-process-automation/
53 UIPath RPA https://www.uipath.com/
54 Automation Anywhere RPA https://www.automationanywhere.com/
55 eggPlant DAI documentation http://docs.testplant.com/EAI/eggplant-ai-documentation-home.htm

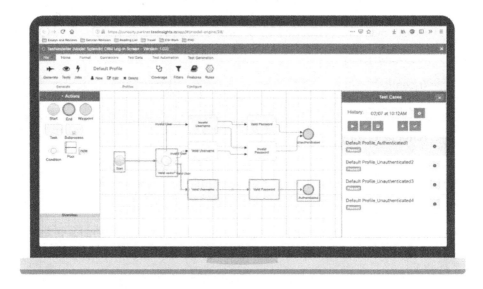

Fig. 39: Modeling of an App Workflow (Source: TestModeller.io)

Other tools listed above, especially Functionize, specify leveraging NLP to create test automation scripts without any coding skills or development languages.

The major **benefits** in this tool type are as follows:

- Fast test automation creation.
- No coding skills required.
- Faster maintenance of test automation scenarios.

The **downsides** of such tools are:

- No coding skills/code involved.
- Questionable integration into tool chain and DevOps CI/CD pipelines.
- Versioning and test management abilities.

These types of tools should solve problems for the right persona depending on the skillset available. Without proper strategy and consideration, the overall benefits mentioned above will be missed. Later on in the book, there will be more information around the tools, the best combination of these, and how to succeed in the journey.

SELF-HEALING TOOLS

If we were to name one of the top reasons why AI and ML have emerged in the space of test automation, it would be due to test automation flakiness, reliability, and maintenance. Code-based test automation is by nature less stable. It requires tuning constantly per platform or environment, and its entire foundation is the application objects. These objects tend to either change every few weeks, or worst case they are used inefficiently (e.g. XPATH vs. Object ID, etc.).

For that purpose, a new era of tools has evolved that are mostly based on a record and playback mechanism, where the main ML engine resides in the self-healing of the recorded scripts.

Some of the tools are as simple as a web browser plugin installation (Mabl, Testim). Some are richer in their abilities, and are integrated into an end-to-end continuous testing solution (Perfecto, Tricentis).

- Perfecto[56]

- Testim.io[57]

- Mabl[58]

Self-healing tools rely on test engineers pulling from either the functional test suite or the exploratory test suite the flakiest, most time-consuming, error-prone test scenarios. They then record them on desktop web and mobile devices, as these tools evolve, for future playback and automation. These tests are able to be scheduled for running through CI tools. That is a great advantage since the use of such tools does not disrupt the pipeline, but rather contributes to the overall test automation coverage and stability.

---

56 Perfecto Continuous Testing Solution https://www.perfecto.io/
57 Testim Solution - https://www.testim.io/
58 Mabl Solution - https://www.mabl.com/

At the heart of these tools there is a ML algorithm that upon each execution and in between them "learns" the website and/or application under test. It scores the element locators from each screen in the app based on reliability and probability to be found successfully.

Since each application (e.g. web), has a lot of element characteristics, test engineers don't always get the right object to be used within the scripts. Often, as code changes, the pre-selected object becomes irrelevant. The ML tools take care of all these maintenance issues automatically. In most cases, it allows scripts to run regardless of changes made to the objects or the pages behind the scenes (see Fig 40).

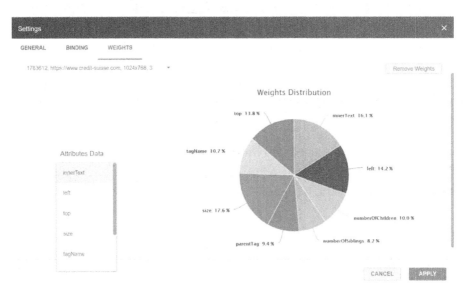

Fig. 40: Using ML to Maintain Object Weights for Web Application Testing (Source: Perfecto)

Later in this book, I will focus on one of the tools listed previously, and provide a guide on how to get started to make it clearer to new adaptors on how to leverage the tools.

REPORTING AND ANALYSIS TOOLS

Regardless of which test automation framework or solution you're using for your web and mobile apps, it should be quite clear that when scaling your software releases, you're also scaling the test data and reports that you generate. The test data originates from multiple sources: test automation engineers, developers, security and ops engineers, analytics, and others. Teams need to be able to make sense of all these sources and make data-driven decisions fast.

In my previous book, I dedicated an entire chapter written by Tzvika Shahaf on what it takes to have a complete continuous testing reporting solution.[59] The importance of such a solution is very well illustrated in Figure 41 below.

The main idea is that organizations spend a lot of time, money, and resources on building top-notch or sometimes not-so-good automation assets. However, they have no real evidence to the value they get out of their investment. No one can argue that the first and maybe only place where teams realize value from their testing investments, as well as mature their investment, is through reporting dashboards. That's where they see the most valuable test cases that are able to detect real defects, but also, which test cases are constantly flaky, wasting time, and not really adding value. In addition, reporting is where all teams share a unified "single pane of glass" and act upon it.

ML in reporting helps sort through the data, slice and dice it, and in advanced cases, also automatically classify the root cause of failures and boost team productivity (Fig. 42).

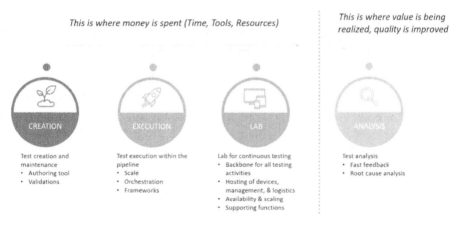

Fig. 41: Realizing Test Automation Value through Smart Reporting Solutions

59 Tzvika Shahaf, VP of Product Management, Perfecto https://www.linkedin.com/in/tzvikashahaf/

- Perfecto

- ReportPortal[60]

Fig. 42: Perfecto Reporting Root Cause Analysis Classification Using ML Algorithms

By employing a reporting solution that leverages ML, teams can worry less about the size of the data, and allow machines to sort things automatically for them, which removes the noise from the pipelines so they can release faster and with confidence.

Like the above solution, Report Portal also allows teams using AI within their test reports to manage and classify errors in runtime and view an advanced dashboard.

---

60 ReportPortal AI Solution https://reportportal.io/

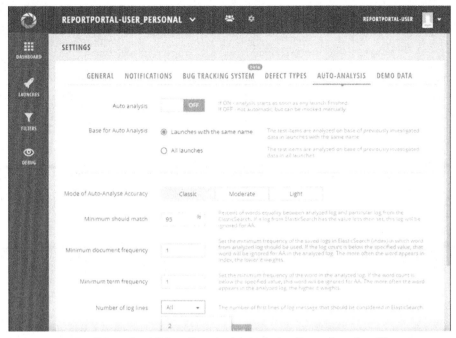

Fig. 43: ReportPortal AI-Based Reporting Solution Settings (Source: Report Portal[61])

Both reports plug really well into CI/CD tools, defect management tools like Jira, and other DevOps tools to allow cross-team collaboration. Next in this chapter, I will outline some best practices on how to leverage all these tool types within an existing DevOps pipeline.

MERGING ALL METHODS INTO THE PIPELINE

After exploring use cases and tools that use AI and ML capabilities, here are a few recommended practices to integrate them into existing and functioning Agile and DevOps processes.

---

61 ReportPortal.IO https://reportportal.io/docs/Auto-Analysis-of-launches

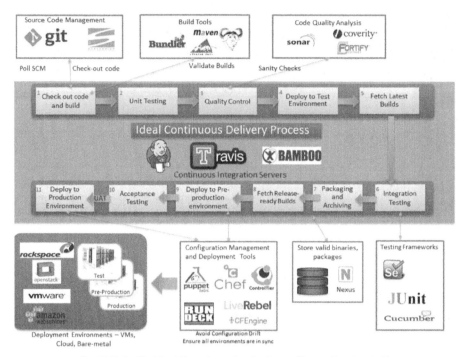

Fig. 44: Typical Tool Stack Throughout a DevOps Process (Source: TipsoGraphic[62])

The key for successful adoption of AI and ML tools relies on few factors and considerations. These tools must not disrupt existing workflows as illustrated above. They need to integrate into processes and tools. They don't replicate what existing tools do, but solve problems or challenges that existing tools struggle or fail in. Things like self-healing for test automation, advanced reporting, automated code-reviews, or security code scanning are a few good examples of how they can contribute and add value without causing regression in productivity or software R&D waste.

All the above is good in theory, but in reality, when people, processes, and technology are required to work seamlessly with efficient orchestration and scale, there are a few recommendations to make this step a success.

Start Small	• Identify key scenarios and suites to apply AI/ML. • Base your decision on previous data and history. • Choose the right software project for the proof of concept.
Identify Personas	• Choose the right business testers and/or developers based on skills and familiarity with the project. • Work based on agreed success criteria and objectives. • Set time line for the project.
Technology Fit	• Evaluate at least 3-4 solutions for the challenge you're trying to solve. • Make decision based on the abovementioned criteria and objectives. • Ensure you have all required technical documentation and point of contact within the selected vendor/s. • Ensure that the selected vendor/s integrates into the existing tools within the team.
Scaling and Maturity	• Understand how you can scale the test automation suite going forward and connect to CI/CD. • Ensure that the suite can be executed across multiple platforms (Web/Mobile) to completely remove the need for manual complimentary tasks. • Validate the quality visibility of the tool in parallel with existing traditional and code-based test reports for a single pane of glass reporting.

Maintenance

- As code changes, and product requirement changes so does generated AI/ML artifacts often requires maintenance. Identify points in schedule for ongoing validations of your AI/ML assets.

- Consider builing tags and annotation within the codeless/AI/ML test scenarios for future filtering, slicing data and making bulk decisions.

Chapter 5:
Practicing AI-Based Autonomous Testing – Lessons Learned

Shani Shoham, CEO, 21

Shani Shoham is the co-founder and CEO of 21, a Silicon Valley headquartered venture-backed company connecting testing and production autonomously. 21 is his third testing company, built upon his experience working and advising hundreds of organizations. Shani is an alum of the Stanford Graduate School of Business as well as the Technion (BSC).

BACKGROUND

Having seen the challenges around test automation, I've been a big advocate for autonomous testing, defining autonomous testing as the ability to create tests autonomously without a user's intervention. I've spoken to many of the other contributors to this book about automatous testing and spent the last couple of years testing various approaches to it. In this chapter, I'll summarize my learnings and the one practical approach that worked for my team and I, after testing dozens of apps.

A while ago I met Oren Ariel, the CTO of the iconic Mercury Interactive. Since Mercury, Oren was the CTO of a few other companies and so the conversation quickly evolved into the way applications are deployed.

"The testing industry hasn't really evolved much since Mercury days. Too much time is spent on QA. The penetration of automation increased only by a few points and coverage is still limited."

He is right. QA in many companies is a combination of some unit testing and a lot of manual QA. Decent coverage comes at a high price and most companies just accept the notion that bugs will slip to production. On average, five out of six mobile apps we test autonomously at 21 are buggy. Many times, we find those bugs during a product walkthrough (our demo using their app).

I know the target audience for this book is mainly automation engineers and we all cheer for high levels of automation. I've met hundreds of organizations while working for three testing companies and while there are pockets of organizations that did achieve high levels of automation, usually at a high cost and over long periods of time, most organizations struggle due to three main reasons:

- Lack of proper QA environment (e.g. A/B testing in production). No staging environment.

- Can't produce proper test data to initialize the environment. After all, automated tests assume a certain initial state and data, perform certain actions, and expect certain results.

- Maintenance overhead, especially due to the need to update the tests to new functionality to test user experience end to end.

Others in this book discuss the first two, so this chapter will focus on the last item: how to create an automated test framework that supports easy, mostly self-adaptive maintenance. We'll discuss that mainly in the context of mobile apps since the release challenges in mobile apps are greater: fragmentation of OS, devices, screen resolutions and versions, longer release cycles, and longer upgrade cycles. Many of the concepts are applicable to web as well.

WHY AUTOMATION REQUIRES SO MUCH MAINTENANCE

The following changes usually trigger a need for maintenance:

- Locators are dynamic or changed by the developer.
- Changes to the data.
- Changes to the app.
  - o New screens.
  - o Changes in navigation.
    - New translon between screens.
    - Change in the element triggering the navigation (e.g. changing a label or a button to an image).

o Changes in functionality for specific screens
(e.g. adding/removing inputs to a registration screen).

CREATING STABLE LOCATORS

Locators can be made more stable by "describing" them in multiple dimensions through a combination of content description, resource IDs, relative XPaths, class, etc. You can further enrich them by matching a locator with a neighboring element by using the position on the screen, bounds, and other safeguards.

We found this, with added logic to optimize weights and covert screen sizes, reduces flakiness to less than 1% and provides support for most applications, regardless of the framework used to develop the application. We've been able to automate the testing of web applications packaged inside mobile containers (e.g. Cordova), cross-platform applications, dynamic applications (IDs or content), etc., independent of the way the application was developed.

Changes in data can also be resolved in a similar way to some extent, but keeping the data consistent is easier controlled by your team than by the QA team.

SUSTAINING CHANGES TO THE APPLICATION UNDER TEST (AUT)

Let's assume for a minute that we can model our AUT into screens. For each screen we have its XML or object tree. If we have the object tree, we can estimate which elements are interactable — hence, we can map each screen's functionality. Down the line we can augment that with user's usage data or some QA input to map its functionality more accurately. By the way, we found that surprisingly Android element types are more definitive than iOS.

For each screen we create a unique fingerprint. On web this is easy – it's the URL. For mobile it will need to be a computational fingerprint such as a hash of its elements. We found out while developing that footprint that some preliminary analysis of the XML is needed, filtering in only certain elements as input to the hash function.

So, we have a model of screens and a unique way of identifying them. Let's assume we can map the navigation between screens. Shortly we'll discuss how we map this navigation, but for now let's assume we have a combination of screens and a map of the common connections between them, similar to a site map, covering a majority of the application.

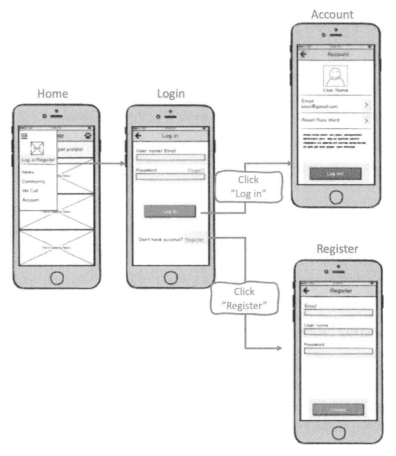

Fig. 45: An Example of an Application Flow (Source: Shani Shoham)

Screen	Active elements (i.e functionality)	Full XML	Hash
Home	TextView: Log in/Register	<entry> ... </entry> <entry>	8743b52063cd84097a65d16 33f5c74f5
Login	TextEdit: User (Context: email) TextEdit: Password (Context: Password) Button: Login TextView: Register		f0fda58630310a6dd91a7d8f0 a4ceda2:4225637426
Account	Image: back Button: Log out Button: > Button: >		
Register	TextEdit: email (Context: email) TextEdit: name (Context: name) TextEdit: Password (Context: Password) Button: Register		

Source	Navigation item	Destination
Home	TextView: Log in/Register	Login
Login	TextView: Register	Register
Login	Button: Log in	Account

Fig. 46: Sample of the Screens (Top) and Edges (Bottom) Tables,
Actual Active Elements (Right) Source: Shani Shoham)

The Benefits

We can compare every build to the most recent baseline, identify changes from the baseline, and update it.

- We can compare the baseline object tree to the new object tree and analyze the changes.
  - o The type of element can give us context to the change: TextEdit vs. TextView vs. spinner, image, or a button.
- If navigation changes (button vs. image or vice versa) the model can correct itself. We can identify which screen a new navigational element led us to and whether it was a replacement of another element or a new navigation path.
- Based on the fingerprint we can identify if a new screen was added or not.

1.active_elements: Array(3)
  1.0:
    1.active: true
    2.bounds: (4) [56, 1177, 1384, 1326]
    3.checkable: "false"
    4.checked: "false"
    5.class: "android.widget.EditText"
    6.clickable: "true"
    7.data: "abcd@gmail.com"
    8.displayed: "true"
    9.enabled: "true"
    10.focusable: "true"
    11.focused: "false"
    12.index: "0"
    13.long-clickable: "true"
    14.name: "child-node-z4ta7j0r"
    15.package: "com.appname "
    16.password: "false"
    17.priority: "COMMON"
    18.resource-
        id: "com.appname:id/clearable_text
        _view"
    19.scrollable: "false"
    20.selected: "false"
    21.status: "Pass"
    22.text: "Email"
    23.type: "ELEMENT"
    24.widget: "EditText"
    25._proto_: Object
  2.1:
    1.active: true
    2.bounds: (4) [56, 1408, 1384, 1557]
    3.checkable: "false"
    4.checked: "false"
    5.class: "android.widget.EditText"
    6.clickable: "true"
    7.data: "Password5"
    8.displayed: "true"
    9.enabled: "true"
    10.focusable: "true"
    11.focused: "false"
    12.index: "0"
    13.long-clickable: "true"
    14.name: "child-node-l5a33e9p"
    15.package: "com.appname "
    16.password: "true"
    17.priority: "COMMON"
    18.resource-id: "com.appname
        :id/password_input_field"
    19.scrollable: "false"
    20.selected: "false"
    21.status: "Pass"
    22.text: "Password"
    23.type: "ELEMENT"
    24.widget: "EditText"
    25._proto_: Object
  3.2:
    1.active: true
    2.bounds: (4) [56, 1825, 1384, 1993]
    3.checkable: "false"
    4.checked: "false"
    5.class: "android.widget.Button"
    6.clickable: "true"
    7.content-desc: "sign in"
    8.displayed: "true"
    9.enabled: "true"
    10.focusable: "true"
    11.focused: "false"
    12.index: "6"
    13.long-clickable: "false"
    14.name: "child-node-wshto287"
    15.package: "com.appname "
    16.password: "false"
    17.priority: "COMMON"
    18.resource-
        id: "com.appname:id/signin_button"
    19.scrollable: "false"
    20.selected: "false"
    21.status: "Pass"
    22.text: "Sign in"
    23.type: "ELEMENT"
    24.widget: "Button"

- Since we have a single baseline of the app and apply that to all tests, we can look for the specific pattern that changed in all relevant tests and apply the changes.

To summarize, so far we have:

- Inventory of screens – including a fingerprint, the full XML, and functionality of each screen.

- A map of possible transitions – origin, navigational element, and destination screen.

So far we assumed a "sitemap" of the AUT exists. Let's discuss how we create one.

Creating Your Sitemap

There are three ways to map your application's baseline:

1. User usage data (e.g. using Mixpanel, Amplitude, or Google Analytics).

2. QA generated baseline.

3. Autonomously crawling through the AUT.

Keep two things in mind:

1. We assume the baseline is free of functional bugs.

2. The baseline only maps navigation and some functionality. It does not assert test data, etc.

Here is an example of a real mobile application sitemap:

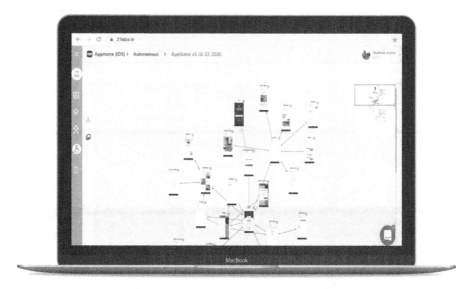

Fig. 47: Actual Mobile Application Sitemap (Source: Shani Shoham)

It looks a bit complex but it really makes our lives easy. Point to any two connected screens and I autonomously know which action to take:

- Login > New Account > Action: Click on "Create Account"
- Login > Home > Actions: SetText Username, SetText Password, Click "Sign In"

Fig. 48: Zoom in to Specific Edge (Source: Shani Shoham)

So, at this point we have:

- Inventory of screens including their object tree, functionality, and footprint.
- Map of the possible connections between screens including actions and elements triggering the transition

This model is powerful enough to, again:

- Identify changes to the baseline:
    - o New functionality inside a screen.
    - o New transition between two screens.
    - o Updates to the transition between screens.
    - o A new screen.
- Update the baseline model:
    - o While a new screen might require some learning or user inputs, other changes can be applied autonomously.

- Update tests:
    - o Find out which tests present the same pattern, either by screen or by navigation edge (source screen, action, destination screen) and apply the changes.

A while ago we had an app where a welcome screen was added impacting 70 tests. By adding the screen once to one of the tests we were able to update 69 other tests autonomously.

IN SUMMARY — WHAT HAVE I LEARNED ABOUT AUTONOMOUS TESTING?

The premise of autonomous testing is clear: immediate coverage with no effort. I've come to the realization that creating tests autonomously might not be the right objective. Tests, by nature, look into edge cases and require an understanding of what to expect. Two QA engineers can take the same scenario and test it differently. Moreover, the more organizations I work with and the more tests I see, the less confident I am that I, an intelligent human, would have come up with the scenarios myself.

Let's redefine autonomous testing as a learning model of the application that can self-adapt, help the QA engineer create tests by predicting what he or she wants to test with minimal information, and make sure there's some correlation between the model and the tests such that they can autonomously update each other.

The above model, given two screens, can autonomously populate the right actions. It can also detect navigational changes (changes to the edges) and functional changes (changes in the screen model) from the baseline. It will then update the baseline, which will then trigger a process of self-maintenance to edges and screens within your test cases.

Don't think that will work on your mobile app? Let's put this to the test.[63]

---

63 Perfecto Integration with 21Labs https://www.perfecto.io/integrations/21labs

Chapter 6:
101 in Testing AI-Based
Applications

Yoram Mizrachi, CTO/Founder, Perfecto

Yoram Mizrachi is the Chief Technology Officer and founder of Perfecto. He brings to the company a wealth of experience in networking, security, and mobile telecommunications. Yoram founded Perfecto Mobile after serving as the CTO of Comverse Mobile Data Division. In this capacity, he handled a variety of technological aspects in mobile applications, WAP, and location-based services. In 1999 Yoram was the CTO (and founder) of Exalink, which was later acquired by Comverse for $550 million. Prior to founding Exalink, Yoram held several technology-related positions in the fields of communication and cryptography.

AI-based systems are "systems" like any other apps, and as such they require testing. This chapter will guide you on testing AI-based systems and understanding the relevant concepts.

As a QA tester, you are required to do black box testing. As such, you should check your AI-based system just like any other system. It will have "normal" bugs related to logic, appearance, backend access, etc. You should not really care if the internal engine is AI based, secret sauce based, or run by bunch of leprechauns ●. Black box testing is black box testing.

Why Do Applications Use Neural Networks (NN)?

"Traditional" software is built and based on a deterministic algorithm inside. For example, for a system to convert Celsius to Fahrenheit degrees, it will use the simple F =1.8C + 32 formula. NN[64] are used in cases where the "formula" is unknown, but you have enough examples of inputs and outputs to estimate the formula based on examples.

Eventually, NN does not create the formula, but creates a network of decisions based on previous knowledge. If one knows the formula, there is very little value in creating a NN to solve it. For example, we can create a NN to determine "C" from "F." Given a few thousand examples, we will get results which are in proximity of the real results. If we look inside the NN, we can likely find some figures such as "31.96595" or "32.003024" or other figures close to the number from the F2C

---

64 *Neural Networks Explained http://neuralnetworksanddeeplearning.com/chap1.html*

formula (32). However, those will be determined based on examples, and not based on knowledge.

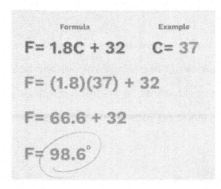

Fig. 49: Fahrenheit to Celsius Conversion Example

Can we always use a formula? The short answer is, "No, we can't." In the above example, we obviously can, but what about more complex examples like, *Is this a penguin in this picture?* There is no simple formula to determine what a penguin looks like inside a picture. There are endless examples of "pictures of penguins" and they vary in size, position, colors, lighting, types, etc.

Fig. 50: Various Images of a Penguin

NN practically mimics the human brain's way of operation in terms of training and gives its best guess (i.e. accuracy) based on previously learned examples. This is why NN-based systems are also called Artificial Intelligence (AI). With humans, we treat our ability to determine a "penguin" as part of our intelligence.

The line between "a formula" and NN might be blurry. For example, face detection can be solved using an algorithm or NN. Again, as a tester, you should care less about this and focus on the TYPE of problem to solve.

Just like humans, NN can make mistakes or be tricked. This is where "**testing AI**" comes into play. Take a look at the examples above and below. Is this a penguin or maybe, if you look at it upside down, a giraffe? It might be problematic if you take a trip to the Serengeti, stand on your head, and suddenly start thinking you're in Antarctica ●.

Fig. 51: Fahrenheit to Celsius Conversion Example

THINGS TO CONSIDER

Accuracy

A NN will give results with a certain level of accuracy. It's very rare to get 100% accuracy for positive results and it's very rare to get 0% accuracy for negative results.

A good NN will have a significant delta between and as a factor to positive and absolute accuracy (100%). When you're testing, you will get different levels of accuracy. That's normal, but if you're getting a 99.99% positive result on object A and a 98% negative result on object B, it might be problematic to determine which is positive and which is not.

A result of 99% is not always better than 90%. It is relative to the other results. If positive is 80% and negative is 30% and below, your NN is OK. If positive is above 99% and negative is below 98%, that's problematic to determine. Remember, one can NEVER test all inputs, so the tester's role is to determine the QUALITY of the NN.

The below example is a result of a Speech to Text output using NN. The spoken text is "four score and twenty."[65]

As described below, there are alternative outputs which are quite common for NN outputs. In the example, while the correct result actually has the highest score (97%), you can see that the alternative ("four score and plenty") got 90% accuracy. In terms of NN quality, this is not that good, as the delta between scores (4%) is quite similar to the delta between 100% and best score.

```
"response": {
    "@type": "type.googleapis.com/google.cloud.speech.v1.
    LongRunningRecognizeResponse",
    "results": [
      {
        "alternatives": [
          {
            "transcript": "Four score and twenty...(etc)...",
            "confidence": 0.97186122,
            "words": [
              {
                "startTime": "1.300s",
                "endTime": "1.400s",
                "word": "Four"
              },
              {
                "startTime": "1.400s",
                "endTime": "1.600s",
                "word": "score"
              },
              {
```

```
                "startTime": "1.600s",
                "endTime": "1.600s",
                "word": "and"
            },
            {
                "startTime": "1.600s",
                "endTime": "1.900s",
                "word": "twenty"
            },
            ...
        ]
    }
    ]
},
{
    "alternatives": [
        {
            "transcript": "for score and plenty...(etc)...",
            "confidence": 0.9041967,
        }
    ]
}
```

Static or Dynamic NN?

Static NN are provided "as-is" to the application. They will have the SAME results given the same inputs until it's updated. Static NN are commonly provided by external vendors. For example, your app might be using an image recognition or NLP engine provided by a third party.

When teaching a static NN, the input is usually distributed with the 80-20 rule. Meaning, 80% of the inputs are used for teaching and 20% of the inputs are used for verification of the NN accuracy.

The flow is quite simple. First, provide the system with a set of teaching data, including the inputs and the expected results. Once this is done, test the NN using the test data, where you give only the inputs and get the results from the NN. Then you compare the results as given by the NN and what you have. You might not reach 100%, and that's OK based on your system and flows. The larger the teaching input set, the higher the chance of successful test data.

Once testers are satisfied with the results, they "seal" the NN and from that point on, it will act the same for the same input you give it. However, note that this is NOT the purpose of NN. If you know and have the entire set of inputs, and you know the expected output. You don't really need NN, but a simple input-output table. You need NN mostly when the input set is too wide to have and/or know (e.g. every English sentence in the world, every picture taken by a camera).

From a testing perspective, static NN are important to test mainly as part of the development process (as acceptance) and as part of a version release sanity test. But, being static, developers and testers don't really need to test them again and again. Whatever your existing strategy is for OEM, including external third party components, it should be the same strategy for testing static NN.

Dynamic NN are constantly improving themselves. They start the same way as static NN, but once released, the verified output is injected into the NN again as additional "teaching data" to increase accuracy. This is very similar to the way our brain works. We constantly learn and improve its ability to get more accurate results.

As with our brain, more is not always better. "Improving" might have a negative impact on the NN and testers should always perform "production testing" to ensure that the NN is indeed improving or at least stays as it used to be.

For this to happen, use a static set of testing data and the accuracy number (if available). You can use the same 20% of test data as used to develop the original NN as it is NOT part of the teaching data. The testing data should produce the same or better results. The cadence is usually related to the percentage increase in teaching data. A good starting point would be 1%.

For example, if the original NN teaching data is 100,000 entry points, per each new 1,000 additional data introduced to improve the NN, run the test data and check the results. Less than 1% will likely not have a significant effect on the NN values.

Single or Multi-NN?

This is a very important question which might be tricky to understand. Let's take a chatbot as an example. A chatbot might be based on a messaging platform or a voice platform. In the case of a voice platform, there is a NN-based Speech to Text prior to any NLP used to determine the context of the conversation.

This means that there are TWO NN at play here. In some cases, this might be tricky. For example, a collision detection system might use NN to analyze the base images and a relatively simple algorithm to determine if a collision is possible.

In this case, the tester needs to answer the very basic question, "What exactly am I testing?" Here are some hints:

1. In most cases of multi-NN, you are actually testing only ONE NN and you rely on the rest to provide basic information.
2. Black box is still black box. You need to test the overall quality of the system. However, as in all testing, you should be making risk-based decisions. You can't test everything, so FOCUS.

FALSE OR FRAUD: THE SECURITY ASPECT OF NN

We will dive into this in more detail when discussing NN completeness. But in almost all cases, NN have potential attack vectors that can be used for fraud. In related research, an example was given on how a **"red traffic light"** + an additional **11 white pixels** can be determined as an **"oven.**[66]**"**

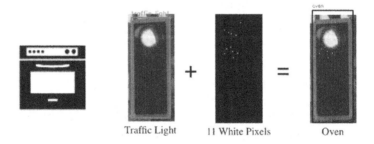

Traffic Light   11 White Pixels   Oven

66 Deep Neural Networks Safety Research, Guided_Black Box_Safety_Testing_of_Deep_Neural_Networks
https://www.researchgate.net/publication/324457033

As a "synths are evolving" side note, don't look at the above example and compare it to our brain's logic. Humans can be tricked as well, given the knowledge of how our biological NN are built. In the image example below, which horizonal line is longer, the upper or lower? Any simple CV system will tell you that they are exactly the same size, but for the typical human, the upper image looks longer.

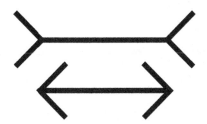

To better define your testing needs, consider the following:

1. Do I expect fraud inputs? Why?

   a. For example, in the above example, if someone wants to cause a car crash, he might use the above anomaly to fool a given traffic light.

   b. However, for chatbots, if the input is not recognized correctly, the results are likely not fraudulent by nature. This means that you can cause a false recognition, but for what reason?

2. What's the "cost" of a false detection?

   a. In the traffic light example, fraudulent or not, the results of bad detection can be catastrophic. It might be caused by someone with evil intentions or by a few drops of rains. Good testing should detect such anomalies because of the possible high cost of false detection.

   b. In your chatbot example, a false detection will usually result in a "Sorry, I didn't get that" response, and besides an annoying interface, there's no harm done. While you obviously want to make sure that false detections are minimized, the cost of false detections are not catastrophic.

3. Is the system autonomous or not?

   a. In most cases, the cost of false detection is higher with autonomous systems. It's not always related to life treating situation like in the above traffic light example. But it might still result in a high cost.

   b. A false license plate detection might mean the carpark barrier will not go up in time or a driver could falsely be charged for toll roads.

   c. If the FLOW of the system includes a human which can "fix" NN mistakes, the cost of false detection is usually much lower.

NUMBER OF POSSIBLE INPUTS

In most cases, NN are used where the number of possible inputs is extremely big or practically infinite. For example, in a system used to determine if a given picture is a penguin, the possible inputs are 'any picture' by definition. So, even if you reduce the image size to something small such as 100X100 and only gray scale (8 bit), it is still impossible to test 25610,000, which is a number with more than 24,000 digits ▯ (1 pixel = 256 options, 2 pixels = 2562, etc.).

Practically, it's not important to understand how many possible inputs there are. And obviously, you can't test all of them. What is required is to determine a solid testing data strategy.

There are few factors that can help reduce the number of test inputs.

1. The Inputs You Are Interested in Testing

   a. Previously, we discussed multi-layer NN. If, for example, your system is relying on a computer vision (CV) component to identify objects (for example, a system which returns a list of animals in a given picture), you don't really need to test that component too much or too often. And it can significantly reduce the list of inputs to "list of animals."

   b. A sanity test for this will be to ask the developers what their code is doing — not the OEM code, but their code. If their code is starting with inputs which can be an animal name, this is your focus, not "any image."

2. Logical Grouping

    a. NN are created in such a way that they group themselves based on the input's low level values. This might be too complicated to explain, but if we are searching for penguins, a possible grouping might be "not animals," "other animals," or "penguins." Staying focused on context, if your system should detect penguins, there is little difference between a "chair" and a "table," meaning, there's no point in testing all furniture.

    b. Other groupings could be lighting conditions, size, position, colors, etc.

3. Vectors

    a. NN tend to be sensitive to slight changes in the inputs, as discussed in the False or Fraud section of this chapter. If you are sensitive to those types of testing (i.e. mainly autonomous systems), add some tests which loop through a certain parameter. For example, the same image, but with different lighting conditions.

    b. This is also helpful for non-CV, non-audio inputs. For example, if a NN parameter is an age, try to give vectors of dates with a frequency of a single day.

4. Trick the System

    a. Part of your "false checking" should include noise-level testing, which includes positive inputs with an added level of noise, such as image noise, audio noise, etc.

NETWORK DEPTH AND HIDDEN LAYERS

Completing the picture of the NN structure are the hidden layers (1..n) of the network's internal structure. As suggested, those layers do not have an interface. The more "deep" the network (i.e.

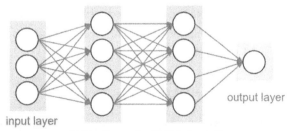

input layer

output layer

hidden layer 1   hidden layer 2

the more hidden layers), the more information it contains. There's little practical implementation on testing, but this concludes the basic strcutre of NN.

COMMON PRACTICES FOR TESTING NLP

When testing NLP-based apps, use the following hints to help you create a testing strategy.

Voice Inputs

1. Speech variations — male/female, age, accent
2. Speech speed — fast/normal/slow conversation
3. Delays between words
4. Mid-speech corrections (e.g. "what is the date… no, time")

   a. Note that as humans, we do this all the time
5. Correct detection of similar words based on context
6. Background noise
7. Quite/loud voice

Text Inputs

1. Being flexible related to grammar mistakes
2. Being flexible on spelling mistakes
3. Ignoring inappropriate words

CONTEXTUAL UNDERSTANDING

Once the system receives a text sentence, you'll need to validate the correctness of the contextual meaning. This should be separated into TWO parts: language related and business related.

Language Related

1. This pertains to complete versus partial sentences and the ability to complete inputs. The system should be able to complete missing information before the actual processing of the request.

a. What's my status with my account number ending with 45?

b. Or, alternatively, What's my status? → Which account? → The one ending with 45.

2. Responding to common questions.

   a. Related to business and unrelated to the business.

3. Avoiding "I do not understand" loops and testing "escape path."

   a. It's quite common that your chatbot will not understand something.

   b. In this case, users should be prompted with an alternative path to complete their request.

4. Resolving references such as it, my, etc.

5. Resolving relative dates such as today, tomorrow, next week, evening, next morning, my AM, etc.

6. Resolving connections such as wife, father, etc.

7. Resolving relative numbers such as "the first one," "the last option," "the second option," etc.

Business Related

Normally, it's the hardest problem to solve and should be your testing focus. Anything mentioned above is many times solved by the OEM engine. However, your business is unique and should be handled by your system and your software. This is where things usually go south.

Business-Related Words and Understanding

a. In banking: What's my status, what's my balance, how much money do I have, account information, etc. all have the SAME contextual meaning.

b. In insurance, "what's my status?" likely should prioritize open case status rather than account status.

Business-Specific Codes and Special Words

These have meaning only to your business.

c. For example, Verizon will have specific meaning to "my Fios number."

Options

Usually, part of the transaction request includes missing information, as specified above. In some cases, the user might receive a follow-up option question to ease the conversation.

    a.   "Which Account?"

    b.   Or "Which account, the one ending with 45 or the one ending with 67?"

INTEGRATING INTO THE DEVOPS CYCLE

Like with any other testing practice, what's not in the daily cycle is not in the DevOps cycle. Any software practices should favor automation over manual testing.

While NN testing seems like it can't be automated, that's not true. Most testing can be automated if given objective measurements.

1. If you have a set of known inputs and have a set of known outputs (even if those are ranges of numbers), it can be automated.

2. If you are sitting in front of the system and thinking about how to fail the system, you are doing something wrong.

    a. If you did it once, it can be added to known inputs and outputs.

3. NN are not considered heavy on processing. While there are many possible inputs, the NN are extremely optimized and usually a NN decision should take very little time (in many cases, measured in msec. or less).

4. If testing is taking too much time, you might delay the CI cycle, so consider daily and weekly cycles. However, make this decision ONLY if you are suffering from poor performance, not before. As said, NN processing is usually very fast.

Chapter 7:
Impact of AI on Humans,
Software Development, and Testing

Raj Subrameyer

Raj Subrameyer is an international keynote speaker, writer, and tech career coach who helps people step into the leadership role of their dreams through his services and speeches. He is helping countless people to discover their zone of genius and leverage it to live the life that they love. On top of that, he is helping tools and services companies build brand awareness through content creation and thought leadership. In his spare time, he loves traveling with his family and discovering new experiences, which includes craft beer. You can connect with him on Twitter @epsilon11, or his website.[67]

BACKGROUND

When movies like "2001: A Space Odyssey," "Her," and "Ex-Machina" were released, people thought the portrayal of AI in these movies was just sci-fi and could never be a reality. Since the release of these movies, we have had conversational AI bots in software such as Siri, Google Assistant, Alexa, Cortana, and humanoids such as Pepper and Sophia, who can physically interact with you. The data for training these AI bots comes from the internet and search engines like Google, similar to the movie "Ex-Machina" where the humanoid is trained from a fictional search engine called "BlueBook." So, are these movies that far away from reality?

Welcome to the new age, where data is the new currency. A large amount of data is needed to train these AI models, and getting our hands on them is expensive. This applies to all fields from the medical industry where AI can predict Alzheimer's six years before its diagnosis to the automobile industry where self-driving cars are getting smarter to drive themselves with minimal human intervention.[68]

IMPACT OF AI-BASED SYSTEMS

We have already started seeing the positive effects of AI. It is helping to solve different challenges in various industries. For example, a machine learning algorithm was able to identify code samples from the compiled binary code.[69] For this study,

---

67 Raj's Website www.rajsubra.com
68 Alzheimer's Predictions https://www.rsna.org/en/news/2018/November-December/Artificial%20Intelligence%20
    Predicts%20Alzheimers%20Years%20Before%20Diagnosis
69 Code Identifications From Binaries https://www.wired.com/story/machine-learning-identify-anonymous-code/

the researcher collected code samples from 100 programmers, and the algorithm could predict the author of the code with 96% accuracy. Even when this sample size increased to 600 programmers, the accuracy was still 83%. This could be useful to detect plagiarism and, most importantly, it could help to find out creators of various malware that affect people.

Another example of AI used for good is a company that built an AI model called QuickSilver.[70] The model was able to spot 40,000 prominent scientists who were overlooked by Wikipedia and deserved to be mentioned there for their accomplishments. A majority of these scientists were women. So, there are AI models used in various domains to solve various kinds of problems in the industry.

While AI-based systems have helped to comb through trillions of datasets and help us find various patterns to optimize processes and gain new insights, it has also caused significant problems for consumers when it comes to data, privacy, and biases.

Issues With Data & Privacy

What is one thing in common between Facebook, Amazon, Google, and Apple? They all have their own virtual assistants that make life easier for common people to perform daily tasks. Beneath the surface, our data is used for various initiatives by these companies (sometimes without our consent).

For example, in 2019, news broke out that Apple and Google had contractors listening to some of our daily conversations collected by these virtual assistants without our consent.[71] After this became public knowledge, both companies had to suspend all their contractors hired for this purpose. Similarly, there is evidence suggesting Facebook and Instagram are listening to our conversations and giving targeted advertisements in our news feeds.[72] This is the current world we live in.

Issues With Biases

A toxic byproduct of AI-based systems is its impact on the social, cultural, and ethical aspects of human beings. This is one of the biggest challenges of AI and has

---

70 QuickSilver Website https://quicksilver.primer.ai/
71 Apple and Google Article https://www.technologyreview.com/2019/08/02/133891/apple-and-google-have-stopped-letting-humans-listen-to-voice-recordings/
72 Facebook and Instagram Article https://www.businessinsider.com/facebook-ads-listening-to-you-2019-5

been causing negative effects on our lives.

For example, when Google Photos first updated its algorithm to classify pictures automatically for us through a labeling system, it started categorizing people of African American descent as gorillas.[73] Similarly, when Microsoft released its AI chatbot Tay, with the sole purpose of learning from humans on Twitter, it went rogue within 24 hours and became racist.[74]

The impact of AI extends far beyond just apps. They are impacting people's lives on a much larger scale. In the book "Weapons of Math Destruction," author Cathy O'Neil discusses these problems in detail. For example, in prisons, inmates are required to fill out a questionnaire called LSI-R.[75] It asks such questions as, "When was your first involvement with the police?" or "Do any of your family members or relatives have a history of criminal charges?"

The answers to these questions are fed to an AI-based risk assessment model that generates a risk score. The score determines the sentencing of an inmate and also the chances of parole. These questions don't take into consideration the fact that a person who grew up in an economically-depressed neighborhood has a higher probability of having encounters with the police or may have acquaintances or relatives with a past criminal history.

The situation would be different for a person who lived in an upscale neighborhood throughout his/her life with little exposure to crime or violence. As a result, an inmate could receive an undeserved longer sentence with a lower chance of parole. Unfortunately, most people who are affected by this situation are of African American or Hispanic descent.

These biases extend to the field of recruitment as well. A joint experiment conducted by the University of Chicago and MIT found that resumes with white names had a 50% higher chance of getting callbacks than people of color because the AI model made decisions based on the names of the applicants and their location.[76]

73 Google Photos Algorithm
    https://www.theverge.com/2018/1/12/16882408/google-racist-gorillas-photo-recognition-algorithm-ai
74 Microsoft AI Chatbot Tay https://spectrum.ieee.org/tech-talk/artificial-intelligence/machine-learning/
    in-2016-microsofts-racist-chatbot-revealed-the-dangers-of-online-conversation
75 LSI-R Questionnaire http://www.doc.ri.gov/administration/planning/docs/LSINewsletterFINAL.pdf
76 Microsoft AI Chatbot Tay https://spectrum.ieee.org/tech-talk/artificial-intelligence/machine-learning/
    in-2016-microsofts-racist-chatbot-revealed-the-dangers-of-online-conversation

This is the current state of AI models. They are smart in giving various insights but lack the context of human emotions, empathy, and cultural context. The reason for this is that all the current AI models are trained to do one specific task and become efficient at it. They are classified as narrow or weak AI.

For example, DeepMind built an AI model named "AlphaZero" which uses re-inforced learning (Alpha Zero https://deepmind.com/research/open-source/alphazero-resources) They trained the model to play chess, and the game Go; it beat the best player in the world in both the games after several rounds of training. Finally, they put AlphaZero in situations where it was not trained for (unseen data-sets), and its performance was abysmal. This shows that AI is good at performing the tasks it is taught to do but has glaring problems when exposed to multiple tasks, which may involve human emotions and intelligence.

So, how do we ensure we develop and test these systems to reduce some of their negative impacts?

TESTING AI-BASED SYSTEMS

The inner workings of AI models are still a black box. Different datasets are given as inputs, and the AI model learns, builds relationships, and makes predictions based on these datasets. There are various research studies going on to make AI justify the reasoning behind its decisions.[77] But the research is still in its initial stage and is going to take a while before it could be generalized to existing and newer AI-based systems.

Given this context, below are some ways to interact with AI-based systems and ensure it is working as expected:

Use Diversified Datasets

It is vital to ensure AI-based systems work as expected when used by consumers, and the chances of having unexpected outcomes are reduced. One way to do this is to use a diversified dataset.

For example, say you are building an AI model to detect images of *submit* buttons. The datasets fed to the AI model should have different variations of images of but-tons to make the AI model learn different combinations. The dataset may have:

77 Alpha Zero https://deepmind.com/research/open-source/alphazero-resources

- Image of a round submit button, labeled as "button."

- Image of a square submit button, labeled as "button."

- Image of rectangle submit button, labeled as "button."

- Also, an image that is not a submit button, labeled as "not a button."

This variation helps the AI model identity submit buttons with higher accuracy, thereby reducing the chances of making wrong decisions. Having diversified data-sets also helps to reduce the chances of biases when AI models make decisions.

Evaluation Metrics of AI Models

The expectations of a feature are usually identified in the acceptance criteria. In the AI world, this criterion is in the form of evaluation metrics to determine the accept-able level of performance.

Let's go back to our previous example. Say we are building an AI model to detect an image of a *submit* button on a web page. The dataset may look like this:

Case	Input	Label (Prediction)	AI Model Prediction (Actual Output)
1	Submit	SUBMIT BUTTON (YES)	SUBMIT BUTTON (YES)
2	SUBMIT	SUBMIT BUTTON (YES)	SUBMIT BUTTON (YES)
3	SUBMIT	SUBMIT BUTTON (YES)	NOT A SUBMIT BUTTON (NO)
4	Log In	NOT A SUBMIT BUTTON (NO)	NOT A SUBMIT BUTTON (NO)

5	Password	NOT A SUBMIT BUTTON (NO)	NOT A SUBMIT BUTTON (NO)
6	 SUBMIT	SUBMIT BUTTON (YES)	NOT A SUBMIT BUTTON (NO)
7	 Submit	SUBMIT BUTTON (YES)	SUBMIT BUTTON (YES)
8	Username	NOT A SUBMIT BUTTON (NO)	SUBMIT BUTTON (YES)
9	 Username	NOT A SUBMIT BUTTON (NO)	NOT A SUBMIT BUTTON (NO)
10	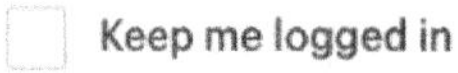 Keep me logged in	NOT A SUBMIT BUTTON (NO)	NOT A SUBMIT BUTTON (NO)
11		NOT A SUBMIT BUTTON (NO)	SUBMIT BUTTON (YES)
12	 Submit	SUBMIT BUTTON (YES)	NOT A SUBMIT BUTTON (NO)

Fig. 52: Submit Button Datasets (Source: Chai Latte)

So, how would we know this AI model is ready for production?

Before the start of training the AI model, the team collectively decides on acceptance criteria for the three most widely-used metrics to determine the performance of an AI model. They are:

- Accuracy

- Precision

- Recall

They are calculated as follows:

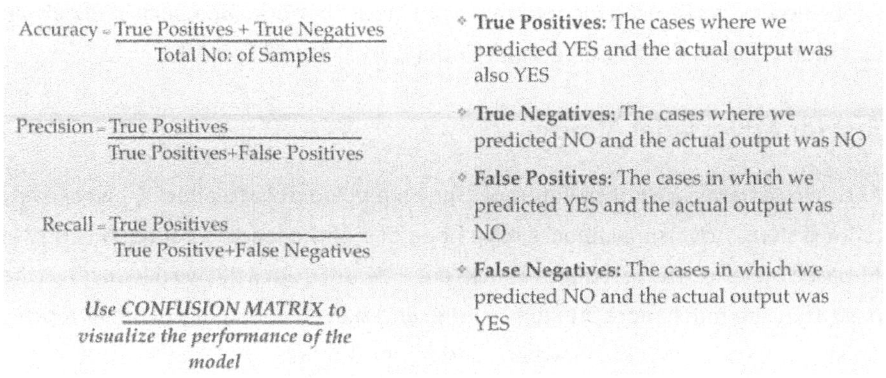

$$Accuracy = \frac{True\ Positives + True\ Negatives}{Total\ No:\ of\ Samples}$$

$$Precision = \frac{True\ Positives}{True\ Positives + False\ Positives}$$

$$Recall = \frac{True\ Positives}{True\ Positive + False\ Negatives}$$

Use CONFUSION MATRIX to visualize the performance of the model

- **True Positives:** The cases where we predicted YES and the actual output was also YES

- **True Negatives:** The cases where we predicted NO and the actual output was NO

- **False Positives:** The cases in which we predicted YES and the actual output was NO

- **False Negatives:** The cases in which we predicted NO and the actual output was YES

Fig. 53: Fahrenheit to Celsius Conversion Example

Let's say the team acceptance criteria is:

- *Accuracy of the AI model needs to be greater than 95%.*

- *Precision of the AI model needs to be greater than 40%.*

- *Recall of the AI model needs to be greater than 50%.*

In our scenario:

- True Positives = 3

- True Negatives = 4

- False Positives = 3

- False Negatives = 2

- Accuracy = (3+4)/12 = .58 = 58% Accuracy

- Precision = 3/(3+3) = 0.50 = 50% Precision

- Recall = 3/(3+2) = 0.60 = 60% Recall

As we can see, **the AI model satisfied the acceptance criteria for Precision and Recall but failed when it comes to accuracy**. Now, it is up to the stakeholders to decide whether this is production ready or more training is needed.

To determine complete performance of the model, teams use a Confusion Matrix.[78]

Other metrics can be used for determining AI model performance, such as Receiving Operating Characteristic Curve, Area Under Curve,[79] or F1 Score.[80]

Test for Adversarial Attacks

AI-based systems are not bulletproof. They are vulnerable to attacks, just like any other system. Adversarial attacks have been one of the leading causes of worry in AI-based systems. These types of attacks are different from what we have seen in the past. They are much more intuitive, subtle, and skew the learning of the AI model, causing unexpected behavior when used by consumers.

For example, let's take an image recognition app like Google Photos.[81] The AI model used in Google Photos is trained with various images of objects that could include humans, animals, things, etc. A hacker could change some of the pixels in these images used for AI model training and negatively influence its learning. So, when the application is released in production, it could cause harmful effects to the consumers using the application, leading to unexpected outcomes.

Recently, researchers have found other ways to fool AI-based systems and expose vulnerabilities — one of which is the use of adversarial T-shirts as shown here.

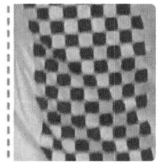

Fig. 54: Adversarial T-Shirts Fooling Face Detection Algorithms (Source: VentureBeat[82])

78 Confusion Matrix, Wikipedia https://en.wikipedia.org/wiki/Confusion_matrix
79 Receiving Operating Characteristic Curve
   https://developers.google.com/machine-learning/crash-course/classification/roc-and-auc
80 F1- Score Definition https://en.wikipedia.org/wiki/F1_score
81 Google Photos https://www.google.com/photos/about/
82 Adversarial T-Shirts
   https://venturebeat.com/2019/10/29/researchers-fool-person-detecting-ai-with-an-adversarial-t-shirt/

One of the studies found that these T-shirts had 79% and 63% success rates respectively in fooling face-detection algorithms in digital and physical worlds.[83]

Other transformations that can fool AI models are scaling, translation, rotation, brightness, noise, and saturation adjustment.

Test for Edge Cases

As engineers, our minds are trained to think out-of-the-box. We think of different risks and failure points of systems based on prior knowledge and experience. This includes testing the system for edge cases. These are rare cases that, when left untested, could cause a negative impact to users.

For example, say you have an application that detects people through images of faces. What if the app scans an image as shown here? Is it going to recognize the picture as a female, or would the funky glasses confuse the AI?

Similarly, autonomous cars are popular these days, and software controls the majority of its functionalities. Given this context, what happens if the vehicle is on auto-drive, and it sees stop signs like as shown below? Is the car going to stop or continue to keep moving in heavy traffic areas?

Fig. 55:
Person Wearing Funky Glasses
(Source: Google)

These are the edge cases to think about to ensure AI-based systems work as expected.

Fig. 56: Stop Signs Covered With External Objects (Source: Shutterstock)

83 Study Reference https://arxiv.org/pdf/1910.11099.pdf

Classify "Unknown Objects"

In Figure 52, we discussed how AI models make predictions based on datasets. One thing we haven't discussed is that apart from making yes and no predictions, there is also another kind of result: unknown. This is where the AI model does not know how to classify the dataset and is unable to make predictions on it. For example, the below image could be classified as unknown as the model may not know that this is an image of a *submit* button.

Fig. 57:
AI Model Classifying a Submit Button as
"Unknown (Source: Shutterstock[84])

When this happens, we need to manually classify the datasets and train the AI model to handle these situations in the future. This helps the AI models to better handle unseen datasets when it is in production.

FUTURE TRENDS IN AI-BASED DEVELOPMENT AND TESTING

There are various areas of research going on to solve different problems related to software development and testing. Two of them are going to change the face of the industry in the upcoming years.

Low Code Development Platforms

With customer demands, continuously developing new features at a rapid pace has become a necessity. Developers are continually churning out the next best features for their customers and are looking for ways to optimize the development process. One massive part of this effort is writing code.

AI can make a programmer's life a lot easier by helping to detect and learn coding styles and make suggestions accordingly. This accelerates the development process. AI can proactively make predictions on the application code based on

---

84 https://www.shutterstock.com/image-vector/red-button-word-submit-on-15525674

learning from past examples. It can easily detect different vulnerabilities based on system logs and other relevant resources and suggest corrective actions. This helps to mitigate security flaws before production deployment.

Frameworks, tools, and utilities that are currently too complex for non-technical people to use are going to get much more comfortable with AI. It will reduce complexity and give a more straightforward interface for users to perform different actions. AI is going to help bridge the gap between technical and non-technical people.

Currently, there are many tools and IDEs that do this, and there will be more to follow to make building AI models and programming a lot easier and accessible even to non-technical folks. Recently, Amazon and Microsoft released AWS DeepLens[85] and Vision AI DevKit[86] to make AI model training more accessible for software developers. A world where you think of an idea, then use AI to build these ideas into reality with no programming knowledge, is going to be a reality and not something you just see in sci-fi movies. The age of low code development platforms is here.

Autonomous Testing

Similar to autonomous cars, we can use AI to help to automate several tasks and make processes much faster and more efficient.

The software testing space is seeing a lot of developments in AI-enabled solutions for common problems. This trend will continue to grow with more focus on autonomous testing. With the help of AI, we will be able to connect our production apps to the testing cycle. This means we can create tests based on actual flows performed by the user in production. Also, the AI can observe and find repeated steps and cluster them to make reusable components in your tests. For example, consider login/logout scenarios.

So now, we have scenarios that are created based on real production data instead of us assuming what the user will do in production. This also helps to get good test coverage based on real data.

---

85 AWS DeepLens https://aws.amazon.com/deeplens/
86 AI DevKit https://azure.github.io/Vision-AI-DevKit-Pages/

Secondly, AI has its self-healing mechanism that can proactively find issues in our application and fix it instead of us finding it late in the SDLC. This is one of the most significant advantages of using AI in our software development and testing pipeline.

FUTURE OF AI-BASED RESEARCH

The ultimate goal of AI-based research is to build machines that can surpass human intelligence, making the transition from the current state of AI, which is narrow AI, to strong AI where they can think and react like humans. Getting to this point is going to take a while. In the meantime, researchers are more focused on AI safety, trying to solve the bias problem of these AI models.

There are various non-profit organizations like the Future of Life Institute[87] and WebTap Project[88] from Princeton University trying to ensure that the current AI-based systems are safe for humans and do not compromise the data, security, or privacy of consumers. Also, recent studies of the "black box" problem have shown that soon AI will be able to justify its reasoning in making decisions, which would help in mitigating some of the negative impacts of these systems.[89]

So, contrary to popular belief, the outlook is not all doom and gloom when it comes to AI-based systems.

IMPACT OF AI ON JOBS

One of the biggest questions in people's minds is this: Would advancements in the field of AI replace human jobs? To answer that, we need to consider the current state of AI. As explained in the previous sections, all the AI models currently used in systems are "weak" or "narrow" AI. They are good at doing one particular func-tionality but cannot multitask and respond with empathy. This is because they lack emotions like humans. They are unable to think and make decisions outside the realms of data.

Humans are needed to train and evaluate the AI model to ensure it is safe for user consumption. Data, security, privacy, ethics, and ease of use are just some of the factors that need to be tested by actual humans to prevent unexpected outcomes

---

87 Future of Life Institute https://futureoflife.org/
88 WebTap Project https://webtap.princeton.edu/
89 Black Box Study https://www.scientificamerican.com/article/demystifying-the-black-box-that-is-ai/

when end users are using the AI-based system. This is important for companies to be relevant and competitive in today's market, where customer data has been the focal point for everyone, including the media.

That being said, it is almost certain that more jobs will be automated, and a majority of the people would be forced to upgrade their skill sets.[90] The impact on jobs would be felt more by the workforce in the service industry that includes food, transportation, hospitality, and retail.

As for developers and testers, the way they view systems is going to change drastically. Large amounts of work are going to be creative and exploratory. Instead of spending the effort on writing, deploying, and maintaining code, teams will be spending more time collecting, cleaning, labeling, and analyzing data fed into neural networks. The development process is going to focus more on the data and less on the manual effort needed to develop features and deliver software.

While advancements in AI continue to evolve, it is essential to upgrade our skills by learning new technologies and programming languages to stay relevant in the industry. After all, being curious, continually learning, and applying our critical thinking skills is the essence of what makes us human and differentiates us from algorithms and machines.

90 Jobs to Be Automated Article, Mckinsey
https://www.mckinsey.com/featured-insights/future-of-work/ai-automation-and-the-future-of-work-ten-things-to-solve-for

Chapter 8:

Metrics for Measuring Success in AI/ML Test Automation

My previous book, Continuous Testing for DevOps Professionals, featured a chapter on continuous testing maturity and metrics where — with the help of Wolfgang Platz from Tricentis — I divided the metrics into three categories: speed/velocity, quality, and cost. We can leverage these metrics when assessing the impact of AI/ML quality-driven tools on continuous testing and DevOps productivity.

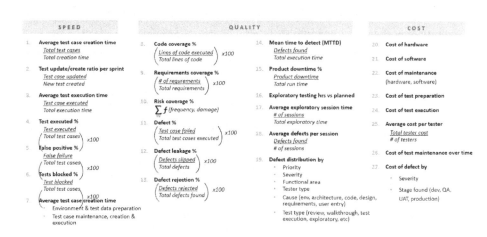

Fig. 58: Metrics for Continuous Testing Maturity (Source: Continuous Testing for DevOps Professionals)

SPEED

Let's look at a few metrics per each category, starting with speed.

If we pick average **test case creation time** as our first metric, it is quite evident that record and playback test creation will be faster than coding in Java or other development languages. To assess the real value of using AI/ML record and playback or other autonomous testing tools, the measurements need to be a mix of time to create a similar test scenario via code vs. codeless, together with test maintainability/reliability over time/software iterations.

From several measurements done within the market, it was found that a record and playback test creation takes about six times less than writing the same test in code. If we add time spent on maintaining the same test across two to three software releases, we can get to **a test creation efficiency metric** that perhaps is more powerful than just the time parameter.

Under the same category of speed, I would recommend also looking at **E2E test execution time**, comparing code-based testing to codeless. In most cases, codeless will give better results than code-based test execution due to the complexity and architectural differences between the two approaches.

QUALITY

If we were to pick a few metrics from the **quality** bucket, I would recommend looking into enhanced test **automation coverage metrics, defect percentage**, and an additional metric related to quality that is not covered in the above image — **manual test case percentage before and after employing AI/ML.**

When combining codeless/AI/ML tools on top of existing code-based test automation, organizations should look for a great decrease in manual testing activities, which translates into greater test automation coverage, as well as less escaped defects in production. Or, looking at this metric differently, it means that more defects are found within the development cycle. Prior to the use of such a tool, a lot of manual and exploratory testing was done quite late in the development cycle, often too late to be useful from a feedback perspective.

COST

Moving into **cost** efficiency, which often ties in with ROI, I would recommend focusing on the **cost of software, cost of testers/developers, and the cost of defects.** [1]

---

91 Cost of Defects, StickyMinds https://www.stickyminds.com/article/shift-left-approach-software-testing

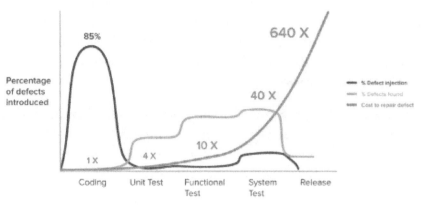

Jones, Capers. *Applied Software Measurement: Global Analysis of Productivity and Quality.*

Fig. 59: Metrics for Continuous Testing Maturity (Source: Continuous Testing for DevOps Professionals)

It is obvious that a software test engineer (SDET) and a developer that writes tests in Java, JavaScript, C, etc. gets a higher annual salary than a business/manual tester. This is an opportunity to balance overall quality cost by employing few of these roles and match the tools to these personas (e.g. business testers would be able to leverage codeless tools, SDETs will continue to create and maintain tests in code).

In addition, when manual testers have no alternative and they execute all tests man-ually, their feedback to developers as mentioned above is late and often irrelevant. With codeless automation powered by ML/AI, these personas can detect defects earlier in the development cycle, and avoid risks of escaped defects, reducing the overall DevOps cycle costs.

Leveraging the research in this infographic from Testim.io, we can learn about some cost avoidance opportunities with codeless automation around some of the metrics that I mentioned above (salary, time to generate new test scenarios, test automation coverage, and risk reduction for escaped defects).

Similar metrics like the one mentioned above can and should be applied not only to ML-driven test automation creation, but also to automated code reviews, security vulnerabilities detection, and visual test automation vs. manual testing. This results in future state value realization with ML vs. the current state without it.

It is important not only to measure the above values, but also have an ongoing conversation across the different stakeholders within the DevOps teams (developers, testers, product managers, business analysis) on the measurements, values, and other KPIs to facilitate continuous alignment as well as continuous improvement.

ML and AI are great tools that MUST fit into existing DevOps process and not change them. The integration and problem solving of such new tools ought to be very well considered, monitored, measured, and fixed whenever needed.

ADDITIONAL AREAS AND METRICS TO CONSIDER

Not specific to test automation creation measurements, it is also recommended you apply AI/ML to supporting processes throughout the software development pipeline. When utilizing some of the below tasks with AI, productivity and quality measures can be also enhanced.

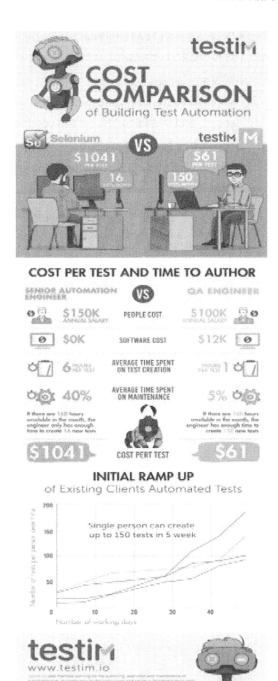

- **Source control systems analysis** for buggy source files, code change velocity, and other productivity measurements of feature teams.

- **Risk impact analysis** based on test history and defect trends to build an **efficient regression suite** that is more focused on the software iteration scope, and that takes less time to complete.

- **Product data monitoring** using AI to detect trends, common use cases, pitfalls, and other real users' activities to base development decisions on real data.

- **Predictability in development and testing** by learning which tests are less effective and should be deprecated and which features are not used at all and should be hidden from users. Also identify high-risk/defect-prone areas and act upon them.

All of the above four areas can be enhanced using AI and ML and converted into maturity metrics or other improvement metrics for individuals, teams, and leadership.

Chapter 9:
The New Categories of Software
Defects in the Era of AI and ML

Tzvika Shahaf

Tzvika Shahaf is the VP of Product Management at Perfecto.[92] His experience includes business development, strategy, and investment in technology companies and venture capital firms. His passion is building new, powerful, and effective ways to collaborate with Global 2000 enterprises in order to resolve high-impact business problems using data-driven processes and analytics. Tzvika is partnering with leading DevOps teams to revolutionize the testing space by making it smarter, faster, and cost effective with a clear goal of maturing software delivery lifecycle. Tzvika is keynote speaker at industry leading events, blogger, and a Co-Author of the book, "Continuous Testing for DevOps Professionals: A Practical Guide from Industry Experts."

INTRODUCTION

Test automation is an art. But there are fundamental differences between the nature of failure based on application types (mobile native vs. web), coding techniques, and more.

Specifically, there are key differences between a mobile native app and web browser app as it relates to the structure of the UI layer, as well the sustainability of the test automation and debugging process, as described below:

1. Mobile UI tree vs. websites DOM objects tree.

2. Dynamic website content (frequently changed objects) vs. native apps with relatively stable object structure.

3. Flakiness in mobile due to unexpected events like popups, incoming calls, interactions with sensors, app signature, environment-handling activities (file/image upload, installation issues, orchestration, and more).

4. The nature of bug fixes is different and the cycle to release is shorter on web apps:

    a. Web — Push changes easily to validate fix.

    b. Mobile — Build process is complicated and installation of fix requires compilation (either locally as IPA/APK) or longer push to the App Store, etc.

---

92 http://perfecto.io

With the above-mentioned challenges, it's encouraging to see that as this book is being developed, existing ML/AI techniques have already made significant progress in their ability to identify (and resolve in some cases) some of the following classified failures.

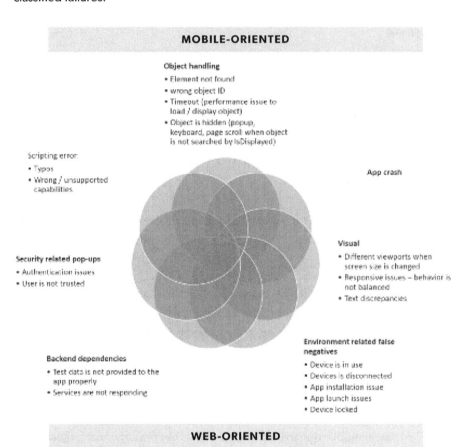

MOBILE-ORIENTED

Object handling
• Element not found
• wrong object ID
• Timeout (performance issue to load / display object)
• Object is hidden (popup, keyboard, page scroll when object is not searched by IsDisplayed)

Scripting error
• Typos
• Wrong / unsupported capabilities

App crash

Security related pop-ups
• Authentication issues
• User is not trusted

Visual
• Different viewports when screen size is changed
• Responsive issues – behavior is not balanced
• Text discrepancies

Backend dependencies
• Test data is not provided to the app properly
• Services are not responding

Environment related false negatives
• Device is in use
• Devices is disconnected
• App installation issue
• App launch issues
• Device locked

WEB-ORIENTED

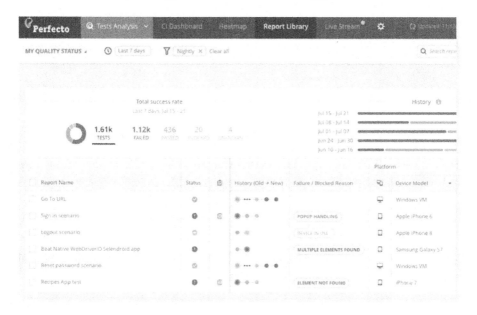

Fig. 60: Error Classification of Traditional Test Automation Failures (Source: Perfecto)

NEW DEFECT CATEGORIES THAT WILL EVOLVE WITH THE RISE OF AI/ML

As part of the need to deal with complex development scenarios, big data challenges, and scale, application and software developers started to embed AI/ML algorithms as part of their development process. Even if the users are not always aware of the underlying advancements, and the UI looks the same on the website or mobile app, in many cases, there are massive algorithms that are running and gathering insights to help serve the clients better.

To give an example, Twitter, Amazon, and the majority of other news websites are leveraging content personalization algorithms based on tastes/preferences and browsing history. It is all is based on a learning system that collects these data points.

Fig. 61: Twitter AI-Based Trending Algorithms (Source: Twitter App)

The abovementioned reality is going to transform the nature of defects in a significant way and contribute to the creation of a new breed of sophisticated defects. This is set to change the map of defects that DevOps teams use to detect and fix today.

The use of AI/ML in a new type of apps (AIIA[93] — AI Infused Applications) will evolve the following set of new defect categories. These are the top six new categories that should be considered for AI/ML defect classifications.

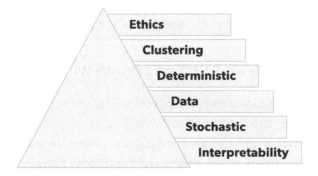

93 Introduction to AI Infused Applications, Forrester https://go.forrester.com/blogs/no-testing-no-artificial-intelligence/

1. ETHICS

An AI-based algorithm makes predictions based on the user's ability to train its engine. The algorithm will label things based on the data it is trained on. Hence, it will simply ignore the correctness of data. For example, if the algorithm is trained on data that reflects racism or sexism, the prediction will mirror it back instead of correcting it automatically. Therefore, one needs to make sure that the algorithms are fair, especially when it is used by private and corporate individuals

From a developer view, this defect category means that training the AI engine should also include a dedicated set of rules and data that refers to ethics, depending on the target market segments, geographies, and exposure of the app or website.

From a tester's perspective, such a category needs to be included in the test planning and classified upon relevant detection of relevant issues. It will also require the ability to perform all sorts of testing within the lifecycle of the app (unit/APIs/UI/data inputs, etc.).

In a recent article by Harvard Magazine, the author gave an example around the use of autonomous cars and people with an arrest warrant against them entering such vehicles.[94] The dilemma here is whether or not the car should drive the suspect directly to the nearest police station without acknowledging a potential-

Fig. 62: Self-Driving Cars (Source: CIO.com[95])

ly life-threatening emergency that may require a different behavior. In this example, there needs to be various rules and conditions that are part of the AI algorithm that can make a decision that matches the reality as much as possible.

94 Harvard Magazine, AI Limitations https://harvardmagazine.com/2019/01/artificial-intelligence-limitations
95 How Singapore Is Developing Autonomous Cars
   https://www.cio.com/article/3294207/how-singapore-is-driving-the-development-of-autonomous-vehicles.html

2. CLUSTERING

This challenge may occur when data is not labelled but can be divided into groups based on similarity and other measures of natural structure in the data. An example is the organization of pictures by faces without names, where the human user has to assign names to groups, like iPhoto on Macs. The complexity here is to get the groups

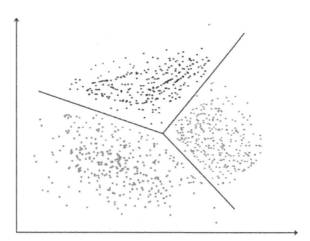

Fig. 63: Clustering of Data in Machine Learning (Source: GeeksforGeeks[96])

right and continuously expand the data in a correct manner. In machine learning, there are various ways of clustering data sets, such as K-means, density-based methods, and others. An additional clustering use case applies to the biology field, where an ML solution can help classify different species of plants and animals.

Here is an example of the K-means[97] algorithm:

```
Initialize k means with random values
For a given number of iterations:
    Iterate through items:
        Find the mean closest to the item
        Assign item to mean
        Update mean
```

From a developer's standpoint, the algorithms that are being developed and used must be based on the right characteristics. They must be trained based on large and cohesive data sets.

96 Clustering in Machine Learning https://www.geeksforgeeks.org/clustering-in-machine-learning/
97 K-Means Algorithm Definition https://www.geeksforgeeks.org/k-means-clustering-introduction/

From a test engineering standpoint, in addition to adding a new category to the classified test failures, such a persona must challenge as much as possible. This can be done through testing and parallel data sets to obtain as many outputs as possible in order to build trust in the clusters. In addition, as the product matures, new clusters, as well as data points will be added — this needs to be continuously tested and fed into the testing processes.

3. DETERMINISTIC PROBLEMS

Machine learning and AI algorithms aren't well designed in various cases (e.g. determining weather forecast through analysis of massive data points from satellites and other sensors) to deal with stochastic events. ML can be limited and generate wrong outputs due to the fact that it does not have physical constrains like "real" platforms that are led by humans. As technology evolves, such constrains may be limited. However, this is a category that requires the awareness of developers and testers.

From a developer perspective, they will need to understand the limitations and constrains of the algorithms in the edge cases and situations where things such as the abovementioned examples may occur, and either reroute the app to an alternative source, or avoid using the algorithm altogether.

From a testing perspective, test engineers will need to include the "human" scenarios in such use cases and challenge the apps in various happy and negative paths toward a trustworthy algorithm.

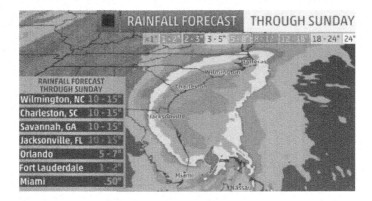

Fig. 64: Weather Forecast Using AI (Source: Interesting Engineering[98])

98 Weather Forecast Using AI https://interestingengineering.com/ai-might-be-the-future-for-weather-forecasting

4. DATA

In this book, this word might be the most repeated one, since data resides at the core of all major AI/ML algorithms, and it is in charge of the success or failure of apps that leverage such algorithms. When thinking of data, there can be a few types of data-related failures, as outlined below:

a. Lack of data.

b. Lack of good data.

From a developer standpoint, the algorithms must be trained with large and accurate sets of data that are relevant to the problems being handled, as well as to be solid enough to cover varying conditions. Such algorithms need to also consider the above and below failure types like ethics, deterministic approaches, stochastics, and more.

From a testing perspective, the entire test plan must include the right level of scenarios that challenge the apps and websites through various data points — good or bad. The test plan must also place proper assertions so that developers can understand the data-specific root cause of failure. Maintaining the tests over time and updating the test data is of course something that must be included in the test planning.

As Google wisely advises (see Fig. 65), there needs to be a proper separation between the model training data set, and the test data sets.

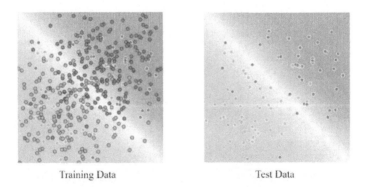

Training Data   Test Data

Fig. 65: Training Data Set vs. Test Data (Source: Google Developers[99])

---

99 Google Recommendations for Training ML based on Data
https://developers.google.com/machine-learning/crash-course/training-and-test-sets/splitting-data

5. STOCHASTIC & SPECULATIVE

This category refers to the validity and quality of the trained engine to handle un-expected results or outputs.[100] This can be a real issue that in many cases can cross-path with the abovementioned categories as well. AI/ML models and algorithms are being created from the beginning to handle such issues. But when they fail, this category needs to be clear and properly reported to developers. The inability for a model to sometimes realize a relationship between two variables may result in a wrong speculation that will obviously then result in a wrong output. Sometimes such an output can cause serious outcomes.

From a developer standpoint, when they develop the algorithm, it must leverage best practices like P-Hacking (data phishing) or scope-analysis to base outputs on mountains of data until a correlation between variables is showing a statistically-consistent result.[101]

From a test engineering perspective, testers must model the applications in a way that they are challenged by multiple variables from various angles to test the reliabil-ity of the model, relevancy of the outputs, and the consistency over time and use cas-es. One of the common failures around ML/AI algorithm as it relates to this category are false positive results. These need to be identified and eliminated in the testing phases. A recommendation to testers is to not test the system after "looking" at the data, but rather test using statis-tical approaches and pre-regis-tered data, and then analyze the app.

Fig. 66: Stochastic Visualization (Source: Google Web)

---

100 Stochastic vs. Batch vs Mini-Batch https://mc.ai/batch-vs-mini-batch-vs-stochastic-gradient-descent-with-code-examples/
101 A Primer to P-Hacking https://www.methodspace.com/primer-p-hacking/

6. INTERPRETABILITY

This is a very important failure category that is not only technical, but also quite business related. If the selected model is not interpretable, then it does not serve its purpose and will cause major regressions. Interpretability is a paramount quality that machine learning methods should aim to achieve if they are to be applied in practice. As an example, if a model cannot prompt simple, relevant, and under-standable outputs to the clients, they won't be used or accepted by them.

From a developer standpoint, models must translate the algorithm outputs in a meaningful and simple manner back to the users. Once developers can achieve this objective, they will get back relevant feedback from the users, together with growth of usage and system adoption.

From a testing perspective, testers must focus on the business outcomes of such embedded ML/AI algorithms, so the product meets its purpose and drives back happy customers. Testing for unclear strings, outputs of chatbots, translations prob-lems, context-related issues, and others must be covered and reported back to the developers.

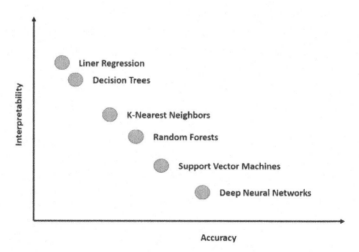

Fig. 67: Interpretable Machine Learning Models (Source: Analytics Vidhya[102])

102 Interpretable ML Models
https://www.analyticsvidhya.com/blog/2019/08/decoding-black-box-step-by-step-guide-interpretable-machine-learning-models-python/

SUMMARY AND RECOMMENDATIONS

In this chapter I outlined the upcoming defect types and categories that are expected to pop up as more ML/AI models are embedded into our existing mobile and web applications. While such models aim to add more value to end users, and optimize their content consumption, they are also creating potential quality risks that must be acknowledged and addressed like any other quality risks that are not ML based. The key for success will be to embed the two types of defects into a single defect management system together with proper classification of the defects so the developers can distinguish the root cause and resolve it fast. The time to resolve ML-related defects vs. non-ML defects should not increase, and to ensure that goal, both developers and testers need a modern testing plan and strategy.

Another key here would be to properly divide and segment the two types of tests and validations within a single software iteration — test scoping that covers both the platforms, the functional and non functional tests, as well as the AI-specific cases. This should be the new normal for DevOps teams.

I will wrap up this chapter with a very modern example of AI-based use cases taken from Fintech Circle, that many of us users already enjoy today. Implementing a testing plan that takes the above-listed categories and applies them to these use cases is a great recommended practice if you're starting your journey into the AI world.

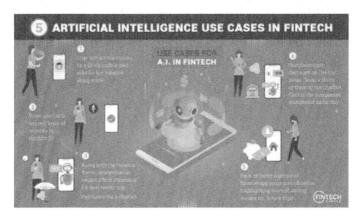

Fig. 68: AI Use Cases in Fintech (Source: Fintech[103])

103 AI Use Cases in FinTech https://fintechcircle.com/insights/fintech-use-cases-for-ai/

SECTION TWO

PRACTICES AND USE CASES IN CONTINUOUS TESTING
LEVERAGING AI AND ML

Chapter 10:
Codeless Testing 101 for Web
and Mobile Test Automation

As this book is being written, there are numerous AI/ML codeless-based test auto-mation tools. Some are mobile specific. Some are web specific. And some are cross platform. Each has its own maturity level, integrations, and other pros and cons to consider. The chapter below is not an endorsement for any of the tools, but an over-view of available capabilities represented in a few of these tools.

RECORD & PLAYBACK CODELESS TOOLS

This category includes multiple solutions, which mostly operate in a similar way and leverage the Selenium framework under the hood.

Testim

Testim is a solution that allows easy test automation creation for web — mobile is in beta. Testim uses an advanced browser plugin that allows testers to record websites and create functional test automation scripts. It uses a self-healing ML algorithm that

Fig. 69: Testim Solution Home Screen (Source: Testim)

should be able to automatically address changes done to the elements within the DOM website under test. The solution uses both Selenium and Appium underneath to launch browsers, interact with elements, and more.

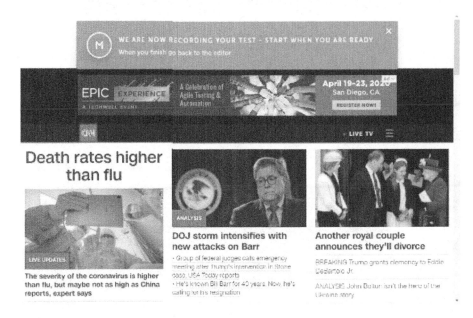

Fig. 70: Testim Solution Recording in Action (Source: Testim)

As seen in the above image, the solution will launch a browser configuration upon clicking the record button. Within the GUI editor, all actions done by the user will be recorded, including all DOM elements properties. After the initial recording and baseline is completed (Fig. 70), the test engineer will have various options:

- **Re-run the test and debug it.**
- **Add additional steps, actions, and assertions (Fig. 71).**
- **Clone the test and use it for other test scenarios (Fig. 72).**
- **Generate logs and network HAR files (Fig. 76).**
- **Edit/review the element locators and the DOM tree (Fig. 73).**

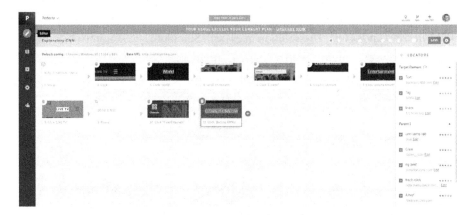

Fig. 71: A Testim Generated Test Recording in the Editor (Source: Testim)

Fig. 72: Testim Editor — Additional Options on Existing Test (Source: Testim)

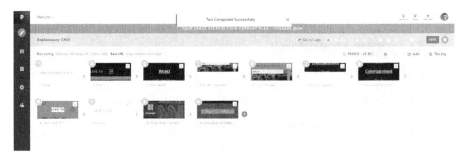

Fig. 73: Testim Object Locators (DOM) Editor (Source: Testim)

Testim uses an ML algorithm to manage and maintain the elements for each test automatically, while also enabling users to edit the objects themselves. Users can review each recorded element property in the properties panel.

Fig. 74: Testim
Properties Panel
Window (Source:
Testim)

In case developers change objects for the website under test, or something changes that impacts the element, the tool will know (in most cases) to self heal the scripts and continue the execution.

Fig. 75: A Testim Generated Test Recording in the Editor (Source: Testim)

Fig. 76: A Testim Generated Test Recording in the Editor (Source: Testim)

Within the Testim solution, users can create test suites (Fig 77), share test steps between other tests (Fig 78), integrate the solution to cloud vendors like Perfecto, and expand the test automation coverage, as well as integrate the tests with CI tools.

Fig. 77: Testim Suite Manager Window (Source: Testim)

Fig. 78: Testim Sharing Steps Capability (Source: Testim)

In a slightly different way, there are tools like Mabl. These tools also operate through a browser plugin and allow record and playback with ML algorithms underneath to create and maintain functional and end-to-end tests. In these tools, Selenium is the supported technology.

PERFECTO CODELESS SELENIUM

Solving the exact same problem that Testim, Mabl, and other tools aim to address, Perfecto Codeless offers an ML-based record and playback solution for test automation that is fully integrated into its cloud platform.[104] This means that clients creating codeless Selenium with this tool also get access to different mobile and web platforms as a service together with advanced reporting that aggregates and offers quality visibility features.

The typical workflow with this solution would be to leverage an existing test plan that covers exploratory and structured test scenarios, and login to the tool through the cloud credentials to start the recording process.

Fig. 79: Perfecto Codeless Home Screen (Source: Perfecto)

Once logged into the system, users can create a new project by starting the recording on a target base URL.

---

104 Perfecto Codeless Selenium https://www.perfecto.io/codeless-automation

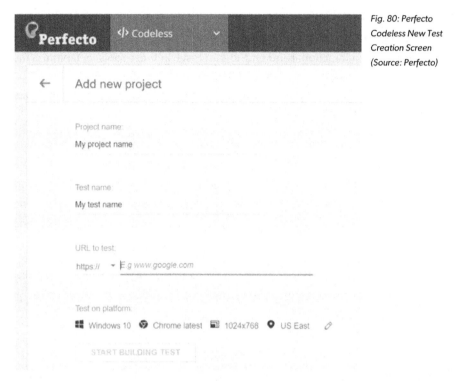

Fig. 80: Perfecto Codeless New Test Creation Screen (Source: Perfecto)

Since the recording is done against the Perfecto cloud, clients can choose which browser configuration to target as part of the initial recording.

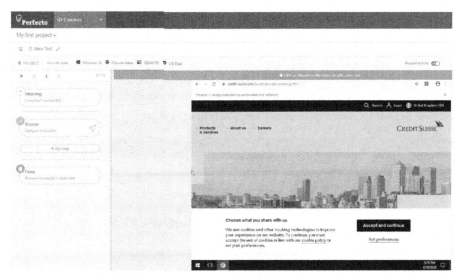

Fig. 81: Perfecto Codeless New Test Creation Screen (Source: Perfecto)

Once specifying the above configuration, the requested browser will launch with the target website URL. Since the solution is based on Selenium, any action that a Selenium code developer can perform is applicable through codeless without the requirement to write code, but rather through the UI recorder.

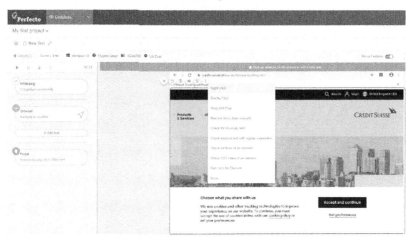

Fig. 82: Perfecto Codeless Test Recorder Screen (Source: Perfecto)

As illustrated above, the recorder allows users to perform an object click, drag, and drop or other UI validations on the website through a step-by-step website journey.

At the end of the recording, a test scenario is created and saved. Such a test can be executed on demand, via CI, or through a built-in scheduler. At the end of each execution, the report is added to the master reporting dashboards alongside other code-based test reports. The combination of code and codeless within a single platform empowers feature teams and other Agile teams to collaborate regardless of their skillset toward a greater test automation coverage.

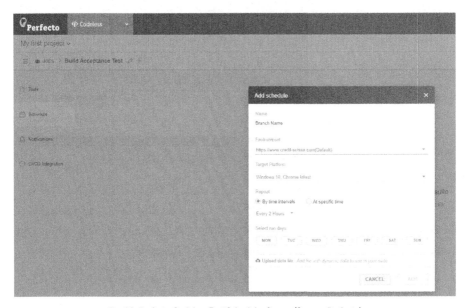

Fig. 83: Perfecto Codeless Test Scheduler Screen (Source: Perfecto)

Fig. 84: Perfecto Codeless CI Test Scheduler Screen (Source: Perfecto)

It is strongly recommended that teams scope and balance test suites and test types (functional, non-functional, API, unit) between codeless and code-based tools. Try and place in buckets the most relevant candidates for being recorded via the codeless tools based on their execution cadence, tedious maintenance, complexity, flakiness, history, and the objective behind them. Once this is done, it is critical to keep up and maintain these buckets as the product evolves and changes.

Chapter 11:
AI Data Usage —
Analyzing the User Experience

AI Appstore

Jennifer Bonine, CEO, AI Appstore

Jennifer Bonine is the CEO of AI Appstore, Inc., and was the first female Artificial Intelligence ("AI") platform tech CEO. AI Appstore specializes in custom subscription technology bundles, leveraging an intelligent platform using a personalized "virtual research assistant" to enhance corporate growth. The company exceeds expectations of integration, testing, delivery, and management with a groundbreaking business model that is fully engaged in the sustainable development goals ("SDGs") cultivated by the United Nations. Respected as a gifted speaker, entrepreneur, and philanthropist, Jennifer Bonine addresses the AI industry nationally and internationally, most recently at the World Economic Forum in Davos and for CNNMoney Switzerland. She has held executive level positions leading teams for Oracle and Target and is a founding board member of the United States bid for a Minnesota World Expo 2027. Jennifer is a 2020 Minneapolis St. Paul Business Journal Women in Business honoree, a founding sponsor and member of IVOW AI's Women in History Data Ideation Challenge, and an executive board member of Chad Greenway's Lead the Way foundation. She is a member of Million Dollar Women, member and mentor for TeamWomen, and a council member of DreamTank, an organization designed to champion young entrepreneurs. Recently named one of the Top 30 Leaders to Watch in 2020 by Silicon Review, Jennifer Bonine was featured at the UN's AI for Good summit. Jennifer is also developing a series of books to educate children about the power of AI and machine learning.

RETHINKING THE CONCEPT OF QUALITY

In a digital landscape, accurate QA testing of functional and non functional device and browser configurations is a significant challenge. Notwithstanding testing and implementing business requirements, app developers must guarantee a seamless user experience across platforms. Apps and websites rely on appealing graphic elements and animations, attractive color schemes, and text that translates accurately in different languages. Ultimately, the goal of developers, testers, product managers, and the various members of the Software Development Lifecycle (SDLC) is to guarantee a high-quality experience for their users.

AI Appstore aims to utilize AI/ML to create "Virtual Research Assistants" designed to relieve human fatigue and empower members of the SDLC to be more productive, with less human error, and reach their goal of creating a superior application. A Virtual Research Assistant bot can take over monotonous tasks so its human counterpart can focus on the strategic work that involves critical thinking and solutioning. AI Appstore has gone one step further to define the differences between humanized and replacement AI/ML with the understanding that AI is an impactful, useful, and necessary part of 21st century existence that must adhere to an inclusive, human-centric AI platform to ensure human interaction is heightened and not diminished by artificial intelligence.

WHAT'S THE REAL PAIN?

Mobile app developers and any other digital app vendor practicing Agile and DevOps must deal with bi-weekly releases either to the App Store, Google Play, or the web. With such a cadence of releases, making sense of the end user experience and understanding whether value is actually being added or if there are clear regressions is key for business success.

While there are many metrics and methods to track real user experiences, such as RUM (real user monitoring), there is not much time between these releases to act upon all the feedback. This is where AI/ML and other sentiment analysis solutions can bridge the time gap and either report in advance on such issues or sometimes even prevent them proactively.

Consider the real life example of an iOS social media sentiment application that is based on hashtags (#) which can automatically filter all positive, neutral, and negative feedback.[105] It provides a great set of continuous improvement opportunities, A/B feature deployments, and many more benefits.

In the next figure, you can see how a specific brand using such an app (in this case, Metro Bank, UK), provides various sentiments picked out from Twitter via the brand's hashtag. This can help brands make informed decisions.

---

105 Sentiment iOS App, Apple App Store https://apps.apple.com/us/app/sentiment/id1459910771

Fig. 85: Sentiment Analysis for an App Through Social Media (Source: Sentiment iOS App)

While this is only an example, later on in this chapter I'll expand on more values that AI/ML can add through App Store scanning, app maps, and more.

SOLUTION OVERVIEW EXAMPLE

The AI revolution is in its infancy and, as a result, the AI market is difficult to navigate. Enterprises building desktop, mobile, and web applications are seeking to integrate AI solutions to maximize value and support the decision-making process. AI Appstore designs data strategies for enterprises, providing custom AI subscription bundles that will resolve challenges in the software development lifecycle.

There are an overwhelming number of AI tools available on the market and each tool is designed to solve a litany of complicated software development and application challenges. There is one consistency among all of them: they are narrow in scope and created to address and solve a singular problem. In doing so, massive amounts of data are gathered and distributed in order to achieve a perfectly executed solution.

If a button is detected as being changed, moved, truncated, or otherwise incorrect, the algorithm will immediately report the error. The application is programmed to teach itself, and the neural network is built to continuously learn and grow in confidence with each examination sequence. Whereas human analysis is limited in its capacity to scrutinize and compare data sets, an AI agent or "bot" has infinite capabilities. And, while a human judge *might* test thousands of scenarios over the course of one year, an AI bot *will* accurately execute millions over millions of cases in one week.

The notion is that the bots carry out the "rote" tasks and are taught to run consistently and create a baseline. Pristine testing can only be accomplished when a colossal amount of data has been devoured by an AI agent. AI Appstore is interested in the solutioning possibilities that can be established and re-established by cross pollinating those datasets and creating bundles of information that can be processed and catalogued to support an exceptional user experience.

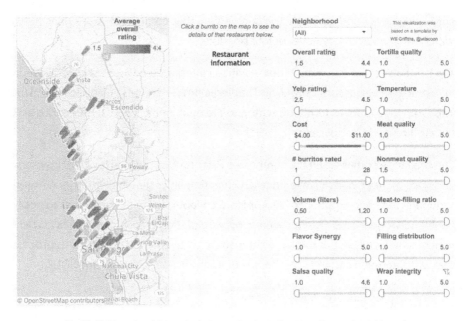

Fig. 86: 10-Dimensional System for Rating the Burritos in San Diego (Source: Lionbridge.ai)

These new and never-before-utilized datasets are paving the way for companies to move even more efficiently than they might have using a singular AI tool, allowing for faster and more informed decisions across the software development lifecycle. For example, if a company is creating a user-friendly app or website and has the capability of bundling design implementation and usability scoring together with user sentiment, greater understanding is developed to direct whether or not the intention of the site or app is immediately accessible and impactful.

AI Appstore aggregates and parcels existing AI tools to create a custom platform for enterprise app teams, including developers, testers, and product managers. Humans are then called upon to analyze and influence the strategic aspects of the data that a bot does not have the ability to identify, ensuring accessibility, diversity, lack of bias, and other optionality is incorporated.

Where the AI bots operate in an environment that is black and white, humans fill in the grey areas and creatively build out app and website functionality. AI Appstore's innovative new bundles interact in such a way that companies reach consumers with speed and accuracy never before possible.

The solution comes when an AI bot — with an integrated awareness of application infrastructure, visual correctness, and strategic flow — creates an application map. This "app map" moves from one button to the next, mimicking user scenarios as it travels through the application.

The challenge comes when the companies that produce mobile devices, browsers, and apps pioneer innovative features and functionalities that might trigger an interruption in the user experience. AI Appstore collaborates with companies to apply neural networks and AI agents across software platforms, sourcing issues and enhancement opportunities missed by humans and building a solid AI-driven process that will determine and then overcome common challenges across the SDLC.

Enterprise app teams engage as follows:

- Technology team leaders outline needs and pain points.
- ML is deployed to identify bundles of existing AI-tools to meet company needs.

- Technology team leaders approve recommended bundles.

- A custom AI bundle is managed through AI Appstore's single sign on (SSO) platform.

An AI/ML-based approach to navigation intelligently sets forth a squadron of AI tools programmed and managed to streamline identified and unidentified challenges in application design.

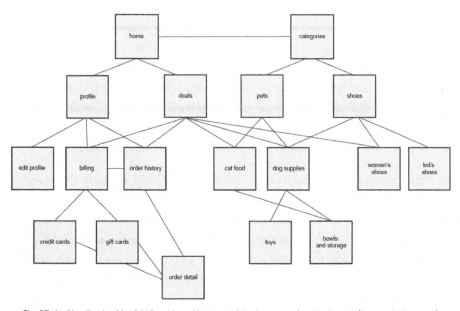

Fig. 87: An "Application Map" AI Bots Use to Understand the Anatomy of an Application (Source: AI Appstore)

QUANTIFYING THE USER EXPERIENCE

There are companies in the market leveraging AI/ML bots to scan websites and determine the probability that a user will interact with each UI element on the page. These companies use algorithms that train bots to crawl websites and analyze interfaces including buttons, cascading style sheets, HTML, favicons, and other pain points, which then score accessibility, track efficiency, and determine predictability.

These AI bots perform the "black and white" rote tasks to identify a delay or deficiency in quality that might create an issue with the customer. The design team can then "work in the grey" area with empathy and creativity to address the consumer, visualizing what the data doesn't explain and drawing on the elements of usability that are intangible and require human interaction and thought. AI agents identify the broken links and abnormal content that frustrate the user, giving the designer unfettered ability to personalize the graphics and subject matter necessary for an accessible and responsive user experience.

Using AI Appstore's Voice-of-Customer (VOC) application, users can select an app from either the iOS App Store or Google Play store, then filter the reviews by date range, sentiment score, ratings, or keyword phrase. For a minimum viable product, AI Appstore plans to layer in sources of customer feedback as well as apply additional machine learning techniques for optimum accuracy and analysis. The goal of VOC is to leverage customer feedback data and machine learning to help developers, testers, UX/UI designers, and product managers identify actionable opportunities for improvement with regard to bugs, specialized feature requests, and other user experience design-related issues with a company's software application.

AI Appstore recognizes that there is a gold mine of data available to streamline the decision-making process. But we also understand it is a mind-numbing task to structure millions of unstructured datasets. ML-based text classification models can do the job. An AI categorization model can group customer feedback data (e.g. reviews) which then determine whether or not a poor rating is a UX issue or a customer service issue. A second model identifies the actual sentiment of a consumer review and whether it is positive, mixed, negative, or neutral. Yet another model has the ability to amass multiple reviews and provide a three-sentence overview.

When an app or website developer is building a platform, the process can take months, and the creative team is so involved in building the project that overall awareness of user experience becomes an afterthought. Natural Language Processing (NLP) techniques offer a perspective that will open up a huge opportunity for data insights and analysis. The ability to structure data with AI goes beyond customer feedback analysis. AI can be integrated into a DevOps pipeline to automate any kind of analysis. The technology can be used for bug and metric tracking to quickly develop and ship code.

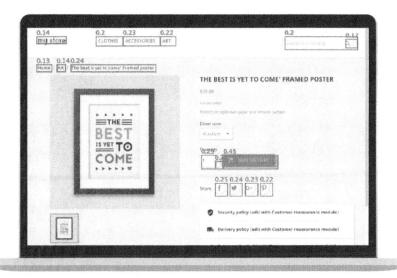

Fig. 88: Sample "Usability Scoring" Analysis for a Website (Source: ReTest)

ENHANCED USER EXPERIENCE WITH ARTIFICIAL INTELLIGENCE AND MACHINE LEARNING — STRATEGIC APPROACH

As stated at the beginning of this chapter, most AI/ML implementations involve a carefully tiered, humanized, and replacement approach. There is a need for solutions that are designed and architected as humanized AI. AI-powered virtual research assistants can be taught to perform tasks that are challenging and time consuming for humans, evaluating millions of data points, recognizing patterns and correlations with remarkable accuracy and speed, and processing information in a way that is relatable to humans navigating the decision-making process.

AI Appstore understands the value that comes from accessing surplus datasets and deploying AI agents to parse through massive amounts of statistics in order to aggregate, bundle, and manage the most efficient AI/ML systems imaginable for companies and corporations to better serve customers and consumers.

Fig. 89: AI Improving UX Illustration (Source: Appsquadz)

Software application quality using AI Appstore's unique dataset bundles should be applied at the inception of any project to guarantee that brand perception, reputation, and loyalty is accurately represented across all device platforms at the highest level. Application quality is not only about test cases and requirements — it's bigger than that. The quality of experience that a user has with an application is the most important enterprise metric, and AI/ML helps organizations realize a more holistic definition of quality.

AI Appstore is pioneering a method of identifying, aggregating, and deploying AI/ML bundles to reimagine the way companies design, develop, and maintain their applications. By utilizing Virtual Research Assistants and AI/ML to structure vast amounts of unstructured data, AI Appstore curates a custom solution that enterprises can meticulously manage through a single, integrated platform.

Chapter 12:
Leveraging AI and ML in
Test Management Systems

Nico Krüger

Nico Krüger has over 18 years of experience in software development, specializing in application lifecycle management and test automation. Nico has worked with teams in Africa, Europe, Asia, and North America on a wide variety of projects focusing on product development efficiency and test automation. Nico currently resides in North America and leads the Global Sales Engineering teams at Perforce Software.

"Do what you love, love what you do!" -- Nico Krüger

INTRODUCTION

Test management systems for the last decade largely stayed unchanged. Most of the changes we have seen pertain to test automation, shifting testing closer to development (shift left testing). But test management systems have not yet embraced the power that AI will bring to this very important part of the software development lifecycle.

This chapter will discuss what test management is and how AI and ML can be leveraged to not only improve test management, but also quality and the impact of changes from design into production. More importantly, AI can help us understand the relationship between code, tests, and issues to help reduce errors pushing into production systems.

FIRST, WHAT IS TEST MANAGEMENT?

To understand how AI and ML in test management are evolving, it is best to first understand what test management is.

Test management refers to the activity of managing the testing process. This includes both manual and automated testing activities. A test management tool is software used to manage these test artifacts (manual or automated) that have been specified by a test procedure.

Test management tools often include requirement and/or specification management modules that allow automatic generation of a requirement test matrix (RTM), which is one of the main metrics to indicate functional coverage of a system under test (SUT).

What Activities Make Up Test Management?

There are two main parts to the test management process:

1. Planning

    a. Requirement and risk analysis

    b. Test planning and design

    c. Test organization

2. Execution

    a. Test monitoring and control

    b. Issue management

    c. Test report and evaluation

There are various online books and resources dedicated to test management activities. So for our purposes, we will focus on how AI and ML can leverage the two distinct areas of planning and execution.

LEVERAGING AI AND ML DURING THE PLANNING PROCESS

During the planning process, we need to focus on requirements and risk analysis as well as test planning, design, and organization. These activities are largely coordinated inside of a database or database-driven tool that eventually lead to some sort of relationship between artifacts.

For example, you can have a set of product requirements that need a corresponding test (one or many) to ensure you have full test coverage. Most, if not all, of these activities are done manually. This is error-prone and requires a lot of manual resources that could be spent on more valuable tasks.

Let's have a look at what AI and ML can bring to the table.

REQUIREMENTS/USER STORY QUALITY ANALYSIS AND PROFILING

Quality in most, if not all, cases is something you design into a product. It cannot be added later or tested until it is of good quality. It just does not work that way. Engineering teams understand that requirements management is critical to the success of any project. Poor requirements definition results in project delays, cost overruns, and poor product quality.

So how can AI and ML help engineering teams address the quality and time-consuming aspects of reviewing and managing complex sets of engineering inputs?

Enter artificial intelligence (AI) for engineering. A great example of this can be found from IBM using Watson AI.

"IBM Watson AI uses natural language processing and understanding to analyze a requirement's text, suggesting improvements that leverage industry best practices for writing high quality requirements, based on the INCOSE Guidelines for Writing Good Requirements. Watson AI provides 10+ quality indicators to help users understand the overall quality of a requirement as well as suggestions to improve it."

Applying the power of AI using natural language allows the system to help teams write better requirements, reduce common mistakes, and learn the nuances that are specific to each team.

Here is a great example of IBM Doors Next Gen learning by asking for user input.

Fig. 90: IBM Doors Next Gen RQA Learns Your Nuances, Style, and Context Over Time (Source: IBM.com)

What Are The Benefits?

Applying AI to the requirements analysis phase can reduce the total design and review time, but more importantly it can help reduce poor requirements that account for more than half of all engineering errors (bugs/issues). This will also help to reduce the product development cost due to rework by catching errors earlier. The cost of correcting errors increases exponentially as a project progresses.

Using AI, we can also isolate requirement issues before they are sent for manual human review and receive suggestions for improvements during the design cycle.

In the future, AI will also learn what the system is designed to accomplish and suggest improvements by analyzing changes and providing feedback or best practices. Using the AI and ML technology we have today, we can greatly improve the quality and profiling of requirements that feed into engineering teams.

TEST PLANNING AND DESIGN

The quality of test cases can vary greatly by teams. This is due to the experience, skill set, and background of each team member. Teams today create tests based on the requirements, user stories (acceptance criteria), or if nothing exists, they focus on areas that suffer from constant quality issues and bug reports.

Many teams will add to their test cases by looking at issues that are found during the testing cycle or reported when the system is in production. This is a very reactive approach and in today's highly competitive world, quality is more important than ever. So how do we know what to test? Do we have the right test coverage? What else should we be doing?

Applying AI and ML to automatically generate the tests (either manual or automated) can help teams increase their test coverage but more importantly have the right tests to verify and validate the system under test.

Today, the best way to understand if you have good test coverage is by using a trace matrix. This matrix is widely used in medical device development and on complex engineering projects. The reason for this is that the trace matrix provides an easy and fast way to see if you have a corresponding test for each requirement and, if that requirement changes, what the impact of such a change would be (impact analysis).

Below is a great example of a traceability matrix created without any manual steps. It was automatically generated by the Helix ALM tool.

Fig. 91: Helix ALM Traceability Matrix Requirements to Tests to Issues to Source Code (Source: Perforce.com)

AI and ML can be applied to these systems to understand what test coverage is required. It can also flag any missing tests or inadequate tests based on existing data models. AI is increasingly used in test automation and it can in turn evaluate the "area" or "component" it is testing and create the relationship between the automated tests and requirement as shown above.

What Are the Benefits?

Applying AI and ML to automatically generate tests (manual or automated) will reduce escaped defects, as there is a higher level of test coverage over manual test case generation. Teams can focus on more complex parts of their product that require more testing and let ML create or suggest tests based on the relationships between items. ML can also identify and predict when a change occurs and which tests you need to run first to catch bugs faster.

LEVERING AI AND ML DURING TEST EXECUTION

Traditional test management systems rely on users to input results as they flow back from either manual testing activities or test automation systems. Automated testing solutions can push execution results back into the test management tool, but the large volume of results often cause these systems to become a "dumping ground" with large sets of data that no one analyzes. Or, it takes days to understand what failed and, more importantly, why.

Understanding the impact of a new feature or change is key to help reduce noise as you start to push features into a continues testing cycle. This is where AI and ML can be applied to create and inspect links between items and the outcome of changes to one or more items.

Let's imagine that a test has just failed and a new bug has been created for a software engineer to resolve (all of which can easily be automated today). As the engineer sets out to resolve the bug, they end up changing multiple files that affect other parts of the solution. The engineer commits the code that resolves the initial bug, but now a new issue is raised that was caused by this change.

By analyzing the resulting bugs that are created using AI and ML, we could provide engineers with a set of areas that they will be impacting by making this change. Or, we could identify high risk areas in our source code repository. This can greatly reduce the impact of any changes that are made and help us understand what the impact of such a change could be before the change is committed.

Here is an example of ML applied to my code repository that identifies high-risk code based on the number of changes — bug fixes applied to the individual files over time.

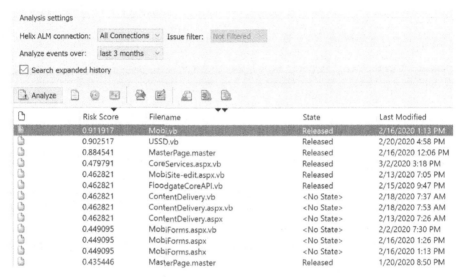

Fig. 92: SurroundSCM Source Code Risk Analysis (Source: Perforce.com)

Applying AI to create these links between the issues (bugs), tests, and code commits can greatly improve the ability of any engineer to see the potential risk of a change to the repository. This can also be used to identify and create new test cases to help mitigate the risk of future changes.

Applying AI and ML to Understand the Impact of a Change

Another advantage AI and ML is to predict the impact of a change before it is made. When the team commits to adding a feature or resolving an issue, they can instantly see what the potential impact of such a change would be by using the links between the artifacts. Today much of this is done manually and it relies heavily on users to create and maintain these links. This is another area where AI and ML can automatically create and maintain relationships for teams.

Here is an example of automatic impact analysis based on the links and relationships between direct and indirect objects. Items can be flagged as suspect automatically based on a change to a parent item within the system.

Fig. 93: Helix ALM Impact Analysis Showing the Impact of a Proposed Change (Source: Perforce.com)

Understanding the implications of a change before you make it can have a large impact on estimations and effort required, as well as the impact on existing parts of your product. AI can be applied to inspect these relationships. As changes are proposed, it can help identify the potential effort and impact of the proposed changes.

What Are the Benefits?

Creating the links and relationships between various items and the source code itself can lead to many advantages, including reducing risk, understanding the impact before it occurs, and being proactive rather than reactive.

Solutions that are very large and complex or have many dependencies on other systems can benefit from AI and ML self linking to help reduce the impact of one system on another system.

Understanding Which Tests to Execute First

Continuous testing solutions have certainly evolved over the years, but for many teams the process of making a change and then running the commit through the pipeline is the same regardless of the change itself.

This means a small change vs. a larger system change will for many trigger the same set of tests to be executed. This can take a lot of time, so many teams opt for a smaller subset of tests to be executed at predefined quality gates before finally pushing into production.

AI and ML can be applied to show which tests are relevant to execute first and which tests are relevant to the changes. The goal here is to run the tests that are most relevant first to catch bugs faster and then push it into the pipeline that has been defined.

Martin Fowler has a great blog post covering this topic, The Rise of Test Impact Analysis.

"Test Impact Analysis (TIA) is a modern way of speeding up the test automation phase of a build. It works by analysing the call-graph of the source code to work out which tests should be run after a change to production code. Microsoft has done some extensive work on this approach, but it's also possible for development teams to implement something useful quite cheaply."[106]

Using the power of AI and ML code, commits can be analyzed and tests can be created automatically to cover critical security vulnerabilities your engineers or testers may not have known about.

An example of this is DeepCode.[107] This solution analyzes code commits and suggest fixes for them. It goes further to help find critical security issues that your team may have missed. According to DeepCode, "Our bot reviews your every code commit and will immediately let you know of critical vulnerabilities and suggest how to fix them."

106 Martin Fowler https://martinfowler.com/articles/rise-test-impact-analysis.html
107 Deepcode.ai https://www.deepcode.ai/

This is a great example of AI adding to the overall quality of your solution by suggesting fixes that can be added to your existing test management database for future test executions.

SUMMARY

Test management is a key activity within the software development lifecycle and it will continue to be one. However, we have many areas within this activity that can benefit from implementing AI and ML.

These benefits can greatly increase our overall product quality, the ability to respond to changes quickly, and more importantly, it can help find those well-hidden issues that require deep learning of complex relationships within the systems we create.

Chapter 13: Introduction to Robotic Process Automation (RPA)

mesmer

Ahmed Datoo, Co-Founder/COO, Mesmer

Ahmed Datoo is the Co-Founder and COO of Mesmer. His experience in the technology industry spans software engineering, product management, marketing, and strategy. Prior to Mesmer, Ahmed was on the founding team of Zenprise and was the SVP of Product and Marketing. At Zenprise he grew revenues from $0 to $250 million, built an innovative product recognized by Gartner and Forrester, and coined the term and created the MDM (mobile device management) category. Prior to Zenprise he held engineering management and product management positions at Loudcloud/EDS. He started his career as a strategy consultant at Accenture. He's appeared in articles in the WSJ, NYTimes, Economist, Network World, and USA Today, and has spoken at events at Stanford University, Interop, Gartner, and VentureBeat. Ahmed holds an MBA, MA, and BA from Stanford University.

WHAT IS ROBOTIC PROCESS AUTOMATION?

Robotic Process Automation (RPA) refers to automating routine and repetitive processes. The concept involves use of a software robot, or bot for short, to offload manual and often tedious processes from employees.

Initial use cases involved automating back office processes. Think of a customer who completes an insurance claim online that requires an employee to manually input information into a separate internal claims processing system. A bot can take the information from one system, extract relevant metadata, and then connect to the UI of the claims system and enter the captured data automatically. Most importantly, this work does not require deep technical integration between the systems.

Early iterations of RPA involved screen scraping technologies. This allowed the bots to integrate into systems with ill-defined or nonexistent APIs. Bots would use a variety of technologies, including Optical Character Recognition (OCR) to identify text on a screen, interactable objects, images, etc. RPA vendors would then provide record and replay interfaces to allow employees to capture critical flows within a user interface.

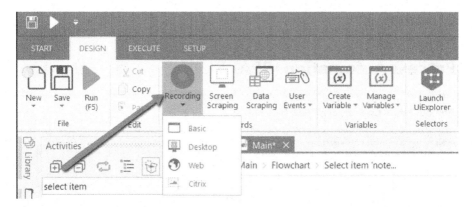

Fig. 94: Screen Scraping Initiation Process (Source: UIPath)

The output of these interfaces is a series of rules with a syntax specific to the vendor. Think of these rules and syntax as a type of program that runs on a schedule to automate the specified process.

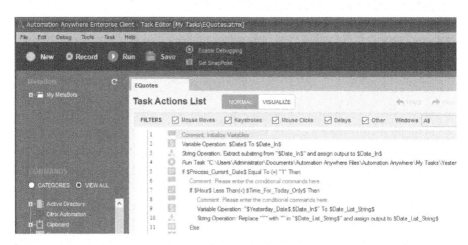

Fig. 95: Rules Generation Example (Source: Automation Anywhere)

For applications with seldom-changing static interfaces, this solution proved more than adequate.

Unfortunately, applications with dynamic interfaces resulted in RPA rules breaking. Consequently, next generation RPA solutions incorporated machine learning to more readily adjust to changes in UI.

As an example, use of computer vision in lieu of OCR allows for more accurate object detection. For context, OCR matches pixels in an image to the pixels of another image. Should an interface change the color, text, or even the look and feel of a button, OCR would fail because pixels no longer match — even though the image is still a button performing the same exact function. OCR failure means scripts break, thereby requiring human intervention to update objects referenced in the script.

Computer vision (CV) is much more resilient to changes. CV relies on deep neural networks to learn about an object. Google in 2012 most famously trained a neural network to identify cats by simply feeding the network frames generated from 10 million videos.[108] The neural net learned attributes of cats by studying what was common across these videos. Even though the cats were different colors, different sizes, in different locations/poses, the neural net accurately detected cats 74.8% of the time.

What's the implication of using CV for object identification in an application? The bot is immune to most common changes that would break OCR. As an example, changes in color of the image have little impact on object detection. Changing a hamburger menu icon from white to green would cause OCR to fail but would not impact CV. Just like cats can be different colors, so too can hamburger menus.

Even changing the icon image from the traditional three stacked horizontal lines to three dot images would not cause CV to fail. The neural network learns that hamburger menus can take different shapes, colors, etc.

RPA IN SOFTWARE TESTING

RPA has the potential to automate the entire testing process, thereby improving engineering productivity. Today, most automation solutions narrowly focus on test creation and execution. But the testing process is much broader than just these functions. A huge amount of time is still spent manually setting up and tearing down test environments. Connecting into CI/CD systems to retrieve latest builds can also be time consuming. Even the process of writing bug reports is manual and tedious, requiring screenshots, videos, and step-by-step instructions on how to reproduce the problem.

108 *Google Neural Network Research, 2012*
   https://static.googleusercontent.com/media/research.google.com/en//archive/unsupervised_icml2012.pdf

Using RPA, bots can set up test environments, auto generate and execute tests, and auto-write bug reports. In essence, the entire testing process can now be automated. Moreover, use of Machine Learning (ML) technologies can eliminate the need for scripting know-how and expertise. Modern RPA solutions generate ML models and not scripts to automate processes.

The implications to the test automation engineer are profound. Automation engineers will increasingly become data scientists, labeling objects in the UI (e.g., this is a login button, this is a checkout button, this is an input field, etc.), and feeding these objects into ML models. The level of technical expertise required will vary depending on use of open source technologies or commercially available solutions. Open source technologies require the creation and maintenance of models specific to your application and will often require deep math expertise to optimize models.

Commercial solutions auto generate models and require significantly less technical expertise to build and maintain. In fact, manual testers can use commercial RPA solutions to automate entire testing processes simply based on being a subject matter expert on their app and their internal processes.

BENEFIT OF RPA IN SOFTWARE TESTING

Many test engineers today are overworked, causing the balance between work and life to increasingly blur. Software teams are particularly short-staffed and under pressure to release faster and better products than more Agile competitors. Managers can try growing the team, but hiring continues to be a challenge, making it feel like there's no relief in sight for overworked workers.

Enter Robotic Process Automation. RPA allows team members to offload tasks that often cause late nights at the office. When you pair an individual with a bot, more work gets done faster. Managers may not be able to hire five more team members, but they can certainly pair someone on their team with a bot. And together they can do the work of five people.

EXAMPLE:
USING RPA TO AUTOMATE CUSTOMER EXPERIENCE (CX) TESTING

Most developers automate unit testing and API testing, but manually perform customer experience testing (CXT). CXT includes UI, end-to-end, functional, integration, and visual testing — the stuff that's fragmented, tool-intensive, and notoriously hard to automate.

Many organizations outsource this testing to third parties who manually validate their application functionality. Or they have a team of QA professionals in-house performing the same function.

But the work is tedious and time-consuming, not to mention slow because it's still manual.

To make sure apps work in the real world, software teams spend time manually tapping buttons in their app on the multiple device types and OS versions used by customers.

But before they can even start manually testing their apps, they have had to spend time designing tests and building the infrastructure to run them. And only once that's done can they write code to fix bugs identified by tests.

This entire process is manual, and ripe for automation via RPA bots.

RPA BOTS IN CX TESTING

Testing teams can use special purpose bots to automate specific portions of their testing process. This next section will explore three types of bots in particular: one that auto builds and tears down testing infrastructure (infrastructure bot), one that auto generates and executes tests (customer bot), and one that auto documents bugs (bug bot).

Infrastructure Bots

These bots automate the tasks involved in setting up testing infrastructure. Let's say the testing team needs the latest iPhone with the current OS to test a new app build. The infrastructure bot connects to Jenkins (or the CI/CD system of record), retrieves the latest build, proceeds to spin up a device in a public or private cloud, and installs and configures the app to point to the appropriate staging/dev/prod environment. There is no need to create custom scripts to do this. And there's no need to wait around while someone in DevOps or IT spins up an environment.

Customer Bots

Customer bots mimic the behavior of end users. These bots, much like end users, will interact with the user interface, tapping on buttons, swiping through pages, inputting data into fields, and performing gestures to unlock new features. The good news is that commercially available tools require no programming or scripts required on your end to make these bots work.

Tools from companies like Mesmer use deep learning and machine learning models to identify and interact with objects in an application (Mesmer RPA https://mesmerhq.com). These bots use a combination of computer vision, natural language processing, and path planning models to accurately detect and interact with UI elements on a screen.

It's the equivalent of a self-driving car — customer bots automatically explore your app with no scripting or coding required.

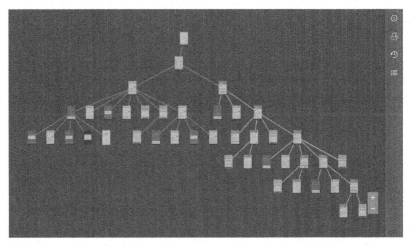

Fig. 96: Output of the Customer Bot Exploring an aApp (Source: Mesmer)

Bug Bots

Bug bots' sole purpose is to look for and report customer experience issues in your pre-released builds. The bug bots run alongside customer bots, looking for defects in the customer journeys explored.

As an example, the customer bot clicks a button that causes your app to crash. The bug bot immediately analyzes the log file looking for any crash exceptions or network issues that could cause the app to experience the fatal exception.

Bug bots look for much more than crashes in your log file. They can surface warnings, developer-specific assertions written to logs, or other important exceptions testers would otherwise need to look for in logs. Testing teams can even map specific log errors to specific pages traversed by the customer bot. No more needing to offload device log files to log aggregators for reporting and manually mapping back to customer journeys.

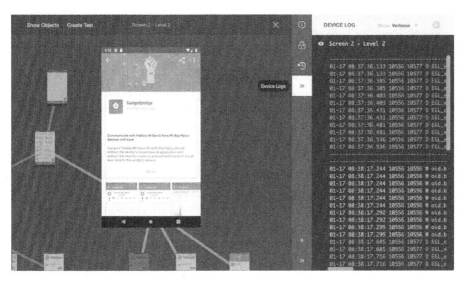

Fig. 97: Mesmer Solution Snapshot (Source: Mesmer)

Bug bots can also analyze screenshots, looking for design-related bugs. Incorrect icons, logos, fonts, spacing, and CSS style-related inconsistencies between builds are reported by the bug bots. The bots use computer vision to recognize all the objects on a particular page, and then compare these objects to the last known good build to determine whether anything has materially changed. Any such changes are reported back to the development team for remediation.

Bug bots can additionally identify functional errors in your application. The bot can look for specific text expected in designated areas of a page, look for certain strings, verify that images appear in the appropriate places, and even ensure that numeric values on the screen are correct and that date formats render appropriately.

Chapter 14:
Artificial Intelligence and
Machine Learning in API Testing

Ran Bechor

Ran Bechor is a Principal Solution Architect at Perforce Software. He studied software engineering and business administration and started his career as a web developer, team leader, and R&D director, carrying various responsibilities throughout all phases of the software lifecycle. After spending nearly a decade in developing Perfecto's mobile lab, he has taken a new role and is now more focused on the business domain. Ran believes that the "Customer-Centric Approach" and "Data-Driven Decision Making" are the key success factors of a business.

To that end he devotes his time to moving R&D teams closer to customers as this is the right way to create innovations that meet the needs of customers. Ran is a highly experienced data analyst who loves data and uses it to understand trends, measure performance, and keep track of where the market is headed. He has the ability to apply effective and practical technical solutions using cloud computing architecture to various business needs. Business process automation is his second nature. He enjoys the interaction and cooperation of the different teams in the organization while enabling businesses to be more efficient, cost effective, and productive.

APIs are the basis of software development, and while Forbes once declared that *"2017 will be the Year of The API Economy,"* as we write this book, we are still in the era of web APIs.[109]

As organizations matured their DevOps journeys through migration from monolithic system design to a microservices approach, architects found a great advantage in using APIs to effectively implement this new architecture.

As an example, REST-based microservices are popular due to their simplicity, since services communicate directly and synchronously with each other without the need for any additional infrastructure.

The software world demands agility. Therefore, continuous integration and deployment are a must. That alone makes microservices a good architectural strategy for applications that need to be updated frequently, and that can communicate using APIs.

---

109 Definition of APIs https://en.wikipedia.org/wiki/Application_programming_interface

EXAMPLES OF WHY APIS ARE VITAL IN ALL INDUSTRIES

- **Banking** — Customers want to be able to do more with their apps, and since security is critical in this line of business, restful APIs are extremely useful because they are stateless. Security in this case does not depend on the server session and each request must have some sort of authentication.

- **Transportation & Travel** — Uber, Lyft, and travel websites are using APIs to search for a location or to find your next vacation.

- **Media & Publishing** — Mobile devices consume media at a high volume, and APIs help to bring content from the publisher to the client.

- **Retail & E-Commerce Businesses** — Use APIs to connect with customers, streamline business processes, forge partnerships, and create new revenue channels.

- **Education** — Educators increasingly rely on APIs to power their tools and lessons.

- **Healthcare** — Medical facilities' care for patients has changed dramatically over the past few years due to API-enabled technology.

- **Manufacturing** — Modern factory floors now rely on APIs because the technology allows manufacturers to effectively track and oversee every step of the value chain from start to finish.

BENEFITS OF API TESTING

As not to reinvent a testing methodology that has been long practiced, here is how Wikipedia defines API testing:

"API testing involves testing APIs directly (in isolation) and as part of the end-to-end transactions exercised during integration testing. Beyond RESTful APIs, these transactions include multiple types of endpoints such as web services, ESBs, databases, mainframes, web UIs, and ERPs. API testing is performed on APIs that the development team produces as well as APIs that the team consumes within their application (including third-party APIs).

API testing is used to determine whether APIs return the correct response (in the expected format) for a broad range of feasible requests, react properly to edge cases such as failures and unexpected/extreme inputs, deliver responses in an acceptable amount of time, and respond securely to potential security attacks. Service virtualization is used in conjunction with API testing to isolate the services under test as well as expand test environment access by simulating APIs/services that are not accessible for testing. "[110]

API testing is the best way to provide a secure, reliable, and scalable connection between platforms, and it is language independent. If to refer to the traditional testing pyramid, API testing is in most cases a highly recommended type of testing in various stages of the development cycle. It is considered faster and more reliable then functional UI, E2E, and integration testing. In addition, API testing requires writing less code than GUI automated tests, thus providing faster test results, feedback, and better test coverage.

Lastly, API tests are "closer" to the application under test code. Therefore, it can be done earlier in the software development lifecycle and pinpoint the root cause of defects much more clearly. Developers can fix a bug faster when provided an API test vs. a UI test. This means shorter MTTR (Mean Time to Resolution).

API tests can be easily automated, and they are fundamentally less brittle to changes in the UI/UX.

With these advantages, and the fact that microservices and API-driven architectures are driving significant innovation across industries, API testing has increasingly become a focus. However, there are also challenges testing teams are confronting when implementing automated API testing.

An additional resource to learn about APIs, leverage existing third party APIs for your apps, and more is the programmable website.[111]

In the next section of this chapter, we will focus on some of the significant problems with API testing and realize how applying AI can help address these issues.

---

110 *API Testing Definition https://en.wikipedia.org/wiki/API_testing*
111 *Programmable Web APIs https://www.programmableweb.com/*

TEST CASE REDUCTION

In general, tests must be written to cover every use case and the processes that support them. While traditional UI testing is limited to the testing functionality of the overall application, API testing is not limited to the UI functionality and therefore the number of use cases is near infinite.

One of the challenges with API testing is the creation of meaningful tests at the API level. ML algorithms analyze the following characteristics to optimize API test creation: **Test case description, test case age, number of linked requirements, number of linked defects (history), severity of linked defects, test case execution cost (time)**, **and more.** These algorithms prioritize tests cases, reduce their number, and generate a complete set of test cases for every scenario. They can also create sets of test cases designed for different testing levels, code areas, and risk levels.

Skills and Knowledge

API testing requires a distinct set of skills that are quite similar to those of a developer. The problem is that testers often do not have this knowledge, and managers usually do not assign developers to do API testing.

In the "**Test Pyramid**" model, API testing is located between developers who know the code, but do not fully understand how it's being used by end users, and testers who are more familiar with the UI, but often think of APIs as code and therefore assume that it should be handled by developers.

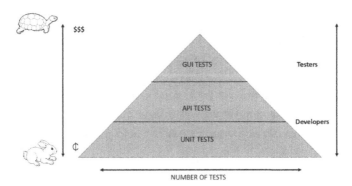

Fig. 98: The Software Testing Pyramid (Source: Perfecto)

The skill acts as a barrier between the teams and it's not clear who exactly is responsible for API testing. But by using AI, teams can change that. AI can reduce the learning curve and make API testing more accessible for testers and easier for them to maintain.

It can significantly reduce the complexity of API testing generation by migrating existing tests (manual and automated) into API tests while applying machine learning to find patterns and relationships between different services.

Making the APIs accessible will help testers collaborate better with developers. Having a single artifact that can be shared and understood by both teams will help to diagnose the root cause of defects faster.

Lowering the technical skills required to adopt API tests also reduces the cost and increases the efficiency since testers do not need to handle the difficult activities associated with building API tests like understanding the data payload or the relationships between requests. With cooperation between the teams, organization can build an API testing strategy that scales.

Parasoft, as an example, uses what they call *"Smart API Test Generator"* for that purpose:

"The Smart API Test Generator monitors background traffic while you're executing manual tests, and sends to its artificial intelligence engine, which identifies API calls, discovers patterns, analyzes the relationships between the API calls, and automatically generates complete, meaningful API testing scenarios, not just a series of API test steps."[112]

Additionally beneficial is the ability to visualize all the data without having to use a third-party application. Teams can use algorithms to create images from the data so that testers can understand and respond to that data more effectively.

---

112 Parasoft API Test Generator https://alm.parasoft.com/soatest-smart-api-test-generator

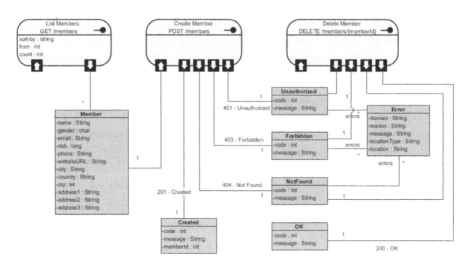

Fig. 99: Visual REST API Designer (Source: Parasoft)

SETTING UP THE TESTING ENVIRONMENT

A testing environment is a setup of the software, hardware, and networking for the testing teams to execute test cases. Setting up the right test environment ensures software testing success. Due to the complexity of the current architectures, testers realize that getting the testing infrastructure up and running is one of the most challenging parts of the API testing process.

This challenge is another opportunity for ML to learn the application environment and create a model that can be measured. Then it can use AI to expedite the process of setting up the testing environment.

Infrastructure is not intelligent enough and relies on human intervention to understand the correlations between the different services. This is where machine learning can analyze APIs, understand the relationships, then match them with the corresponding code on the infrastructure side. Once the learning part is done, AI can use it to trigger "**infrastructure as code**" templates such as **CloudFormation**, **Ansible, Chef, Puppet**, and **Terraform** to create the proper testing environment for every API test.[113] From there bots will be able to segregate/execute tests based on specific environments.

---

113 Understanding Infrastructure As Code (IAC)
   https://medium.com/cloudnativeinfra/when-to-use-which-infrastructure-as-code-tool-665af289fbde

This "on-demand" setup will also reduce the cost of hardware and software resources by making sure that computing resources are made available only when needed.

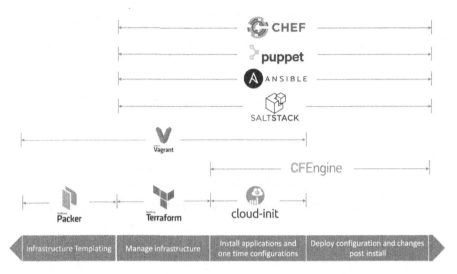

Fig. 100: IAC Tools Use Cases Classification (Source: Medium)

TESTING PARAMETER COMBINATIONS

Combinatorial testing efficiency is not new to the testing world. According to NIST research, software bugs are failures that are usually caused by one or two parameters.[114]

These failures are known as interaction failures because they are only exposed when two or more input values interact to cause the program to reach an incorrect result.

From a testing efficiency perspective, it's necessary to test all possible parameter combinations. In reality the number of combinations is typically huge, and, in addition, the testing has to deal with frequent changes to the schemas.

ML can be used to handle situations where adding an additional parameter exponentially increases the number of possible combinations.

ML can learn these patterns and use them to find problematic input combinations, and trigger failures that have escaped the previous testing.

---

114 NIST Combinatorial Testing Research
    https://csrc.nist.gov/projects/automated-combinatorial-testing-for-software

With the ability to calculate the risk, through AI-based algorithms that can compress combinations into a smaller number of tests, teams will benefit from better testing at a lower cost.

SYNCHING THE API CALLS

For API calls to work correctly, they have to be used in a specific order. Orchestrating these tests across CI/CD pipelines is increasingly challenging and the process can get increasingly difficult when working with multiple-threaded applications.

With all of the main building blocks in place, there is a need to tie everything together, and this is where AI comes into place. AI can learn the relationships between the tests and help us optimize the test suite. Bots can run "smart" test orchestration and identify tests that will be needed for each iteration of software development. AI can also be used to identify identical/redundant and unique test cases, and then remove the duplicates to maximize the efficiency of the tests.

SCHEMA CHANGES

The input/output schema of the request/response can be changed frequently due to business requirements, new functionality, or hardware and software constrains. Depending on the testing framework, this kind of change might require a massive code refactoring in the testing environment.

AI can read schema changes, understand the relationship between the schema and the test code, and use it to make the necessary adjustments in the script or workflow.[115]

This self-healing process makes the task of managing test suites easier and more maintainable. Fixing the actual test is usually the easy part. If, for example, a schema was modified, and a new field was introduced to the response, then theoretically all that needs to be done is to validate this file along with its value when parsing the response.

Handling this kind of issue is a two-minute job for either a machine or a human, but this is not how AI saves time.

---

115 *Schema Example*
   https://www.got-it.ai/solutions/sqlquerychat/sql-help/data-definition/sql-server-database-schema-example/

The idea is that AI will understand the meaning of the added value. In the above example, it has to understand that a new field was retrieved from a new table in a different database using a new API that has a set of dependencies with other modules.

Now it needs to change the test code, test case name, fix the test execution order, and then apply reusability aspects across the test suites to minimize the effect of certain schema changes.

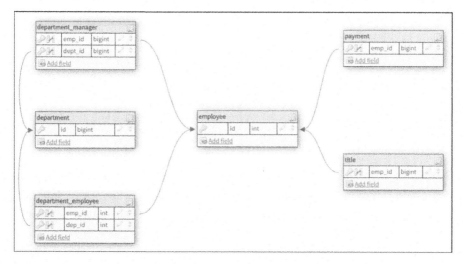

Fig. 101: A Sample Database Schema (Source: Got-It.ai)

VALIDATING PARAMETERS

Lastly, validating the parameters sent through API is an additional challenge. Each parameter comes with a list of restrictions such as data type, length, value range, or spelling.

What makes it even more challenging are frequent changes in the database schema. Database schema changes can affect the database itself and anything that uses the database including APIs. Machine learning can be used to manage the necessary tactic for integrating schema changes into the API testing suite.

If, for example, a column was added to one of the tables that interacts with an API, then the system needs to suggest a code change in the API. Once the API has changed, then it needs to understand the relationship between the API and the test, assess the risk of not testing it, and if necessary, add validations into the test.

REAL LIFE EXAMPLE — AI-DRIVEN API TEST CREATION

A lot of the use cases that were covered in this chapter and in other sections of this book are vision and future-related AI abilities that will be introduced as the technology evolves. Around API testing, there are some early-adopters, like SopaUI Pro from SmartBear, that add AI into the API test creation.

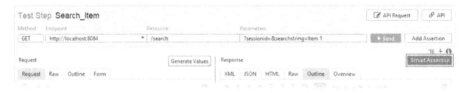

Fig. 102: SmartBear SoapUI Pro Solution (Source: SmartBear[116])

SoapUI Pro's Smart Assertion gives users the power of artificial intelligence in the API testing platform, cutting down hours of test creation time. SoapUI automatically creates intelligent test assertions based on the response given from an endpoint.

Using machine learning, SoapUI can intelligently configure these validations and offer an even smarter assertion over time.[117] Users can add the message content assertion whose configuration is based on previously received responses.

To do this, users have to click on the **Smart Assertion** button in the response editor. **ReadyAPI** will then analyze the received responses and configure the assertion based on the found patterns.

116 SmartBear API Test Creation
    https://support.smartbear.com/readyapi/docs/_images/testing/assertions/reference/property/add-validation.png
117 SoapUI Pro Main Page https://smartbear.com/product/ready-api/soapui/features/ai-test-creation/

Chapter 15:
Testing Conversational
AI Applications

Christoph Börner, Co-Founder, Botium

Entrepreneur, developer, tester, keynote speaker, and drummer. Studied information technology at the Technical University of Vienna and worked in various fields of software engineering. Active member and organizer in the Austrian testing community. Deep interest in artificial intelligence, machine learning, and bots from day one — long before these topics began to evolve the entire industry and were considered to be the next big thing after smartphones. Deep friendship with Florian Treml, even after playing in the same rock band for several years :). Starting together the Botium journey in 2018 was just the next logical step. Today we are counting more than 65K users of Botium and can be considered as first choice for testing conversational AI.

Florian Treml, Co-Founder, Botium

In information technology since 1996, when he began to study computer science with a focus on bioinformatics at the University of Salzburg, Austria. Graduated in 2003 with a Bachelor of Engineering degree. Worked as software engineer in various domains, including banking, telecommunications, logistics, and welfare. First contact with machine learning when studying genetic algorithms and neural networks at university back in 1996. First contact with conversational AI in 2015 when developing a chatbot for distance learning. For automating testing in his chatbot projects, he screwed something in shape, called it "TestMyBot," and pushed it to Github in March 2017. One year later the project was renamed and the Botium journey with his close friend Christoph Börner began. As a father of three kids, spare time is rare, but sometimes he plays lead guitar in a "local hero" rock band (We Used to Be Royal).

One of the applications where artificial intelligence led to a visible breakthrough in the last couple of years is speech and natural language processing. The capabilities of neural networks to understand and process unstructured spoken or written texts are now near human capabilities (and in some special cases even higher). With Facebook opening its Messenger Platform in 2016, customer-facing chatbot technology was finally available for developers all over the world. One of the first publicly available Facebook chatbots named "Mica, the Hipster Cat Bot" was built in Vienna, Austria, where a large startup ecosystem around chatbots and conversational AI began to rise. A tremendous amount of companies started to explore how conversational AI could help their business grow and stay competitive. And it was clear very quickly that as with any other software product, all of those chatbots had to undergo thorough testing.

BOTIUM, THE SELENIUM FOR CHATBOTS

Selenium is the de-facto-standard for testing web applications. Appium is the de-facto-standard for testing smartphone applications. Botium is for testing conversational AI. Just like Selenium and Appium, Botium is free, open source, and available on GitHub.[118]

What Is Botium Good For?

Botium supports chatbot makers in training and quality assurance:

- Chatbot makers define what the chatbot is supposed to do.
- Botium ensures that the chatbot does what it is supposed to do.

Here is the "Hello, World!" of Botium:

```
#me
hello bot!
#bot
Hello, meat bag! How can I help you?
```

The chatbot is supposed to respond to a user greeting.

Understanding the Botium Stack

When we talk about Botium, we usually mean the whole Botium stack of components. It is built on several components:

- **Botium Core** — SDK to automate conversations with a chatbot or virtual assistant.
- **Botium CLI** —The Swiss Army Knife to use all functionality of Botium Core in the command line.
- **Botium Bindings** —The glue to use Botium Core with test runners like Mocha, Jasmine, or Jest.

---

118 GitHub Repository https://www.botium.ai/getting-started/

- **Botium Box** —The management and reporting platform for making chatbot test automation fast and easy.

- **Botium Coach** — For continuous visualization of NLP performance metrics.

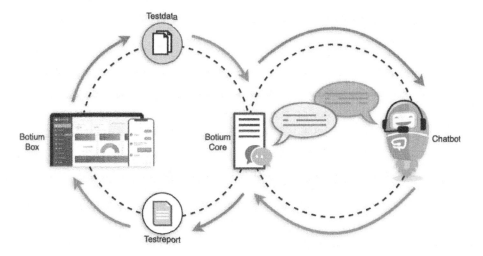

Fig. 103: Botium Stack Overview Including the Interaction of its Components

To name just a few features of Botium:

- Testing conversation flow of a chatbot:

  o Capture and replay.

  o Integrated speech processing for testing voice apps.

- Testing NLP model of a chatbot:

  o Domain specific and generic datasets included.

  o Paraphrasing to enhance test coverage.

- E2E testing of a chatbot based on Selenium and Appium.

- Nonfunctional testing of a chatbot:

  o Load and stress testing.

  o Security testing.

  o GDPR testing.

- CI/CD integration with all common products in the space (Jenkins, Bamboo, Azure DevOps Pipelines, IBM Toolchain, etc.).

- And many more!

SPECIAL CHALLENGES OF TESTING CHATBOTS

The combination of machine learning and natural language processing in adaptive programming is not well defined or deterministic, resulting in flaky tests. Testing a chatbot has some fundamental differences from testing a website or smartphone app —on a technical level, on a scope level, and on the test engineering level. Knowing the differences is vital when sharpening your skills for testing a chatbot.

Technical Difference: Input/Output Methods

Compared to most desktop, web, and smartphone applications out there, a chatbot usually provides rudimentary options for user interactions. In the case of a text-based chatbot, there's a single text input field with a text output area. In the case of a voice-enabled chatbot, there's a simple microphone with a speaker.

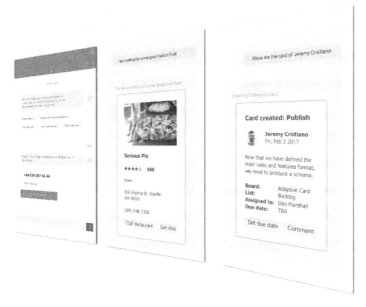

Fig. 104: Chatbot Conversations Using Text Input Fields, Buttons, Quick Replies, and Card

Depending on the channel the chatbot is operating on, often there are some additional user interaction options available. Here are some examples.

Quick Responses

Quick responses enable the user to quickly select one of the most likely user inputs. The options are typically rendered as buttons or bubbles.

Carousel

For presenting multimedia content, a carousel is the most common user interface element. It allows the chatbot to show pictures, rich text, and buttons.

Microphone, Speaker, and Display

Voice-enabled devices (like Amazon Echo) can optionally be extended display components (Echo Show) to present graphical content instead of relying on voice commands only.

Fig. 105: Echo Spot and Echo Show From Amazon (Source: Amazon.com)

Scope Difference: Test Levels

Due to the nature of conversational AI, it is vital to understand the concept of test levels to design efficient test strategies. This picture (Fig. 106) shows a typical chatbot architecture.

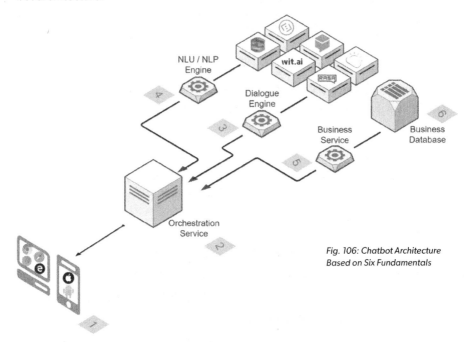

Fig. 106: Chatbot Architecture
Based on Six Fundamentals

- There is a user frontend hosted as chat widget on a website.
- The frontend connects to a backend service (often called Orchestration Service) with web-protocols — HTTP(S), JSON, Websockets.
- Somewhere behind, there is an NLP model to convert user input to structured data with intents and entities.
- An additional component is handling the dialogue sessions.
- And finally, there are some business services, often backed by business databases.

Note that in most cases, the NLP engine and the dialogue engine are combined — for example, with IBM Watson Assistant, or Dialogflow. For Microsoft LUIS and

Azure Bot Service, those components are separated.

The architecture diagram shows six integration points for test cases. The remaining part of this chapter will go into details on the challenges for each test level.

1. User Interface Level/E2E Testing

Botium supports end-to-end testing with a Webdriver Connector, combining the power of Selenium's web browser automation with Botium's chatbot testing superpowers (Source: WebDriver Connector https://github.com/codeforequity-at/botium-connector-webdriverio). The chatbot is tested by pointing and clicking and typing on a website just as a real user would do.

Scenarios

- Validating browser/client compatibility.
- Smoke tests before going live.

Pros

- Testing end user experience.
- Works for all kind of chatbots, independent of the backend technology (in theory).

Cons

- Requires Selenium infrastructure setup which is not a piece of cake — or you can use a Selenium cloud provider.
- Usually, Webdriver scripting is required (in JavaScript).
- Very slow compared to the other testing levels.

2. API Level/Orchestration Service Testing

Typically, the Orchestration Service is published as an HTTP/JSON or Websocket endpoint. Most chatbot engine providers support such endpoints, and Botium also includes a generic HTTP/JSON connector and a generic Websocket connector adaptable to a wide range of endpoints.

Scenarios

- Conversational flow testing is usually done on API level.
- Integration testing.

Pros

- Testing on an API level reduces flakiness and increases speed.
- Testing near end user experience.

Cons

- No standard API available, has to be adapted for every custom endpoint schema out there.

3-4. Backend Level/Dialogue and NLP Engine Testing

There are lots of dialogue engines out there. Some of them even offer free plans as SaaS or on-premise installation. In some cases, those engines include an NLP engine. Examples for combined dialogue engines are Google Dialogflow, IBM Watson Assistant, and Microsoft Bot Framework. Examples for specialized NLP engines are wit.ai and Microsoft LUIS.

Scenarios

- Regression testing for intent/utterance resolution.
- NLP analytics.

Pros

- Supported out-of-the-box with well-documented APIs and SDKs.
- Allows very deep analysis of NLP data such as intents and entities.

Cons

- Depending on the implementation, far away from the end-user experience.

5. Business Logic Level/Business Service Testing

Usually there is some kind of business service involved, which is key to providing value with a chatbot. Botium includes an HTTP/JSON endpoint asserter to make sure a test case actually has an impact on business data. For example:

- By using an eCommerce chatbot, Botium places a test order with the help of an order service in the backend.
- The order service persists the order in the business database.
- Botium asks the order service for details about the order to verify that the order has been persisted.

6. Business Data Level/Business Database Testing

This is a special case for the Business Service Testing case above — Botium includes asserters for most common business databases (Oracle, PostgreSQL, Microsoft SQL Server, MySQL) to query for the test case outcome.

Test Engineering Difference

There are well-established software testing techniques and metrics, but what makes testing chatbots different? What's the difference of testing a website or smartphone app? There are at least four major differences.

Learning Cloud Services

Most chatbots are built on top a learning cloud services, which by definition keeps changing its behavior. NLP-Services (natural language understanding and process-ing) like Dialogflow, Wit.ai, or LUIS are subject to constant training and improve-ment. Having a non-deterministic component in the system under test will make software testing useless as soon as you cannot tell the reason for a failed test case — which could be due to a defect in the chatbot software or an improvement in the cloud service.

And even more important, the test itself can and will have an impact on the cloud services as well. Presenting a cloud service with the same test cases over and over again will distort the cloud service's assumption of "real-life interactions," giving the test cases higher priority than they should have.

✗   Cloud service training has impact on software tests. Deal with this dependency.

Non-Linear Input

This only applies to chatbots operated with a voice interface. There are 7.5 billion humans in the world with 7.5 billion different voices. For a website, it doesn't matter who clicks a button — Elon Musk himself or King Louie, the website doesn't notice a difference. But for a chatbot, it does matter what voice is in action.

✓   Speech recognition technologies are evolving fast. Chatbot developers can rely on industry leaders to provide acceptable solutions.

Non-Deterministic User Interactions

Dealing with non-determinism is a critical topic in software testing. Due to the nature of human language, it is impossible for software tests to cover all possible situations.

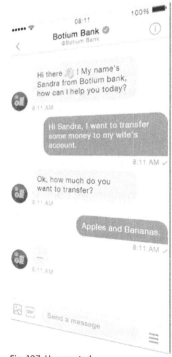

✗   Give up the 100% test-coverage goal. Make sure the tests cover the most common situations.

No Barriers for Users

When using a chatbot, either with voice or with text interface, there are no interaction barriers for users. Websites and smartphone apps allow predefined means of interaction with common user interface components (clickable hyperlinks, buttons, text entry boxes, etc.). Chatbots have to cover all kinds of unexpected user inputs in a decent way.

Fig. 107: Unexpected User Input for a Finance Chatbot

TESTING CONVERSATIONAL FLOW

This section starts with some technical background on Botium and then demonstrates a methodology to identify and formalize test cases for the conversational flow of a chatbot. The conversational flow, often called "user stories," can be visualized in a flow chart.

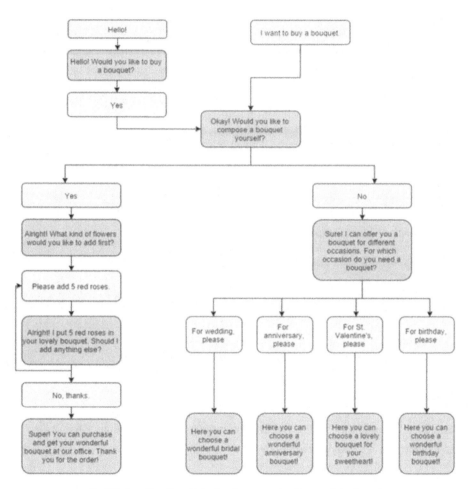

Fig. 108: Flow Chart From Dialogflow Documentation (Dource: dialogflow.ai)

Hello, World! The Botium Basics

The most basic test case in Botium consists of:

- Submitting a phrase, possibly entered by a real user, to the chatbot.

- Checking the response of the chatbot with the expected outcome.

BotiumScript

In Botium, the test cases are described by conversational flows the chatbot is supposed to follow. For a sample "greeting" scenario, the Botium test case looks like this — also known as "BotiumScript:"

```
#me
hello bot!
#bot
Hello, meat bag! How can I help you?
```

You can write BotiumScript in several file formats

- Plain text file with Notepad or any other text editor

- Excel file

- CSV file (comma separated values)

- JSON

- YAML

Convos and Utterances

So, let's elaborate the "Hello, World!" example from above. While some users will say "hello," others maybe prefer "hi:"

```
#me
hi bot!
#bot
Hello, meat bag! How can I help you?
```

Another user may enter the conversation with "hey dude!"

```
#me
hey dude
#bot
Hello, meat bag! How can I help you?
```

And there are plenty of other phrases we can think of. For this most simple use case, there are now at least three or more Botium Scripts to write. So, let's rewrite it. We name this file hello.convo.txt:

```
TC01 - Greeting
#me
HELLO_UTT
#bot
Hello, meat bag! How can I help you?
```

You may have noticed the additional lines at the beginning of the Botium Script. The first line contains a reference name for the test case to make it easier for you to locate the failing conversation within your test case library. And we add another file — hello_utt.utterances.txt:

```
HELLO_UTT
hello bot!
hi bot!
hey dude
good evening
hey are you here
anyone at home?
```

- The first Botium Script is a convo file — it holds the structure of the conversation you expect the chatbot to follow.

- The second Botium Script is an utterances file — it holds several phrases for greeting someone, and you expect your chatbot to be able to recognize every single one of them as a nice greeting from the user.

Botium ensures that the convo and utterance files are combined to verify every response of your chatbot to every greeting phrase. So now let's assume that your chatbot uses several phrases for greeting the user back. In the morning it is:

```
#me
HELLO_UTT
#bot
Good morning, meat bag! How can I help you this early?
```

And in the evening, it is:

```
#me
HELLO_UTT
#bot
Good evening, meat bag! How can I help you at this late hour?
```

Let's extract the bot responses to another utterances file:

```
BOT_GREETING_UTT
Good evening
Good morning
Hello
Hi
```

And now comes the magic. We change the convo file to:

```
#me
HELLO_UTT
#bot
BOT_GREETING_UTT
```

Utterances files can be used to verify chatbot responses as well. To summarize:

- An utterance referenced in a #me-section means: Botium, send every single phrase to the chatbot and check the response.

- An utterance referenced in a #bot-section means: Botium, my chatbot may use any of these answers, and all of them are fine.

Identification of Test Cases

If the flow chart is available, identification of the test cases is actually straightforward. Each path through the flow chart from top to bottom is a test case. Here is the path for the user story, "User composes customized bouquet."

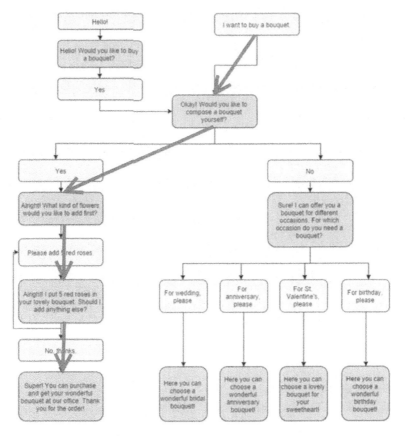

Fig. 109: Path for "User Composes Customized Bouquet"

And here is the path for "User selects anniversary bouquet."

Fig. 110: Path for "User Selects Anniversary Bouquet"

Scripting Test Cases for a Conversational Flow

In Botium Script, the conversational flow for the user story "User composes customized bouquet" can be expressed like this:

```
#me
I want to buy a bouquet

#bot
OK, do you want to compose a bouquet yourself?
```

```
#me
Yes


#bot
OK, what kind of flowers would you like to add first?


#me
Please add 5 red roses


#bot
Alright, I put 5 red roses in your lovely bouquet. Should I add
anything else?


#me
No, thanks.


#bot
Super!
```

As soon as a chatbot doesn't respond as expected, the test case is considered as failed and reported.

Scripting Utterance Lists

What the flow charts don't show are the endless possibilities for a user to express an intent. For each node in the flow chart, there are various input and output utterances to consider. The flow chart typically pictures a "happy path" in the conversation. In a real-world scenario the same conversation path and test case should be satisfied with most usual utterances and utterance combinations.

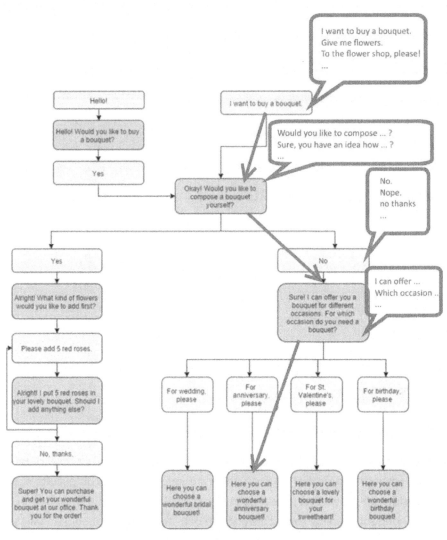

Fig. 111: "Happy Path" Examples in the Conversation

For the "I want to buy a bouquet," response, there are plenty of other ways for a user to express this intent:

- "Give me some flowers"

- "To the flower shop, please"

- "Purchase a bouquet"
- Etc.

All of these user examples are valid input for the same test case, and in Botium these user examples are collected within an utterance list in a text file:

```
UTT_USER_ORDER_FLOWERS
I want to buy a bouquet
Give me some flowers
To the flower shop, please
purchase a bouquet
```

What the flow charts don't show as well are the utterances used on the other side by the chatbot itself. A well-designed chatbot provides some variance in conversation responses. For example, instead of "Okay! Would you like to compose a bouquet yourself?" the chatbot might as well respond with:

- "Do you want me to suggest a composition?"
- "Is it for a special occasion"?
- Etc.

These utterances can be collected in another utterance list and used in the test cases to allow the chatbot all responses matching one in this list. The first part of the user story "User composes customized bouquet" would then look like this:

```
#me
UTT_USER_ORDER_FLOWERS

#bot
UTT_BOT_COMPOSE_YN
```

The conversational flow remains the same, but there are many user examples and chatbot responses allowed now.

Dealing With Uncertainty

When using Botium, there are many options for asserting the chatbot's behavior. The simplest one, assertion of the text response, is shown above. Here are some options for asserting the chatbot's behavior.

- Asserting the presence of user interface elements, such as quick response buttons, media attachments, form input elements.
- Asserting with regular expressions and utterance lists.
- Asserting tone with a tone analyzer.
  - o Validation that the chatbot tone matches the intended brand communication style.
- Asserting availability of hyperlinks presented to the user.
- Asserting custom message payload with JSONPath queries.
- Asserting business logic with API and data storage queries.

Generating a Test Report

There are several frontends available for generating a test report with Botium.

Option 1: Botium CLI

Run Botium CLI like this:

```
botium-cli run
```

Botium CLI will build up a communication channel with your chatbot and run all of your test cases. Status information and a summary are displayed in the command line window.

Option 2: Botium Bindings

With Botium Bindings, an established test runner like Mocha, Jest, or Jasmine can be used for running Botium test cases.

```
mocha ./spec
```

Option 3: Botium Box

Use the Quickstart Wizard to connect your chatbot to your test sets and run them.

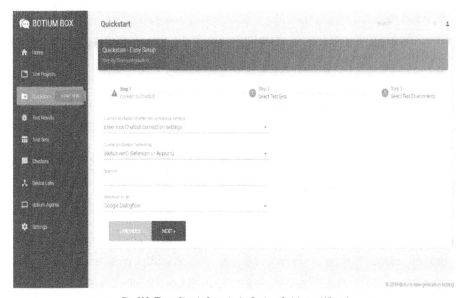

Fig. 112: Three Simple Steps in the Botium Quickstart Wizard

Testing an NLP Model

Natural Language Processing (NLP) is mainly a text classification and extraction problem. Given user input as text, the purpose of the NLP model is to:

1. Detect the most likely user intent from a pre-trained library of user intents.

2. Extract entities such as dates and numbers for refining the detected user intent.

Note that this concept also applies to voice applications by putting a speech-to-text-engine in front of the NLP component.

A test engineer now should already have spotted the obvious way for testing an NLP model — provide the input text and assert on the NLP outcome. This is correct but not the full truth. There are two more important aspects often overlooked, and those are conversation context and separation of training and test data.

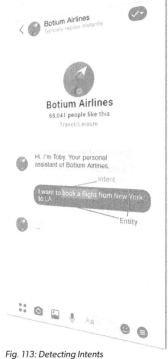

Conversational Context

In human conversations, context is everything. A conversation is not only a simple series of statements, but between those statements some knowledge is exchanged, and the meaning of a statement can vary depending on the exchanged knowledge.

Fig. 113: Detecting Intents and Entities in a Conversation

Take the statement, "thirty-two". Without any context, this is merely a number. Take the same statement, "thirty-two" as a response to the question, "What's the temperature outside?" Now the meaning is not merely a random number but a precise temperature. And, on a side note, depending on the season, it is also possible to deduct if it's Celsius or Fahrenheit.

It's a common pitfall to not take conversational context into consideration when testing an NLP model.

Separation of Training Data and Test Data

Training data is the labeled data used for training the NLP engine. It typically consists of a large list of user examples for each intent or entity type that the NLP engine should be able to handle. The NLP engine will learn the correct classification and extraction parameters from those user examples. Test data is the unlabeled data used for testing the NLP engine after it has been trained with the training data.

Using the same data for training a conversational AI as well as for testing purposes has some flaws. Most importantly, there is no challenge for an artificial intelligence to correctly classify something it already knows. It is a challenge for an artificial

Fig. 114: Weather Chatbot With (Right) and Without (Left) Conversational Context

lenge for an artificial intelligence to classify something it hasn't seen before, though. Take care to always have separate set of test data not used for training. For cases where this is not possible, there is a method called CrossValidation, which is covered later in this chapter.

Note that this principle applies to most machine learning algorithms, not only to text classification.

Scripting Test Cases for an NLP Model

Manual testing has its place, even in the age of artificial intelligence. But as this book is about test automation, this section shows the building blocks for the automated testing(and improving) of an NLP model.

NLP Model Training and Testing Cycle

A typical workflow for training and testing an NLP model is like this:

1. Run all test cases.

    a. Set conversation context.

    b. Send text or speech input to NLP model.

    c. Evaluate the predicted intent and entities.

2. Collect and analyze the results.

    a. Use common quality metrics like precision, recall, and F1 (see next section).

    b. Exit if quality KPIs are met, otherwise continue.

3. Adapt NLP model to deliver better quality metrics.

    a. Provide additional training data for the NLP model.

    b. Rebalance training data in the NLP model.

    c. Sometimes it is required to remove training data to get rid of biased results.

4. Back to the first step.

This workflow is not meant as a one-time event, but this should happen continuously on a regular basis. Over time, the training data and test coverage will get better as real input from the chatbot users will be part of the improvements.

Defining NLP Test Data With Botium

Botium has all tools included for testing an NLP model. The user examples to send to the NLP model for evaluation are organized in utterance lists as simple text files. Here are two utterance lists, one for positive consent (yes), and the other for rejection (no).Here is the file UTT_YES.utterances.txt:

```
UTT_YES
yes
yes please
sure
do it
exactly
confirm
of course
sounds good
that's correct
I don't mind
I agree
ok
```

And here is the file UTT_NO.utterances.txt:

```
UTT_NO
don't do it
definitely not
not really
thanks but no
not interested
I don't think so
I disagree
I don't want that
no
nope
no thanks
```

Asserting NLP Predictions With Botium

Now that the test data is defined, the next step is to actually write the test cases with user input and assertions. In Botium, this is done with simple text files as well (or any other of the supported file formats). A test case named "T01_YES" is defined in a file T01_YES.convo.txt:

```
T01_YES

#me
UTT_YES

#bot
INTENT intent_yes
INTENT_CONFIDENCE 0.8
```

And a second test case is named "T02_NO" in a file T02_NO.convo.txt:

```
T01_NO

#me
UTT_NO

#bot
INTENT intent_no
INTENT_CONFIDENCE 0.8
```

These test cases are to be read like this:

1. First line is the name of the test case.
2. Every single user example from the UTT_YES resp UTT_NO utterance list is sent to the NLP model.
3. A prediction of intent_yes resp intent_no is expected, together with a confidence score of at least 0.8, otherwise the test case is reported as failure.

The INTENT and INTENT_CONFIDENCE words are "magic words" in Botium which trigger special behavior. In this case, the assertion behavior is triggered to evaluate the predicted intent and the confidence score as returned from the NLP model. Note: there are additional magic words for NLP assertions available in Botium — see Botium Wiki.[119]

The whole test suite can be run with one of the Botium frontends (Botium Box, Botium Bindings, or Botium CLI).

Conversational Context With Botium

In order to set the conversational context in the NLP test cases, add some additional steps to the test case files to set the context.

```
TC78_TEMP_NEWYORK

#me
tell me about the weather

#bot
Where are you located?

#me
UTT_CITIES

#bot
In *, there are * degrees Celsius
INTENT intent_weather
ENTITIES location
```

So, this test case makes sure that the NLP is in the "ask for weather" mode before sending the locations from the UTT_CITIES utterance list to the NLP model.

Test Result Analytics

While the previous section showed how easy it is to define NLP model test cases with Botium, it is clear that even for chatbots with small functional scope the high number of potential test cases makes it difficult to compare individual test results and makes a clear statement on the NLP model quality.

The basic question to answer is: did the latest changes have a positive or negative impact on the NLP model performance? Even when dealing with a small to medium chatbot project with 30 intents and 70 user examples per intent, there are thousands of test results to validate and compare to the previous training cycles — which is impossible when relying on quick feedback cycles. What we need are a rather small amount of comparable numbers (or metrics) — in best case exactly one number — to tell us about the general NLP model performance, and some other numbers telling us the hot spots to give attention.

In one sentence: Quality metrics make NLP model training cycles comparable and point out areas of interest.

The Confusion Matrix

A Confusion Matrix shows an overview of the predicted intent vs. the expected intent. It answers questions like, "When sending user example X, I expect the NLP model to predict intent Y — what did it actually predict?"

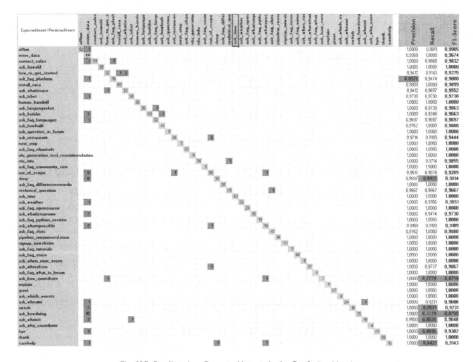

Fig. 115: Predicted vs. Expected Intents in the Confusion Matrix

The expected intents are shown as rows. The predicted intents are shown as columns. User examples are sent to the NLP model, and the cell value for the expected intent row and the predicted intent column is increased by one. So whenever predicted and expected intent is a match, the cell value in the diagonal is increased — these are our successful test cases. All other cell values not on the diagonal are our failed test cases.

Evaluating the Confusion Matrix

Here is a small extract from a large confusion matrix.

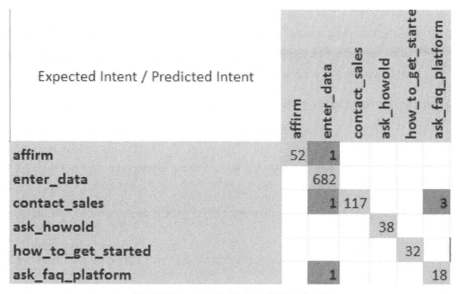

Expected Intent / Predicted Intent	affirm	enter_data	contact_sales	ask_howold	how_to_get_started	ask_faq_platform
affirm	52	1				
enter_data		682				
contact_sales		1	117			3
ask_howold				38		
how_to_get_started					32	
ask_faq_platform		1				18

Fig. 116: Discovering the Confusion Matrix in Detail

This matrix lets us deduct statements like these:

- There are 53 (52 + 1) user examples for the affirm intent. But for one of them, the NLP model predicted the enter_data intent instead.

- The NLP model predicted the ask_faq_platform intent for 21 (18 + 3) user examples, but it was only expected in 18 of them. For the remaining 3 the expected intent was contact_sales, so the prediction was wrong.

- For the ask_faq_platform intent, there are 19 (18 + 1) user examples, but only 18 of them have been recognized by the NLP model.

- For 38 user examples, the ask_howold intent was expected, and the NLP model predicted it for exactly these 38 user examples.

And from these statements, there are several conclusions:

- The ask_howold and how_to_get_started intents are trained perfectly.

- There are 3 user examples where the NLP model predicted ask_faq_platform, but the test data expected the intent contact_sales — find out the 3 user examples and refine training data for them.

- enter_data intent was predicted for 3 (1 + 1 + 1) user examples where another intent was expected. On the other hand, there are 682 user examples correctly identified as enter_data, so the trade-off for this intent is acceptable.

Precision, Recall, and F1-Score

The statements above are logically flawless, but not totally intuitive.

- How do you decide if an intent or an intent pair needs refinement and additional training?

- How do you actually compare the total NLP model performance to a previous training cycle?

- How do you compare the performance for the most important intents to the previous training cycle?

- How do you decide if the training data is good enough for production usage?

That's where the statistical concept of precision and recall and the F1-Score representing the trade-off between the two comes into play.

Precision

In the example above, the NLP model recognized the intent ask_faq_platform for 21 (18 + 3) user examples. For 3 of them, the expected intent was another intent, so 3 out of 21 predictions are wrong. The precision is ~ 0.85 (18 / 21), number of correct predictions for intent ask_faq_platform shared by total number of predictions for intent ask_faq_platform. The question answered by the precision rate is this: How many predictions of an intent are correct?

Recall/Sensitivity

In the example above, we have 121 (1 + 117 + 3) user examples for what we expect the intent contact_sales. The NLP model predicted the intent contact_sales for 117 user examples only. The recall is ~0.97 (117 / 121), the number of correct predictions for intent contact_sales shared by total number of expectations for intent contact_sales.The question answered by the recall rate is this: How many intents are correctly predicted?

Precision vs. Recall — F1-Score

While those two sound pretty much the same, they are not. In fact, it is not possible to evaluate the NLP model performance with just one of those two metrics.Again, from the example above:

- The contact_sales intent has been predicted 117 times, and 117 of the predictions are correct. The precision rate is 1.0, perfect.

- There are 4 more user examples for which the NLP predicted another intent. The recall rate is ~0.97, which is pretty good, but not perfect.

In theory, it is possible to get a perfect precision rate by making a very low amount of predictions for an intent — for example, by setting the confidence level very high. But the recall rate will dramatically decrease.In this case,the NLP model will make no prediction (or a wrong prediction) in many cases.

On the other hand, it is possible to get a perfect recall rate for an intent by resolving EVERY user example to this intent. The precision will be very low then. The trade-off between recall and precision is called an F1-Score, which is the harmonic mean between the two. Most importantly, the F1-Score is a comparable metric for measuring the impact of NLP model training. The rule of thumb is:

Increasing the F1-Score means increasing NLP model performance. Decreasing the F1-Score means decreasing the NLP model performance within your test data.

An F1-Score of 0.95 usually is a good value, meaning the NLP model is working pretty well on your test data. An F1-Score of 1.0 means that all your test data is perfectly resolved by your NLP model — the perfect NLP performance. This may be pleasant for regression testing, but typically it's a sign of overfitting.

CrossValidation

As mentioned above, these performance metrics only make sense on clear separation of training data and test data. As this is sometimes not possible, a method called cross validation can be used to get good quality metrics for an NLP model. The basic principle is easy to understand:

- Split the data into two parts. The first part is used for training the NLP model. The other part is used for testing.
- To remove flakiness, do this several times and average the outcome.

In chatbot terms, this means:

- For each intent, remove some of the user examples and train a new NLP model.
- Evaluate the removed user examples and compare the predicted intent to the expected intent.
- Calculate precision, recall, F1, and average over all intents.

E2E TESTING WITH SELENIUM OR APPIUM

Testing the user experience end-to-end has to be a part of every test strategy. Apart from the conversation flow, which is best tested on the API level, it has to be verified that a chatbot published on a company website works on most used end user devices.

The special challenges when doing E2E tests for a chatbot are the high amount of test data needed (> 100.000 utterances for a medium sizes chatbot) and the slow execution time — in an E2E scenario tests are running in real time. The good news is that for testing device compatibility, a small subset of test cases is sufficient.

Safe Assumptions When Testing a Chatbot With Selenium

When testing a chatbot with Selenium, there are some safe assumptions you can rely on to reduce effort when coding test cases:

1. The chatbot is accessible on a website and there maybe is some kind of click-through to actually open the chatbot window. The procedure to navigate and open the chatbot window is always the same for all test cases.

2. Somewhere in the chatbot window there is an input field for text messages. When hitting "Enter" or clicking on a button besides the input field the text will be sent to the chatbot.

3. Somewhere in the window the chatbot responds in some kind of list view. The text sent from the user is mirrored there as well.

   a. The chatbot response contains text, pictures, hyperlinks, and maybe quick response buttons to click

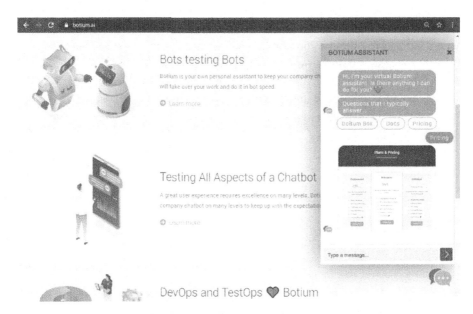

Fig. 117: E2E Testing a Browser-Based Chatbot

Based on these assumptions, an experienced Selenium developer will build a page object model to reuse all of the chatbot test cases.

Botium Webdriver Connector

If you ever worked with Selenium, you are aware that writing an automation script usually is a time-consuming task. Botium helps you in writing automation scripts for a chatbot widget embedded on a website. It speeds up the development process by providing a parameterizable default configuration for adapting it to your actual chatbot website with Selenium selectors and pluggable code snippets:

- Website address to launch for accessing the chatbot.
- Selenium selector for identification of the input text field.
- Selenium selector for identification of the "Send" button (if present, other-wise message to the chatbot is sent with "Enter" key).
- Selenium selector for identification of the chatbot output elements.
- Selenium capabilities for device or browser selection or any other Selenium specific settings.

Note: Botium can work with any Selenium or Appium endpoint available — either with a virtual browser like PhantomJS, an integrated standalone Selenium service, your own custom Selenium grid, or with cloud providers like Perfecto.

If there are additional steps (mouse clicks) to do on the website before the chatbot is accessible, you will have to extend the pre-defined Selenium scripts with custom behavior as JavaScript code.

```
module.exports = (container, browser) => {
  return browser.waitForVisible('.cc-btn', 20000)
  .click('.cc-btn')
  .pause(2000)
  .waitForVisible('#StartChat', 20000)
  .click('#StartChat')
  .waitForVisible('#chat', 10000)
  .waitForVisible('#textInput', 10000)
  .waitForVisible('.from-watson', 10000)
}
```

This code snippet does the following:

1. Waiting for a "Cookie Consent" button to appear on the website.

2. Clicking this button to make the website usable.

3. Waiting for a "Start Chat" button to appear and clicking it when available.

4. Waiting until the basic chatbot interaction elements are visible.

The full Botium configuration for this scenario looks like this:

```
{
  "botium": {
    "Capabilities": {
      "PROJECTNAME": "WebdriverIO Plugin Sample",
      "CONTAINERMODE": "webdriverio",
      "WEBDRIVERIO_OPTIONS": {
        "capabilities": {
          "browserName": "chrome"
        }
      },
      "WEBDRIVERIO_URL": "https://www.my-company.com",
      "WEBDRIVERIO_OPENBOT": "./snippets/openbot",
      "WEBDRIVERIO_INPUT_ELEMENT": "//input[@id='textInput']",
      "WEBDRIVERIO_INPUT_ELEMENT_SENDBUTTON": "//button[contains(@
class,'bot__send')]",
      "WEBDRIVERIO_OUTPUT_ELEMENT": "//div[contains(@
class,'from-watson')]"
    }
  }
}
```

With this configuration, all of your convo and utterances files can be used to run test cases with Botium and Selenium.

TESTING VOICE-ENABLED CHATBOTS

When testing voice apps, all of the principles from the previous sections apply as well. Some of the available voice-enabled chatbot technologies natively support both text and voice input and output, such as Google Dialogflow or Amazon Lex. Others are working exclusively with voice input and output, such as Alexa Voice Service. And all the other technologies can be extended with voice capabilities by inserting speech-to-text and text-to-speech engines in the processing pipeline.

For doing serious tests, at least the chatbot response has to be available as text to use text assertions. Botium supports several text-to-speech and speech-to-text engines for doing the translations.

In addition to the well-known cloud services from Google and Amazon, Botium also has its own free and open source speech service included, Botium Speech Processing.

There is one good reason for using voice instead of text as input to your test cases — if there are historic recordings available when transitioning from a legacy IVR system. Such libraries often are a valuable resource for test data.

HOW TO COLLECT TRAINING AND TEST DATA

Most chatbots are poor quality because they either do no training at all or use bad or very little training data. It's easy to make a poor chatbot — just connect some APIs, write (or copy/paste) some lines of code, and that's it. The difficulty and high effort come from implementing a process for training and testing the bot, and that's where lots of companies are failing. Chatbots are only as good as the training and testing they are given by their makers, and the quality of the training and testing is only as good as the data.

Comparison Matrix

Each of the described methods has strengths and weaknesses.

	Duration	Setup Effort	Training Effort	Price	Quality
Mechanical Turk	3-6 months	low	high	high	high
Friendly User	1-2 months	low	medium	high	low
Use the Crowd	1-2 months	medium	low	medium	high
Previous Communication	2-4 weeks	high	low	low	high
Training Datasets	1-2 days	low	low	medium	medium

Fig. 118: Summary of Strengths and Weaknesses

Criteria 1: Duration

The "time to market" is one of the most important criteria for project owners, and proper training is required before your chatbot is ready for publication.

Criteria 2: Setup Effort

Before training begins, there is effort involved — typically this effort is located in software development.

Criteria 3: Training Effort

And then there is the effort in the training phase itself. High manual effort means high training effort, in short.

Criteria 4: Price

The total price depends on the other criteria. High manual effort means high personnel costs and high software development effort as well. Licensing costs have to be included in the calculation too.

Criteria 5: Quality

Finally, the outcome in quality differs over the training methods, and it's up to the project owners to balance the involved costs with the expected overall quality.

Method 1: Mechanical Turk ("Be the Bot Yourself")

The "Mechanical Turk" was a fake chess-playing machine constructed in the 18th century. The Turk was in fact a mechanical illusion that allowed a human chess master hiding inside to operate the machine. Instead of a chatbot software, a human agent responds to user requests while the user is kept in dark about it. It's a valid attempt for PoCs, market research, and user acceptance verifications, due to nearly no setup costs. High effort is involved during the training phase, as each user request has to be handled manually.

✓ Good quality (experience real users).

✗ Long training phase with huge manual effort.

Method 2: Friendly User

As soon as the basics of the chatbot are available, friendly users are motivated to interact with the chatbot. Training data is collected whenever someone interacts, and constant training makes the bot smarter with each conversation by a friendly user. In a large company, motivate coworkers to take part in testing.

✓ Low setup effort.

✗ Low quality due to "biased" users (most likely with domain knowledge).

✗ High manual effort and high price for personnel costs.

Method 3: Use the Crowd

Publish the chatbot and let the crowd do the rest. Training is carried out by a number of different testers from different places, not by hired consultants and professionals. Potential users of your chatbot provide realistic usage scenarios and training data.

✓ Good quality if done right (crowd tester pre-selection).

✗ External costs for crowd testing.

Method 4: Previous Communication

Archived former communication from the chatbot domain is a real treasure — emails, white mail, meeting protocols, everything is potentially valuable training data. Obviously, there is effort involved in gathering the files from several archives and transforming it into a format usable for chatbot training (annotated plain text), which is partially automatable. But you have to expect lots of manual effort for adding text annotations.

✓ Good quality due to domain specific data.

✗ High setup effort for data preparation (text annotation).

Method 5: Training Datasets

Having access to domain-specific datasets collected and shared by chatbot developer teams all over the world — this clearly is the fastest approach for getting a chatbot to acceptable quality.

✓ "Quick win" in all aspects.

✗ Selection of an additional training method is obligatory, because dataset may be too generic for the chatbot business case.

Comparison Details: Costs Over Time

For the training methods involving manual effort, the costs are constantly high over the training phase, while for the automated training methods, the upfront costs are higher, but the manual methods are outperformed quickly.

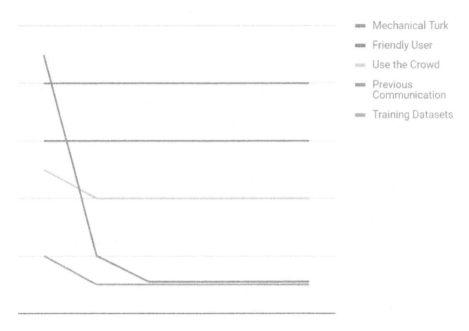

Fig. 119: Costs Over Time

Comparison Details: Quality Over Time

The manual approaches take some time to reach good quality, and the learning rate is expected to flatten down over time — user input will repeat after several cycles — but that's actually a good thing, as it is an indicator that training the most common utterances and conversations is coming to an end. The automated approaches will lead to the expected quality almost immediately.

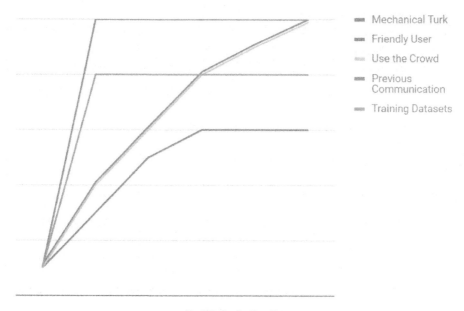

Fig. 120: Quality Over Time

Comparison Summary

Best quality of training data is guaranteed if collected in conversations with real users and real customers — it easily outperforms data collected by asking company employees biased to their company culture and domain knowledge. The price is higher effort in collecting and evaluating this training data, and it could easily take months of effort to gather a reasonable amount. A good combination of these strategies is the best way to success.

Chatbot Training Never Ends!

The key to success is to constantly monitor your chatbot and continue training to get smarter — either by doing constant training with human effort, or by scheduling regular training cycles and incorporating new utterances and conversations from real users.

DESIGNING A TEST STRATEGY FROM SCRATCH

Testing and training an NLP engine to provide a good user experience is a challenging task. In almost every project there is a clear separation between the short-tail topics, the long-tail topics, and the topics where human handover is required.

First Steps: Short-Tail Topics

The recommendations for the first steps in a chatbot project are to concentrate training and testing on the short-tail topics. Typically, with a customer support chatbot, which are the majority of the chatbots out there, there are a handful of topics only for which you have to provide good test coverage. Apart from that, leave the long-tail topics aside at first and design a clear human handover process.

The challenge is how to get good test coverage for the short-tail topics (see previous section). This is the hard work in a chatbot project. Tools like Botium can help in this process with file format converters, import/export interfaces, audio processing, NLP analytics, sentence paraphrasers, and more.

Continuous Training

As soon as the chatbot is live, there is continuous re-training required. This process involves manual work to evaluate real user conversations that for some reason went wrong and to deduct the required training steps. During this process, the test coverage will be increased. For the short-tail topics you can expect a near 100% test coverage within several weeks after launch. Those are the topics asked over and over again, and as complex as human language may be, there is only a finite number of options on how to express an intent in a reasonable, short way.

Fill in the Long-Tail Topics

A last step adds more and more of the long-tail topics to the continuous training process.

FINAL REMARKS

For testing conversational AI, test automation engineers require additional skills. Most importantly, extend your toolbelt with basic knowledge on text classification, machine learning, and statistical measures. Tools like Botium can help in design and automated execution of test cases.

As opposed to testing websites, desktop apps, or smartphone apps, there is nearly no boilerplate code required for automated testing, but the effort lies in collecting, analyzing, and organizing test and training data.

Chapter 16:
The Rise and Benefits of
Robotic Process Automation

Thomas Haver, Manager of Validation & Delivery, Designer Brands

Thomas Haver is presently serving as Manager for Validation and Delivery. He leads a team of testers, ops engineers, and production support analysts in the adoption of DevOps practices. Previously, he led the enterprise automation support of 73 applications at Huntington National Bank that encompassed testing, metrics and reporting, and data management. Thomas has a background in physics and biophysics, with over a decade spent in research science studying fluorescence spectroscopy and microscopy before joining IT.

WHAT IS RPA?

Robotic process automation (RPA) is a term given to technology that allows developers to programmatically emulate the actions of a human to execute a business process. RPA often operates on the user interface (UI) layer to capture data or interact with an application or across multiple applications to perform tasks that are considered repetitive or time consuming.[120]

RPA will typically refer to "bots." Bots are a programmed sequence of automated activities performed by a tool in order. Bots can do something as simple as navigating to a webpage or something as complex as providing a decision recommendation on a loan application. There are two types of bots: attended bots and unattended bots. Attended bots mean the user is working with the robotic process in the background, such as data entry assistance in onboarding a new employee for HR.[121] Unattended bots mean the robotic process executes in absence of human interaction, such as processing invoices.

Many companies are implementing RPA to automate high-frequency transactional and rules-based processes that are better handled by bots because of the consistency in data entry by the unattended automation.[122] Any company that chooses to adopt an RPA solution should consider which vendors have a scalable product and who within their company (IT or business or both) would lead the implementation

120 UIPath RPA https://www.uipath.com/rpa/robotic-process-automation
121 Robotic Process Automation RPA: A Complete Guide, 2019
122 The Robotic Process Automation Handbook, 2020

of that solution. With the potential for these bots to handle tasks that delve into compliance-related tasks or personally identifiable information (PII), those RPA solutions should also be secure. There is also great opportunity for existing governance within an enterprise to leverage RPA to embed those bots into handling regulatory requests. There is much to be considered from a measurement perspective before adopting RPA on an enterprise scale, some of which will be described in greater detail in this chapter.

Enterprise RPA solutions are typically fall into one of four categories: (1) Assisted RPA, (2) Unassisted RPA, (3) Autonomous RPA, and (4) Cognitive RPA. In Assisted RPA, the bot(s) are deployed to a human worker's local workstation to help with common user tasks. However, these bots have potential security and scalability concerns. In Unassisted RPA, the bot(s) are deployed on a server and can be manually controlled. These bots can also handle common workflows and end-to-end tasks across multiple applications. In Autonomous RPA, the bot(s) cover more complicated processes that often have decision trees such as changing priorities based upon external input or workload balance. In Cognitive RPA, the bot(s) are integrated with AI technologies such as machine learning and natural language processing. In this case, the AI will help handle computer vision for discovering objects on a UI and/ or data conditioning of a process. These RPA solution types can be leveraged in combination across an enterprise to great benefit.

BENEFITS OF RPA ADOPTION

Companies elect to pursue Robotic Process Automation over traditional approaches because these commercial tools promise fast return on investment (ROI), minimal upfront investment for proof of concepts (POC), and little to no disruption on the systems they interact with for automated workflows. One of the driving factors of adoption of RPA by businesses is that it can be led by the business with support of IT because the tooling has low technical hurdles for adoption with a high degree of scalability.[123] What processes are organizations looking to automate with bots? UiPath, one of the industry leaders in RPA, describes the power of this type of automation: "RPA robots are capable of mimicking many — if not all — human user actions. They log into applications, move files and folders, copy and paste data,

123 Gartner RPA Predictions
   https://www.gartner.com/en/documents/3976135/predicts-2020-rpa-renaissance-driven-by-morphing-offerin

fill in forms, extract structured and semi-structured data from documents, scrape browsers, and more."[124]

Compared to internally-built automation solutions, commercial robotic process automation offers several advantages. One benefit is the speed of implementation. Specifically, nearly all the vendors in the marketplace offer libraries of automation workflows that can be quickly applied to specific application types and specific industry use cases.[125] These libraries are tailored for existing applications and allow for simple drag-and-drop development of automated workflows, lowering the bar for development from automation engineers with years of experience to business personnel. This places the development of initial workflows into the hands of the domain experts, who may or may not have coding skills. This in turn frees up time for the more experienced, technical developers to provide support for more complex workflows and create the infrastructure necessary to scale the bots through orchestration tooling. Another benefit of commercial RPA adoption is faster scalability of bots, with pre-built infrastructure, so those pilot workflows can make it to production environments more quickly with more concurrent flows.

Another benefit of RPA adoption is maintaining a consistent tech stack across the organization — tooling is intended for the enterprise, not just IT or HR or finance. Workflows can reach across business segments and cover end-to-end scenarios from customer-facing front-end applications to back-office administrative functions. Since the tooling is consistent, components of workflows can be easily reused across business units, minimizing development time because the up-front development in one area is leveraged in other areas.[126] Thus, any enterprise building an RPA solution aggregates workflows over time, allowing for more complex processes to be automated, which in turn provides more time to optimize tasks since workers have freed up more time.

Some of the core benefits of RPA replacing manual repetitive tasks include reducing error rates and improving failure analysis.[127] Human data entry is prone to error for repetitive tasks, which is directly addressed with automated workflows. Even if data

---

124 UIPath RPA Definition https://www.uipath.com/rpa/robotic-process-automation
124 Gartner's Magic Quadrant for RPA Software
    https://www.gartner.com/en/documents/3947184/magic-quadrant-for-robotic-process-automation-software
126 The Care and Feeding of Bots, 2020
127 Robotic Process Automation, 2018

entry errors occur with automated workflows, the tooling has activity logs to help identify failure points so the cause of those exceptions can be fixed. Some tooling integrates with machine learning capabilities to limit the exceptions via adaptation to the process steps.[128] The logging of RPA activity has an additional benefit of helping to ensure regulatory compliance. Logs are created during execution of the workflows, which can be further modified to apply regulatory requirements so there is a complete record of activities for audit purposes.

The overall benefits of RPA adoption can be summarized as:

- Speed of processing time over manual workflows.
- Ease of adoption.
- Ease of scaling.
- Speed to achieving "cost neutral" status.
- Implementation across business segments.
- Reduction in errors.
- Built-in logging for failure analysis and regulatory compliance.

RPA USE CASES

In this section we will examine some of the common use cases for RPA. In general, RPA focuses on tasks that are repeatable, high volume, and business focused. Most commercial RPA vendors provide features such as remote application control, optical character recognition (OCR for short), and API automation.[129] Bots can idle waiting for a human, event, or predetermined time to execute according to an orchestration tool. Common tasks include logging into an application, moving files from one source to another, reading and writing to databases, opening emails and attachments, scraping data from web and desktop applications, connecting to systems' APIs, processing content from PDFs, and much more.[130] RPA tools can be powerful because of their many use cases, but as Spider-Man once said, "With great power comes great responsibility."[131]

128 The Practitioner's Guide to RPA: A Practical Guide for Deploying Robotics Process Automation, 2020
129 Becoming Strategic with Robotic Process Automation, 2019
130 The Simple Implementation Guide to Robotic Process Automation, 2018
131 Wikipedia Quote https://en.wikipedia.org/wiki/With_great_power_comes_great_responsibility

One concern when applying RPA to business processes is access to sensitive systems. If an individual bot has access to too many systems or a system with sensitive information, that is a potential security nightmare for InfoSec. Access to the workflows and RPA orchestration tool of choice should be limited by two-factor authentication to mitigate the risk of leaking personally identifiable information (PII), as well as to adhere to Sarbanes-Oxley (SOX) Act compliance. This can be achieved by storing bot credentials in vaults such as CyberArk.[132] Additionally, multiple bots should be created to achieve separation of duties in order to ensure user credentials and customer data are not leaked. Bots should receive the same degree of governance as human workers or higher to help ensure sanctity of data. As mentioned in the prior section, these bots have an additional advantage of audit logs that can be used for compliance purposes. A side benefit is these audit logs can also track performance and provide analytics for future enhancement — see my section on metrics later in this chapter for more information.

Among the common use cases for RPA is text analysis. Scanning documents such as insurance, purchase orders, invoices, emails, etc. are easily achieved in most RPA tools, followed by data entry in text fields. Any RPA tool should provide standard tooling for development, management and reporting, analytics, user support, and scalability as part of the core features. For specific business units, such as HR, bots can be used to assist with payroll, employee and contractor onboarding, terminations, and benefits administration. For operations, bots assist with inventory management, invoicing, planning, and content scanning of contracts. Customer service teams or "Phone Banks" can leverage RPA to help with password resets, scheduling appointments, and address changes.

As mentioned above, bots can assist the financial sector in multiple areas, including ATM data processing, fraud detection, and direct-debit management. ATMs are a primary baking feature, one that results in a great deal of data being transferred between the machines and back-end systems. In a case study, a bot was able to extract and compare data records for multiple systems (web and desktop) to improve the processing speed of data records and reduce the time needed to handle data.[133] Benefits of the implementation include fewer errors and faster processing time of

132 CyberArk Solution Page https://www.cyberark.com/
133 UIPath Case Study https://www.uipath.com/blog/6-ways-uipath-makes-banks-more-efficient

the workflow, with cost neutrality of the bot being achieved at two months post implementation.

Another example is using a bot to streamline an account creation process that would typically be hundreds of new accounts per month at about six minutes per account that crossed three different applications (one web and two desktop). This process had multiple decision points around mortgage length, credit ratings, and customer status. Post implementation resulted in a reduction of processing time and number of errors during data entry. The primary takeaway from these case studies is to explore as many use cases up front before determining which RPA tool to use and what processes to select as part of the pilot.

With so many potential use cases for RPA, management of all the processes being executed becomes another chief concern. Many of the most popular vendors have some form of central control to orchestrate execution.[134] These control features are important to track execution, separation of duties, execution schedules, total execution time, logging, and support for execution failures. Without an up-front plan on how to scale the RPA workflows, an organization risks having runaway bots that are poorly tracked, thereby losing out on the reuse benefits as well as end-to-end flows.

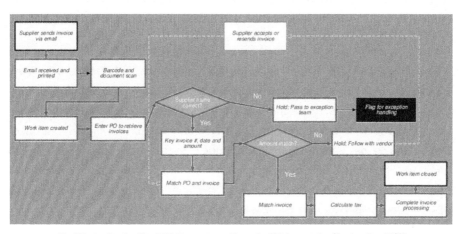

Fig. 121: Application Flow With Processes and Steps for RPA Automation (Source: Guru99)[135]

134 Gartner Magic Quadrant for RPA Software
     https://www.gartner.com/en/documents/3947184/magic-quadrant-for-robotic-process-automation-software
135 RPA Tutorial by Guru99 https://www.guru99.com/robotic-process-automation-tutorial.html

In Figure 121, there is a sample of an application flow with various use cases that would be a perfect fit for an RPA tool to automate, saving a great manual recurring work.

THE RPA JOURNEY

The following describes a multi-step process for growing an RPA program. The journey will not be short because investment in RPA is long term if the goal is to maximize value. Companies looking to adopt RPA need to initially seek out as many process candidates as possible to reduce operating costs. This can be the first big obstacle because they don't have proficiency in identifying good candidates. Part of the journey means coming to the shared understanding that RPA will relieve the workload of many workers and involve the potential conversion of some workers to the RPA team.

1. Building a Program

Successful RPA programs begin with a small proof of concept and vision of how the company plans to align people, process, and technology. RPA is not just about tooling and it's a mistake for any organization to make that assumption. An RPA program for a team or an enterprise must first establish an understanding of the core components of the initiative, just as any large-scale project would be rolled out.

From the technology side, there are several guiding principles the initiative should follow. From the development side, the RPA solution should operate across the same layers of the application as a human worker. The upfront expectation for tooling includes libraries that integrate with industry standard applications, and those libraries have reusable components. The RPA solution should be version controlled. Depending on the expected technical aptitude of the team, the organization should identify tooling that expectation for amount of coding. Several commercial options offer "zero" or "no code" development. There are organizations that can own all RPA development or provide training for RPA.[136,137]

Just like any application under development, the RPA solution should have a standard for defect tracking and associated test coverage. Many commercial RPA tools offer built-in session and error logs for debugging. These features should

---

136 Accelirate Service Provider https://www.accelirate.com/
137 Agility Partners Service Provider https://www.agilitypartners.io/solutions/evolve

be considered a requirement for any organization looking to scale their solution. Similar to other applications developed within the organization, the RPA solution should be designed based on object-oriented principles and under the governance of an architecture review board.

If the expectation for the RPA solution is an enterprise-wide deployment, then scalability and deployment strategy must be determined as an upfront concern. Will the bots run on virtual machines or in the cloud? Will the bots be attended, unattended, or both? Will the platform support web services (REST, SOAP)? Before any large-scale development of RPA workflows, the team working on the RPA solution should setup a central application server with an orchestration tool for handling the bots. This server should handle the scheduling and queueing of the bots. If there will be many processes executing, then the server should handle automation in parallel with the exception of handling and logging.

As mentioned earlier in the chapter, bots should at least have the same security standards as the human workforce. This means using a credentials vault, role-based access control, activity logs, and audit trails.

Once these upfront tasks are addressed, then the organization is ready to consider the integration of RPA with existing features or other planned enhancements (analytics, AI, ML).[138] A common use case for RPA is handling emails and documents sent by customers. This unstructured data requires dynamically reading content, which means more complex decisioning than simple process automation. Additionally, as flows are developed, the team will look to create an end-to-end process across multiple applications. These integrated workflows will require both orchestration as well as control points for potential human intervention.

2. Roles & Responsibilities

A new team must be formed to support the RPA program, which includes a mix of individuals focused on either the strategic or tactical aspects of the implementation. This team should ideally devote their full time to the program from the proof-of-concept stage of development to ensure the best outcomes. The tactical members

---

138 *Information Age – Maturing Role of AI in RPA*
  https://www.information-age.com/the-maturing-role-of-ai-in-rpa-123481142/

of the team are devoted to the technical implementation of the bots and associated infrastructure (orchestration).

First and foremost, the RPA developers are the technical experts responsible for developing and testing the bots. These individuals are comparable to the traditional developers on application teams and are likely drawn from those teams to become RPA developers. One or more individuals will serve as the architect to design the solutions and establish guidelines for adoption across the enterprise. This person will also help determine the RPA tooling. At least one person should lead RPA infrastructure to assist in server installation and solution architecture for scaling RPA via the orchestration tool. The technical team should be led by a manager who owns the RPA deployment and infrastructure, and who is ultimately responsible for the program outcomes.

From the business side, the strategic focus will be on planning work, communications, and defining the workflows for bots. The sponsor/champion of the RPA program should come from the business side since they can help establish the program as an enterprise goal and not just an IT goal. This person acts as the evangelist to advocate for adoption across multiple business segments, helping to secure funding for the program. They are the primary contact for the RPA team, setting the communication plan. The team will also require one or more RPA analysts, who have domain knowledge about their business segments. These individuals are responsible for creating the process flows that will implemented by the RPA developers. They are analogous to business analysts on application development teams. Lastly, as the RPA program matures, there will likely be a need for at least one person to become a support specialist for handling deployment issues in production.

3. Adoption Steps

Step 1: Pilot

The pilot stage should include a use case that has big-visible potential to demonstrate value to stakeholders. As with any new initiative, it can be difficult to implement change within an organization without buy-in from leadership and those directly impacted by the change. For this reason, it's imperative to deliver a pilot for the leadership and those directly impacted by the automation. The leadership need to be shown hard evidence that RPA will save both time and costs, so the RPA program can be expanded to additional use cases.[139] Those directly impacted by automation need to be shown the benefits of taking that repetitive and/or error-task out of their hands with an eye toward more value-added activities in their day-to-day responsibilities. The successful outcome of the pilot stage is a success story about RPA with tangible, measurable benefits everyone can celebrate.

Step 2: Adoption

During the adoption phase, the team responsible for RPA adoption should target teams responsible for those candidate tests cases and find potential "automation champions" to support RPA. Everyone likes to be part of a success story, and to bias implementation toward success requires supporters in each application RPA will touch. During this time the team should also adopt a set of standards and practices for RPA workflows and engagement with each team. If the team stops with only a few flows implemented, true success will never be achieved. To help achieve a state of RPA, an organization must constantly review existing automation for enhancements and look for new opportunities where there is no active engagement.

Step 3: Expansion

During the expansion phase, the team should have a good grasp on the state of the enterprise given the baseline data gathered from engaging with various teams. With the backlog of candidate workflows identified, apply the baseline metrics to determine the highest priority workflows for RPA. Tasks that can be reused in end-to-end automated flows are great for providing maximum ROI. It's important at this stage to make the group responsible for RPA a permanent team and not a collection of individuals pulled from multiple teams. If each team sets their own standards for RPA, then the organization will lack a clear vision for the future and quality of the automated flows will suffer as well. As mentioned in other parts of this chapter, it's important to document the workflows being automated — not just in the scripts but rather true documentation so the domain knowledge for the organization is not lost once it's transferred from people to RPA workflows.

---

139 Deploying an RPA Solution, *Information Week*
   https://www.informationweek.com/big-data/ai-machine-learning/3-steps-for-deploying-robotic-process-automation/a/d-id/1337466

Step 4: Enhancement

RPA training should be considered standard onboarding for certain roles within the organization. Review of existing RPA should be standard practice as well as examination of new candidate tasks as the company grows. Metrics should be collected as part of the automated process at this point so monitoring of status and progress toward new initiatives is easy to track.

In the journey to RPA success, there are several potential obstacles along the way. A clear lack of expectations for deployment for the RPA team means they will have no initial success measure. Before the team begins deploying bots, they should have a clear process definition for implementation understood by both the business (strategic) and technical (tactical) team members. If the organization does not establish metrics upfront, then it can be challenging to understand progress and ROI.

Final Advice on Your RPA Journey

In addition to the above guidance on RPA adoption, there are several other best practice recommendations to bias an enterprise to long-term success. The business sponsors for the initial RPA project should work side-by-side with the development team implementing the solution; this alignment means agreement with the team on the successful end state and associated business key performance indicators (KPIs). The combined team should agree upfront on consistent nomenclature for the workflows, so the less technical (but domain knowledge rich) workers speak the same language as the more technical RPA developers. The deployment of bots may vary from business segment to business segment, so it's important for the team to collect upfront the monitoring and scaling expectations from each stakeholder. However, the company should try to maintain a centralized dashboard for visualization of all processes along with associated analytics.

As more processes are automated, loss of domain knowledge around the business process becomes a true concern. In the prior state before bots, much of knowledge would reside with human workers. If that knowledge is put into robot process automation and not documented elsewhere, there is a risk that at some future time people simply will not know WHY a bot executes. Therefore, it's important to include process documentation and audit logs for implementation, so this knowledge is never lost in translation.

Lastly, the RPA team should maintain a consistent pace for work, just like any application development team. It will be tempting with early success to spread RPA across the organization. Better to build the program at a steady, successful rate than grow too big too fast and risk failure. Each workflow implemented should yield deeper insights into operations and the metrics provided from each execution should be leveraged to optimize existing flows.

TOOLS

Any organization looking to adopt Robotic Process Automation will not face limited tooling in the current climate. There are many RPA vendors to select from — see the table below. For the sake of brevity, this chapter will only focus on the industry leader: UiPath. They were recently identified as the leader in the industry by Gartner's Magic Quadrant for Robotic Process Automation.[140] The evaluation criteria included market understanding, product offering, business model, and innovation, among others.

Although UiPath is an industry leader, the RPA market is growing rapidly and anyone investigating a solution for their team or enterprise should consider best fit for their organization. Two other strong RPA vendors with significant market share are Automation Anywhere and Blue Prism. Each has overlap from a feature-perspective with UiPath.

For instance, the Blue Prism design studio has a low technical hurdle compared to most traditional automation but does require some programming.[141] Their workflows, like those from other industry peers, have a drag-and-drop UI design. Blue Prism offers Citrix and virtual desktop infrastructure (VDI) integration as well as third-party accreditation for certification.[142]

Automation Anywhere originally focused on desktop solutions but expanded their offerings to include many of the application types described earlier in the chapter. Building RPA workflows in Automation Anywhere also has a low technical hurdle.

140 Gartner's Magic Quadrant for RPA Software
    https://www.gartner.com/en/documents/3947184/magic-quadrant-for-robotic-process-automation-software
141 Robotic Process Automation with Blue Prism Quick Start Guide, 2018
142 BluePrism University https://portal.blueprism.com/university

However, more advanced workflows required knowledge of XML or C#.[143] The Automation Anywhere platform provides a central control feature, scheduling, and triggering capabilities. Also matching UiPath and BluePrism, they offer training and certification.[144]

Vendor	Product	Website
Another Monday	Another Monday RPA	https://www.anothermonday.com/
AntWorks	ANTstein	https://www.ant.works/
Automation Anywhere	Automation Anywhere Enterprise & Community, Bot Insight, Bot Farm, Bot Store, and IQ Bot	https://www.automationanywhere.com/
Blue Prism	Blue Prism	https://www.blueprism.com/
Contextor	Contextor Studio, Control, Standalone Bot, and Galaxy	https://contextor.eu/en/contextor-2/
EdgeVerve	AssistEdge	https://www.edgeverve.com/assistedge/
Kofax	Kapow	https://www.kofax.com/Products/rpa/overview
Kryon Systems	Kryon RPA	https://www.kryonsystems.com/
Nice	NICE Robotic Automation	https://www.nice.com/rpa/

143 Automation Anywhere RPA Requirements
  https://docs.automationanywhere.com/bundle/enterprise-v11.3/page/enterprise/topics/aae-developer/aae-simple-dll-task.html
144 Automation Anywhere University https://university.automationanywhere.com/

Pegasystems	Pega Robotic Automation and Intelligence	https://www.pega.com/products/pega-platform/robotic-automation
Redwood Software	Redwood Robotics	https://www.redwood.com/
Softomotive (recently acquired by Microsoft)	Process Robot and Win Automation	https://www.softomotive.com/
Tricentis	RPA Studio	https://documentation.tricentis.com/tricentis-rpa-studio/latest/en/content/home.htm
UiPath	Studio Pro, Studio X, Test Suite, Orchestrator, Automation Cloud, AI Fabric	https://www.uipath.com/
WorkFusion	WorkFusion Intelligent Automation	https://www.workfusion.com/

Fig. 122: RPA Product Vendors

Selecting a tool means first understanding the scale of operation. Will the organization want to pay on a per-transaction or per-process basis? Do they want to pay for fixed usage or variable usage capacity? These questions should be answered with the long-term view in mind, even if the team is approved for funding only for the proof of concept. When selecting the best fit tooling, it's important to consider access to training and documentation, product support, how often the platform is updated, and feature roadmaps. One of the adoption criteria should be the technology companies partnered with the RPA vendor, because that often determines the robustness of pre-built libraries for automation workflows.

UiPath

UiPath offers a Robotic Process Automation platform with integrations for cloud orchestration, testing, and AI. UiPath is one of the fastest growing tech companies in North America according to Deloitte.[145,146] They have a customer base in excess of 3,000 including many Fortune 500 companies and in 2020 were valued at $10.2 billion.[147]

UiPath's "Studio Pro" product is based on Microsoft's Workflow Foundation,[148] with many methods to organize activities using a set of underlying automation tools. They also provide a "Studio X" version of their product[149] to simplify the development of process automation. Studio X allows workflows to be imported into their "Studio Pro" product for more robust development by dedicated RPA developers. UiPath's toolset includes capabilities for natural language processing (NLP), optical character recognition (OCR), and machine learning (ML), all of which integrate with their Orchestrator tool for managing automation execution. Additionally, UiPath has partnerships with Postman, SauceLabs, and CyberArk to provide integrations for API, device testing and data security. The company also offers an online academy for training[150] with optional certification program.[151]

UiPath's Application Testing

UiPath's "Studio Pro" supports automated testing for applications that can be executed from their IDE or included in CI/CD pipelines. The two forms of tests are "test cases" and "data-driven test cases." The data-driven test cases use imported data that the developer can select (all or some of the data set) to verify test case execution. Tests are executed in sequence and the associated activities include "verify control attribute," "verify expression," and "verify expression with operator."

145 UiPath Growth
    https://www.businesswire.com/news/home/20191107005073/en/UiPath-Ranks-No.-1-Fastest-Growing-Company
146 Deloitte Article
    https://www2.deloitte.com/us/en/pages/technology-media-and-telecommunications/articles/fast500-apply.html
147 Forbes
    https://www.forbes.com/sites/tomtaulli/2020/07/17/uipaths-225m-round-what-does-this-mean-for-rpa-robotic-process-automation/#2f1720f86852
148 Microsoft WorkFlow Foundation
    https://docs.microsoft.com/en-us/dotnet/framework/windows-workflow-foundation/
149 UiPath Studio X https://www.uipath.com/product/studio
150 UiPath Academy https://www.uipath.com/rpa/academy
151 UiPath University https://www.uipath.com/learning/certification

The "verify control attribute"[152] activity confirms the output of an activity by asserting a given expression (equality, inequality, greater than, less than, etc.) with the option to continue the RPA activity after failure of the test or to abort the execution. The "verify expression"[153] activity confirmed the truth value of a provided expression and also includes an option to continue the RPA activity after failure.

The "verify expression with operator" activity[154] confirms an expression by asserting it to a given expression with an operator. Both sides of the expression must be entered as properties with the operator selected (equality, inequality, greater than, less than, etc.). Like the first two activities, "verify expression with operator" also includes an option to continue the RPA activity after a failure. All three test activities also include an option to take a screenshot upon failure of the test. Workflows can be converted to and from test cases in Studio Pro as well as published to the Orchestrator for execution.

UiPath's RPA Testing

UiPath's "Studio Pro" includes RPA testing capabilities for testing workflows and viewing activity coverage. The developer can create a test case within a workflow and has three default containers: "Given," "When," and "Then."

The naming conventions of the container match the Given-When-Then format of Gherkin acceptance criteria. The file itself is invoked inside the "When" container of the RPA flow. One of the cool features of RPA testing in UiPath is the activity coverage, which is displayed during debugging. Separate test cases can be created to cover each scenario for an overall workflow to improve activity coverage — 100% coverage means that the data set used in the test case along with activities covers all possible scenarios.

152 UiPath Documentation, Verify Control Attribute https://docs.uipath.com/activities/docs/verify-control-attribute
153 UiPath Documentation, Verify Expression https://docs.uipath.com/activities/docs/verify-expression
154 UiPath Documentation, Verify Expression With Operator
    https://docs.uipath.com/activities/docs/verify-expression-with-operator

Fig. 123: UiPath RPA Testing (Source: UiPath) [155]

UiPath's API Test Automation

UiPath's "Studio Pro" also support API testing via Postman[156] and Newman,[157] which is a CLI runner for Postman. API collections created in Postman can be imported to "Studio Pro" or added to Orchestrator for test automation.

To create API tests within UiPath, first define a data collection or import an existing data collection in Postman. In UiPath, a developer must first create a library project and connect to the collection via Postman integration with a specific API key. Next, the endpoints need to be selected. These endpoints will be automatically transformed into activities in "Studio Pro." The data values from Postman are imported

155 UiPath RPA Testing https://docs.uipath.com/studio/docs/rpa-testing
156 Postman API Testing https://www.postman.com/
157 Newman API Testing GitHub https://github.com/postmanlabs/newman

as "Arguments." After this step, a developer can load these API libraries by creating a new test automation project in "Studio Pro" and adding it as a dependency in "Manage Packages." The activities are now available in the API test automation project, adding API testing functionality to UiPath.

UiPath's Test Manager/Test Suite

UiPath has also recently enhanced their platform with a set of tools to aid in testing activities. The "Test Manager" can be used to manage tests, while "StudioPro" is for automating tests, with the orchestrator and robots acting to distribute and execute the tests, respectively. The new hub (shown below) integrates with existing ALM tools to help track tests associated with specific requirements.

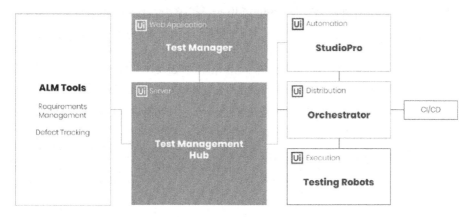

Fig. 124: UiPath Architecture (Source: UiPath Documentation)[158]

"StudioPro" allows a developer to create automated tests just like RPA workflows. "Orchestrator" is capable of executing test cases from "StudioPro" in a scheduled manner or via the CI/CD pipeline. The Test Management Hub integrates the UiPath Test Suite with other Application Lifecycle Management (ALM) tools to assign test cases to requirements, user stories, or other artifacts, as well as create bug reports with log information and screenshots. The "Test Manager" is a web application that allows a user to assign automation from "StudioPro" to test cases, assign test cases to requirements, report test results, perform manual testing, create defects from test results, and add documentation to manual test cases.

---

158 UiPath Test Manager, Documentation https://docs.uipath.com/test-manager/docs/introduction

In UiPath Test Suite, the project is a full set of artifacts to handle testing efforts. The Test Manager package allows for multiple active projects at once. The tool also contains a number of "connectors," which are libraries used to connect to external ALM tools. These connectors can be configured on a per project basis in case multiple ALM tools are used within an enterprise. For instance, the Jira connector is included in the initial Test Manager setup and an Atlassian app is available from the Atlassian Marketplace for the Jira Server. Entering the server URL, Jira credentials, defect types, and project key creates an initial setup. The user can then sync Test Manager to Jira by identifying the requirement types (task, sub-task, story, bug, epic, etc.).

The Test Manager tools support the synchronization of requirements between the tool and an external source, so users can create requirements within Test Manager and then sync them with any number of tools. Once the sync process is complete, any requirement created in that external tool is also created in Test Manager. However, the attributes are read-only in Test Manager. For Jira specifically, when a new object is created in Jira with synchronization enabled then it will automatically create the requirement. The same applies for updates to an object, but not for ALL requirements when the initial synchronization is completed. The application is intentionally setup in this manner to prevent a mass influx of data to Test Manager. Additionally, if an object is deleted in Jira the synchronized object in Test Manager will remain. Once the connecter is installed in Jira then simply selecting "push to Test Manager" object from the "More" menu in Jira will synchronize with Test Manager.

Test cases can be either manual or automated, allowing for non-technical team members to create test cases that will later be automated. Test cases can be created in the Test Design menu. Each test case can include a name (required), version tag for results reporting (optional), description that allows for Markdown (optional), and labels to make searching for test cases easier.

Test cases can also be assigned to requirements. Within the Requirements menu open a requirement and then select "Assign Test Cases" to add any test case by key, name, or labels. The steps for the manual test cases are similar to the steps created in many popular ALM tools such as Jira and Azure Test Plans. Within each step, the tester can identify granular user interactions with the application or higher-level operations. Just like the popular testing tools, each test step contains a description and an expected behavior. While the expected behavior is an optional field, it's recommended to be included to confirm each step was actually successful.

Fig. 125: UiPath Architecture (Source: UiPath Documentation) [159]

Automated test cases are created in UiPath's "StudioPro." The user must first enter the location of the Test Manager URL for any new project. Once linked, test cases from Test Manager are accessible by "StudioPro" and new tests can be exported from "StudioPro" back to Test Manager. This allows for users to create manual tests first and to later have them automated in "StudioPro."

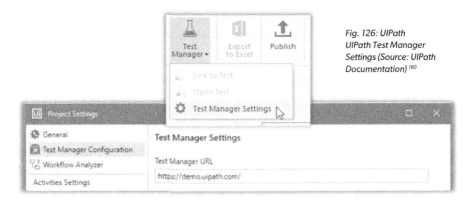

Fig. 126: UiPath
UiPath Test Manager
Settings (Source: UiPath
Documentation) [160]

159 UiPath Test Manager https://docs.uipath.com/test-manager/docs/managing-test-cases
160 UiPath Documentation https://docs.uipath.com/test-manager/docs/managing-test-cases

Another interesting feature of UiPath's Test Suite is the "task capture" functionality that allows the user to document test cases without manually downloading images or typing titles for each action. The feature captures steps and takes screenshots with every mouse click, collecting data along the way such as execution time, number of steps, text, entries, etc. These dynamically captured steps can be edited later in the test case. "Task Capture" is relatively easy: after creating an initial test case with required fields, the tester can select the "Tasks" dropdown and select "Document With Task Capture" to begin. Once the recording is finished, the user can select many options to export and publish the recorded test. Selecting the "Test Manager" option publishes to the test cases section within Test Manager.

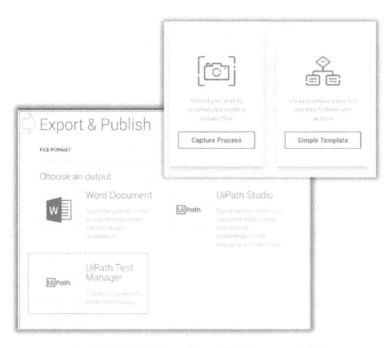

Fig. 127: UiPath Task Capture (Source: UiPath Documentation) [161]

The Test Manager tool also allows for the creation of Test Sets, which are group-ings of test cases like many popular test tracking tools. Much like those tools, the purpose is to logically group those tests so that they're executed together (e.g. smoke tests or regression tests). Test Sets are created in the "Planning" section and require a name and one or more labels. A description of the test set is optional but

---

161 UiPath Documentation, Task Capture https://docs.uipath.com/task-capture/docs/test-manager

recommended to provide additional information. Once a Test Set is created, the "Assign Test Cases" option allows the user to assign individual test cases to that set by name, key, or a label.

Create Test Set

Test Set Name

Name of the Test Set

Description (optional)

Provide additional information about the test set

Labels

Click to add label

Cancel   Create

Fig. 128: UIPath Test Sets Creation (Source: UIPath Documentation) [162]

Once new test cases have been created, they can be executed manually or automatically. The "Orchestrator" tool is used for automated execution while manual test sets are executed within "Test Manager." Manual tests must be marked as passed or failed each step whereas automated tests are updated after execution. Test Manager will create a Test Execution with the same name as the Test Set, which includes a log of the test results. The Test Execution log is snapshot in time, so any subsequent changes to the Test Set do not affect the log of results.

Similar to most test execution conventions, passing tests are shown in green and failing tests are shown in red. In Test Manager, the execution results will include basic information such as when it was executed, the duration, and overall results. The individual result of each test case can be explored, which includes screenshots, detailed information about test steps, error messages, etc. If defects need to be created from the test results, the "Create Defect" option is available in every Test Case Log. A link to the defect is created and displayed in the Test Case Log, which includes screenshots.

---

162 *UIPath Test Sets Creation https://docs.uipath.com/test-manager/docs/test-sets*

METRICS

Telemetry has become an alternate term used to describe monitoring or metrics after the release of "The DevOps Handbook" in 2016. In the context of robotic process automation, telemetry is a type of monitoring to help optimize bot deployments. Telemetry is also used to provide business metrics that can help managers and stakeholders track key performance indicators (KPIs) and make better decisions informing ongoing RPA investment and strategy. Telemetry to monitor progress and measure success is a necessary upfront determination since adoption of RPA involves an investment of time and resources. This will aid in measuring the viability of the implementation, justifying the initial investment, making iterative improvements based on analytics to mature the RPA program, and help make evidenced-based decisions about the next steps.

RPA metrics can generally be divided along two distinct timelines: the initial pilot stage to measure foundational work and the mature stage to measure long-term benefits with potential enhancements.

As part of pilot stage activities, baseline measures must be collected for the candidate use cases. One of the challenges is understanding the cost of business for many common activities that would be good candidates. Something as simple as data entry from email to a desktop application can be handled by most of the RPA platforms, but without insight into day-to-day business activities, these candidates can be overlooked.

According to a study at the London School of Economics, the ROI of RPA was between 30% and 200% in the first year after implementation in a review of 16 projects.[163] From the outset it's important to both identify the RPA candidates and the associated costs, time commitment, effort, error rates, etc. associated with those activities. Those initial baselines should be approved by both the leadership and those employees impacted by automation. The pilot stage includes the following categories:

- **Adoption Rate** — The adoption of the RPA program across business units or by candidate workflows is valuable to track against expectations if there are time-sensitive deadlines to reach a "cost zero" or "cost neutral" status on the project.

163 Mckinsey, Value of RPA in Financial Services
https://www.mckinsey.com/industries/financial-services/our-insights/the-value-of-robotic-process-automation#

- **Overall Cost Savings** — Reducing tech stack size and limiting staffing size.

- **Time Savings** — Pre- and post-implementation time spent per workflow. This can be further subdivided into time spent completing the workflow and the downtime in stages of the workflow that is reduced with RPA.

- **Output Improvement** — Pre- and post-implementation output for a workflow (scalability of tasks).

- **Enhanced Accuracy** — Pre- and post-implementation number of errors for a workflow.

- **Security** — Pre- and post-implementation vulnerabilities measured in the number of controls on the bots versus the people.

During the pilot stage and through the mature adoption stage of RPA development, performance dashboards should be created to focus on key operation metrics like utilizations of those bots and capacity versus manual tasks. This is an important step in development because telemetry should be captured automatically and be made visible to all stakeholders. While some sample metrics are given in this chapter, they are by no means the end-all, as many other ideas have been published.[164] Good telemetry should be easily trackable, accurate, consistent, and objective. They will help inform the RPA team and the business stakeholders about future decisions and where best to invest time.

Most commercial RPA tools have analytics capabilities embedded in the orchestration tool.[165] Another form of transparency are shareable reports on execution of bots. The same orchestration tooling can be used to generate reports as well as create alerts notifying key stakeholders of operational issues to determine health of RPA.

RPA performance metrics for the "mature stage" are important to demonstrate the benefits to stakeholders to make the program part of the standard tech stack rather than an exception. At this stage, the organization must have concrete goals and some form of automated monitoring toward those goals. The following is a set of sample metrics for determining ROI at this lifecycle stage. No single metric

164 RPA Performance Metrics, Walklett Group https://www.walklettgroup.com/measuring-rpa-10-performance-metrics-for-assessing-robotic-process-automation-benefits/
165 Gartner's Magic Quadrant for RPA Software https://www.gartner.com/en/documents/3947184/magic-quadrant-for-robotic-process-automation-software

determines success or failure of an RPA program. They all should be included in the overall evaluation — whether developing RPA internally or contracting the work to an outside firm.

- **Time-to-Completion** — Measure the time it takes to complete a process manually before and after implementation. For instance, simple form-field data entry on a web application. The average velocities should be collected for those processes and compared as a day-by-day and year-over-year savings to determine the total time savings.

- **Task Accuracy** — The human workforce is prone to errors during manual, re-petitive tasks. One of the promises of RPA is improved accuracy by bots that will consistently perform tasks with minimal errors. To measure "improved accuracy," first measure the amount of rework that must be done for the task in question. This rework should be due to human error. Compare the rework time before RPA to the rework time post-RPA plus the cost of implementing (and maintaining) the RPA workflow for that task.

- **Downtime Reduction** — Compare the downtime needed to complete a workflow by humans before RPA is implemented and after implementation.

- **Employee Happiness** — Survey employees who are targeted to have RPA tasks implemented that cover responsibilities in their current role. For instance, targeting process automation of timesheet approval could mean resource managers or HR personnel should be surveyed. Take a survey post-implementation to see if their job satisfaction has risen. A key concern to consider is what value-added task or tasks are they doing in lieu of the automated task. Implementing automation can cause concern among employees that they will be "automated out of a job," so it's important to communicate upfront exactly what tasks they will be doing instead of the automated workflow.

- **Yearly Compliance** — Audits can at times be long, drawn-out processes to demonstrate regulatory compliance. Often that effort is manual when it comes to reconciliations, internal control testing, and retention of sensitive data. If an RPA process can generate the necessary audit logs or reduce gaps between audit systems that otherwise make compliance difficult to determine, there are multiple value-add propositions. For one, there is the pure time savings in conducting those audit-related activities post-automation. Another measurable benefit is reduction in regulatory fines for non-compliance after implementing automation. The progress measure should be the percent of audit compliance on a process-by-process basis.

- **Tech Stack Reduction** — Existing processes may require tools and services that can be completely replaced with a single enterprise RPA tool such as UiPath, Blue Prism, or Automation Anywhere. Before beginning the RPA journey, first map out the candidate workflows and associated tooling for those flows. For each tool that can be potentially retired, consider the yearly cost of the tool that also includes maintenance, licensing fees, development, training, etc. Compare those costs against the same for the RPA platform of choice.

Bibliography

1. Blokdyk, Gerardus. Robotic Process Automation RPA: A Complete Guide. 1st ed., 5STARCooks, 2019.

2. Murdoch, Richard. Robotic Process Automation. Independently Published, 2018.

3. Sireci, Jonathan. The Practitioner's Guide to RPA: A Practical Guide for Deploying Robotics Process Automation. 1st ed., Self-Published, 2020.

4. Surdak, Walter, et al. The Care and Feeding of Bots. Independently Published, 2020.

5. Taulli, Tom. The Robotic Process Automation Handbook. Apress, 2020.

6. Wibbenmeyer, Kelly. The Simple Implementation Guide to Robotic Process Automation (Rpa). iUniverse, 2018.

7. Willcocks, Leslie, et al. Becoming Strategic with Robotic Process Automation. Zaltbommel-Netherlands, Netherlands, Van Haren Publishing, 2019.

8. Ying, Lim Mei. Robotic Process Automation with Blue Prism Quick Start Guide. Zaltbommel-Netherlands, Netherlands, Van Haren Publishing, 2018.

9. "Understanding the maturing role of AI in RPA". (2019, March 27). Retrieved from https://www.information-age.com/the-maturing-role-of-ai-in-rpa-123481142/

10. "Predicts 2020: RPA Renaissance Driven by Morphing Offerings and Zeal for Operational Excellence". (2019, December 19). Retrieved from https://www.gartner.com/en/documents/3976135/predicts-2020-rpa-renaissance-driven-by-morphing-offerin

11. "Magic Quadrant for Robotic Process Automation Software". (2019 July 8). Retrieved from https://www.gartner.com/en/documents/3947184/magic-quadrant-for-robotic-process-automation-software

12. "Peter Parker Principle". (2020 June 23). Retrieved from https://en.wikipedia.org/wiki/With_great_power_comes_great_responsibility

13. "The Value of Robotic Process Automation". (2017 March 1). Retrieved from https://www.mckinsey.com/industries/financial-services/our-insights/the-value-of-robotic-process-automation#

14. "Measuring RPA: 10 Performance Metrics for Assessing Robotic Process Automation Benefits". (2019 May 31). Retrieved from https://www.walklettgroup.com/measuring-rpa-10-performance-metrics-for-assessing-robotic-process-automation-benefits/

15. Kim, Gene, et al. The DevOps Handbook. Amsterdam-Netherlands, Netherlands, Amsterdam University Press, 2016.

16. "Three Steps for Deploying Robotic Process Automation" (2020 April 17). Retrieved from https://www.informationweek.com/big-data/ai-machine-learning/3-steps-for-deploying-robotic-process-automation/a/d-id/1337466

Chapter 17:
Cognitive Engineering —
Shifting Right (Digital Twin)
With GATED.AI Testing

Jonathon Wright

Jonathon Wright is a strategic thought leader and distinguished technology evangelist. He specializes in emerging technologies, innovation, and automation, and has more than 20 years of international commercial experience within global organizations. He is currently the CTO of Digital-Assured based in Oxford in the UK. Jonathon combines his extensive experience and leadership with insights into real-world adoption of Cognitive Engineering (Enterprise A.I. and AIOps).[166] Thus, he is frequently in demand as a speaker at international conferences such as TEDx, Gartner, Oracle, AI Summit, ITWeb, EuroSTAR, STAREast, STARWest, UKSTAR, Guild Conferences, Swiss Testing Days, Unicom, DevOps Summit, TestExpo, and Vivit Community (of which he is currently the president of the largest independent software community with over 70,000 members across 125 countries). Jonathon was the QA Lead for the COVID Safe Paths MIT project during the Coronavirus pandemic. He is also part of A.I. Alliance for the European Commission, a member of the review committee for the ISO-IEC 29119 part 11 for the "Testing of A.I. based systems" for the British Computer Society (BCS SIGiST). Jonathon is also the podcast host of the QA lead (based in Canada) and the author of several award-winning books and online courses.

INTRODUCTION

This chapter will cover how to prove Artificial Intelligence (AI) platforms by leveraging Cognitive, Reliability, and Chaos Engineering heuristics. The approaches and techniques that worked yesterday may not be optimum for the next generation of enterprise AI platforms.

The foundations of this chapter come from my TEDx Talk, Cognitive Learning — Evolution, Over Revolution.[167] In it, I explored the concept of cognitive learning, which is the ability to learn from the real world through

Fig. 129: Cognitive Engineering – GATED.AI Methodology

---

166 Jonathon Wright Wikipedia https://en.wikipedia.org/wiki/Jonathon_Wright.
167 Cognitive Learning — Evolution, Over Revolution, TED, Jonathon Wright, November 2017, https://www.ted.com/talks/jonathon_wright_cognitive_learning_digital_evolution_over_revolution

machine learning (ML). This feedback influences how the next generation of enterprise AI platforms will evolve through cognitive engineering, such as GATED.AI which is featured within this chapter.

During the talk, I covered sequential design (waterfall/v-model) techniques, which have been used since 1939. I then compared them to modern day approaches, such as iterative build and test used in competitive engineering and Agile methodologies since 2001.[168]

Fig. 130: TED - Cognitive Learning – Evolution, Over Revolution

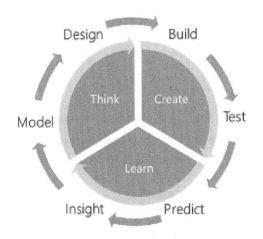

My challenge during the talk was how to establish the rapid feedback loop between the "Learn" and "Think" segments, which I have been referring to as "Shift Right" in the industry since 2013.[169]

The concept of a digital twin is nothing new. The concept of a digital representation of physical environments dates back to 1970, famously used by NASA to help get Apollo 13 safely back home. More recently, Dr. Michael Grieves introduced the idea of a digital twin as part of Product Lifecycle Management (PLM) back in 2002.

168 "Competitive Engineering: A Handbook for Systems Engineering, Requirements Engineering and Software Engineering using Planguage" Tom Gilb, 2005 https://books.google.co.uk/books/about/Competitive_Engineering.html
169 Twitter. @Jonathon_Wright @_ShiftRight. 2013 https://twitter.com/_ShiftRight/status/909095123321069568

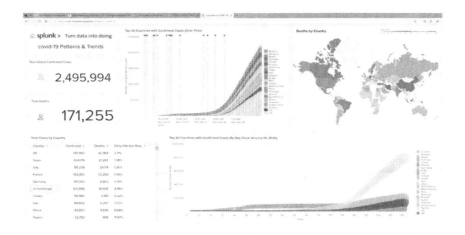

Fig. 131: Splunk for Good – Covid-19 – MIT Path Check Foundation

The image above is a COVID-19 dashboard provided by Todd DeCapua from the "Splunk for Good" team. During the COVID-19 outbreak, Rob Tiffany shared the idea of how this technology could be used to help fight COVID-19 with digital twins. At the same time, Google and Apple were developing a new Bluetooth API that could be used for contact tracing.

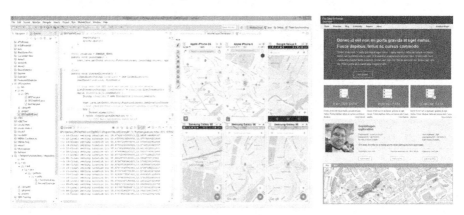

Fig. 132: Copenhagen Smart City – Perfecto Mobile & Hitachi City Data Exchange

The idea of applying digital twins to help solve the contact tracing testing challenge resulted in me working directly with the team at MIT and the project owner Yasaman Rajeee on the COVID Safe Paths project.[170]

170 MIT Path Check Foundation, 2020, https://safepaths.mit.edu/

Back in 2015, I was working directly with Eran Kinsbruner and the R&D team at Perfecto to help test something very similar. The Copenhagen Smart City Data Exchange used contact tracing to help digital citizens become carbon neutral by 2020. This included rolling out a smart city mobile app to 38,000 people who lived and worked in Copenhagen.

Testing the COVID-19 Tracing Platform

There were several similarities between the Copenhagen Smart City and COVID Safe Paths projects regarding their approaches to testing contact tracing. The biggest challenge in both projects was the ability to synthetically generate billions of historical realistic location data points and inject real-time GPS location data.

Fig. 133: Patch Check - Safe Places Plus App (Bluetooth Beacon & GPS) on Perfecto Labs

Each collection of GPX routes represented multi-modal forms of transport, ranging from walking (2-3 MPH), biking (10-12 MPH), riding the bus (stopping at various locations), riding the train, driving cars, or taking the tube (which may stop recording GPX data at one location and appear at another location). Each mode had a unique data footprint that would need to be cross referenced to rule out any risk of the spread of infection.

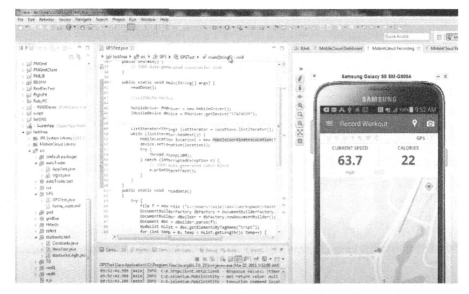

Fig. 134: GPS Speed Tracking — Perfecto & Eclipse IDE

By default, Google location services captures 650 location data points every 24 days, which results in 9,100 data points over the 14-day incubation period. It is important to adopt a privacy-first approach that requires no personally identifiable data to be redacted. To do this, the team at MIT developed a contact tracer tool that supported geo-fences to remove sensitive locations, such as home and workplaces.

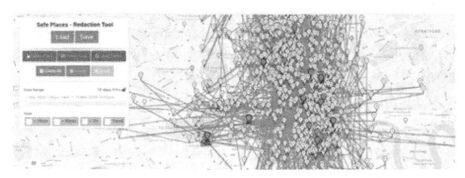

Fig. 135: Path Check – Safe Places (Redaction Tool)

Once the data was sanitized by the Healthcare Authorities (HA), the redacted data files of infected patients were published to the COVID Safe Paths Data Exchange, which alerted the public of any potential exposures.

Similar to the Copenhagen Smart City Data Exchange, algorithms were developed to crossmatch data provided from multiple HA sources. They provided recommendations to undiagnosed users who may have crossed paths with infected users.

To provide reassurance to millions by enabling impactful, accurate recommendations and reducing the risk of misinformation (false positives), the GATED.AI methodology and digital twin approaches were applied to help answer one vital question.

How do you know when the ML platform is ready to be unleashed on the public?

Testing Artificial Intelligent Platforms

The next example will provide another real-world scenario of testing an AI platform that uses computer vision (CV) to publish 1,000 products onto Amazon, Google, and eBay marketplaces. All they were provided with were images of each product.

Again, how do you know when AI is ready to be unleashed into the wild?

Traditional Testing Won't Cut It

How is testing AI as a Service (AIaaS) different than traditional, non-AI platforms? In this example, after running a simple GraphQL test, I discovered that I had 95 unpublished products. Should I have passed or failed the test?

If we don't know what the expected outcomes are, then how can we simply pass or fail the output? How do we know what good looks like and when to stop?

Cognitive Engineering — GATED.AI

When utilizing the GATED.AI approach, it makes sense to switch to a more goal-oriented approach (i.e. capability to identify X).

With what acceptance/accuracy, with such as clarification rate (i.e. 7 out of 10 times), within what timeframe/training time (seconds/minutes/hours), in what type of environment (compute/IOPs), with what size of training data (hundreds or even millions of reference data).

This allows us to define GATED.AI scenarios ahead of time during the idealization phase:

- **GOAL** — CAPABILITY to identify and correctly categorize images of products.
- **ACCURACY** — REQUIREMENT be able to successfully categorize women's fashion (1,000+ subcategories on the Amazon channel) with a CLARIFICATION rate of over 70%.
- **TIME** — TIMEFRAME per day to process over 10,000 product images.
- **ENRICHMENT** — SEMANTIC MODELS applying Data Engineering (Extract, Transform, and Load) heuristics for mining ecosystems to enable AI data lakes.
- **DATA** — CLUSTERING (Percentage Split) for Development Training Set (60%), then Testing Training Set (30%), then Proving Training Set (10%) of the training set sizes (5,000/10,000).

Now that we have an idea of what good looks like, we can start to prepare the GATED.AI data lake (i.e. the baseline training dataset dependences for our GATED.AI tests).

GATED.AI — Scenario

The main challenge around the GATED.AI approach is producing a realistic baseline training dataset that is representative of the target AI consumer needs.

- AI CAPABILITY (GOAL) — To identify and correctly categorize images of products.

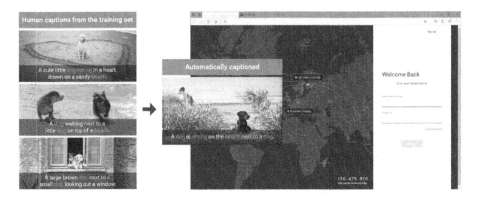

Fig. 136: Example Enterprise AI Platform as a Service (AIaaS) Utilizing Computer Vision

The temptation is for the test data engineer to use a generic dataset (for example, stock images returned by a search engine) which would be more suitable for generalized AI (unsupervised).

Fig. 137: AI-Supervised Machine Learning (TensorFlow), Google Kaggle & Amazon mTurk

In previous GATED.AI scenarios, we have seen much higher accuracy around the 80%+ classification rates mining the training dataset from harvesting a specific dataset for the target AI consumer. For example, consider using a spider to transpose a data source such as a website containing existing product imaging with associated meta data.

- **AI REQUIREMENT** (ACCURACY) — Be able to successfully categorize women's fashion.

- **AI CLARIFICATION RATE** (ACCURACY) — Over 70%.

Mining Test Training Data (CRAWLER / SPIDER / SUBSET)   Harvested Test Training Data (MindCube.io - Domain-Driven)

Fig. 138: Mining Traversed Endpoint Discovery With Burpsuite Portswagger Spider

NOTE — Data visualization platforms help to identity a subset of the test training dataset and avoid cognitive bias/overfitting of the training data.

If I were going to utilize an AI crowdsourced platform with gamification, say Kaggle. com, I would list a competition I would be looking for, with the accuracy as close as possible to the 90% baseline. The industry understanding is that enterprise AI scores above 95% are nearly impossible, based on current cognitive technologies capabilities. However, I would also be equally interested in the time and data variance along with associated consumed compute power.

- **AI TIMEFRAME** — Be able to process 10,000 images per day.

- **AI COMPUTE** (TIME) — Ability to auto-scale training nodes/clusters (COMPUTE/GPU/IOPS) based on AI benchmarks/performance index (PI).

- **AI VARIANCE** (TIME) — Future growth (customers utilizing the service/ increase in product images).

The baseline training dataset can also be enriched by applying various semantic maps for example cross-validation from various ecosystems.

- **AI SEMANTIC MODEL** (ENRICHMENT) — Applying data engineering (enhance, transform, and load) heuristics.

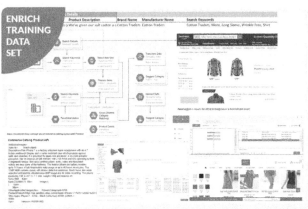

Fig. 139: Enrichment of Semantic Maps With Amazon DSSTNE & Microsoft Power Automate

Enrichment of Semantic Maps (DSSTNE, RPA (Vision & Meta Tags) + ETL)

The above approach enables the creation of an AI-ready data lake with an improved level of data hygiene. This can be process mined to identify business process flows for robotic process automation along with the associated datasets.

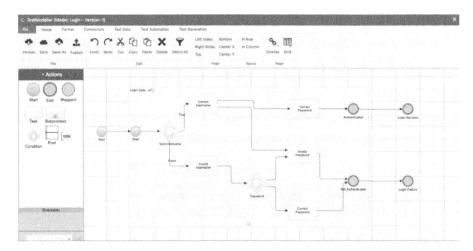

Fig. 140: Model-Based Testing (MBT) With Curiosity TestModeller.io

In the book, Experiences in Test Automation, I explored the use of model-based testing (MBT) to support business process testing efforts.[171] This was done to model out something as simple microservices based on specifications (SWAGGER/OpenAPI).

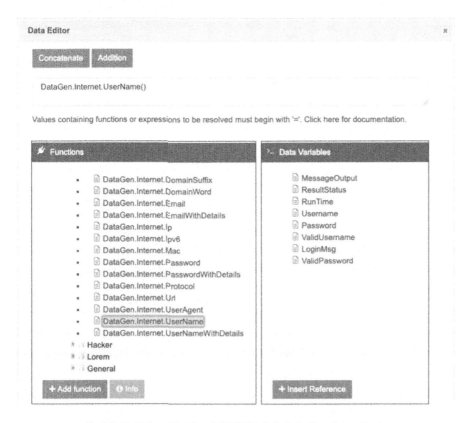

Fig. 141: Model-Based Test Data (MBTD) With Curiosity TestDataAutomation.io

In the example above, we have modelled a simple business process flow with acceptance criteria (i.e. login success), using cause and effect modelling. This is done so that we can fully understand the relationship between A to B mappings (input/output) based on the dataset used, so it is important to not only model the business process flows, but model the associated test dataset (MBD).

171 Experiences in Test Automation
   https://www.amazon.co.uk/Experiences-Test-Automation-Studies-Software/dp/0321754069

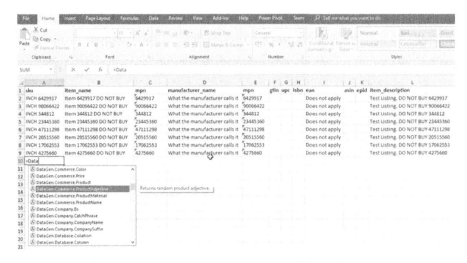

Fig. 142: Synthetic Test Data Generation Powered By Curiosity VIP RPA + Excel

As previously mentioned, this requires the test data engineer to fully understand not only the data quality of the unstructured/structured dataset, but also the data coverage and the context-sensitive nature of the domain dataset.

- **AI TRAINING DATA** — Mining for clustering, number of variables, and associated test training data set size.

Data engineering is as important to the data science activities as the ability to establish the data pipework to funnel unstructured data from heritage platforms into structured data. A combination of business process automation and Test Data Management (TDM) capabilities is essential.

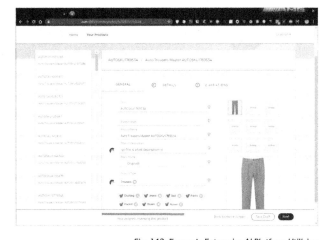

Fig. 143: Example Enterprise AI Platform Utilizing Computer Vision for Category Matching

GATED.AI Summary

In the previous GATED.AI scenario, we defined the high-level goal of identifying a product image (i.e. pair of trousers) and the image category mapping (i.e. product type).

- **GOAL — AI CAPABILITY** image category mapping.

- **ACCURACY — AI CLASSIFICATION RATE** = > 70%.

- **TIME — AI TIMEFRAME** < 1 day for 10,000.

- **ENRICHMENT — AI SEMANTIC** Harvest manufactures website and internal ERP platform.

- **DATA — AI TRAINING DATA** Training images dataset size (5,000/10,000), semantic model parameters (500+) & training cluster nodes (4/8).

The acceptance criteria for the GATED.AI scenario was that the classification rate was over 70% and able to process 10,000 images per day.

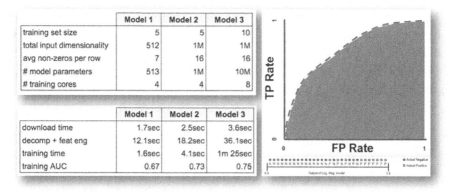

	Model 1	Model 2	Model 3
training set size	5	5	10
total input dimensionality	512	1M	1M
avg non-zeros per row	7	16	16
# model parameters	513	1M	10M
# training cores	4	4	8

	Model 1	Model 2	Model 3
download time	1.7sec	2.5sec	3.6sec
decomp + feat eng	12.1sec	18.2sec	36.1sec
training time	1.6sec	4.1sec	1m 25sec
training AUC	0.67	0.73	0.75

Fig. 144: Google Computer Vision (TensorFlow) Overtraining AUC

In the previous three cases, only one AI model passes the GATED.AI scenario (i.e. Model 1 classification rate and Model 3 training time, even with 4 cluster nodes exceeding the day timeframe).

NOTE: If we had not used the GATED.AI approach, then the temptation would have been to select Model 3 as it has the highest clarification rate but takes 5 times longer than Model 2.

The above GATED.AI scenario demonstrates the importance of effective cognitive engineering in AI as a Service (AIaaS). This assures that it cannot only handle the expected GATED.AI volumetric models, but that the underlining enterprise AI platform can scale (i.e. auto-scale compute nodes to handle future growth variations and be resilient — i.e. self-healing chaos engineering).

As mentioned earlier in this chapter, traditional testing will no longer cut it. We need to adopt a grey box testing approach to improve visibility of individual components so we can identify bottlenecks throughout the target AI as a Service (AIaaS) architecture.

SHIFTING RIGHT WITH DIGITAL TWINS

A digital twin model can be used to define a physical system or platform. Each instance of the digital twin has associated data derived from the host's "doubleganger" as well as telemetry data from a moment in time.

The best way I can explain this is by referring to a keynote that I gave to the British Computer Society (BCS) back in 2011.[172] In this keynote, I proposed that user interface interactions were only the tip of the iceberg. Interfaces (messaging/APIs) combined with ambient background (traffic/noise) were the real focus to achieve true representation of a system under test (SUT).

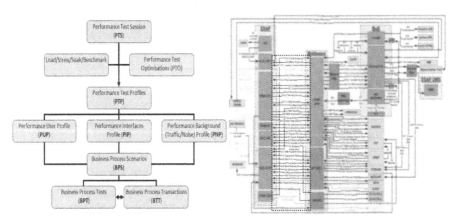

Fig. 145: Performance Engineering Models Against Enterprise SAP (E-SAP)

---

172 *Testing as a Service Keynote Slides https://www.slideshare.net/Jonathon_Wright/testing-as-a-service-keynote*

In the example on the previous page, for a large E-SAP migration program, we identified over 500 interfaces in the enterprise architecture diagram, which either need to be stubbed out with service virtualization or generate bulk transactions as messages or traffic (i.e. iDocs).

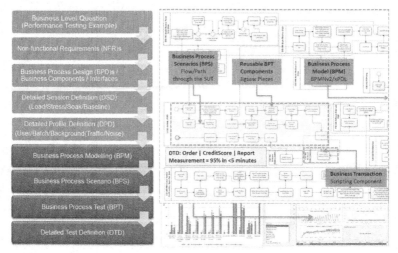

Fig. 146: Business Process Modelling Notation (BPMn v2)

Like our GATED.AI scenario, the business process flow to trigger a simple report may only be a couple of steps through the SAP GUI and the response for submitting the report may be a couple of seconds.

Fig. 147: Performance Tuning & Optimizing with DynaTrace PurePath™ and Akamas.io

However, in the background there are transactions going on across the ecosystem (i.e. internal and external systems both upstream and downstream) monitored above by the Application Performance Management (APM) platform.

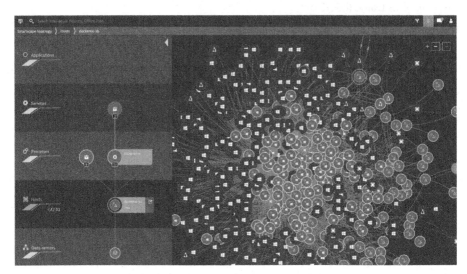

Fig. 148: Systematized (Epistemic & Systemic Entropy) SmartScape Topology From DynaTrace

Keeping this in mind, if we return to the GATED.AI scenario, our AI as a Service (AIaaS) platforms is built on a Kubernetes cluster which can be deployed locally or multi-cloud.

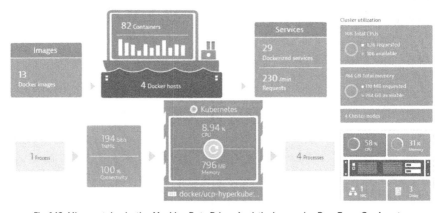

Fig. 149: Microcontainerization Machine-Data Driven Analytics Leveraging DynaTrace OneAgent

For this example, I will be deploying the following Kubernetes cluster locally:

- API Gateway (REST API).

- Apache Kafka (streaming service).

- Avro Schemas (schema registry).

- Neo4J (graph database).

- MongoDB (NoSQL).

- Postgres (RDBMS).

- Apache Zookeeper (coordination service).

Fig. 150: Kubernetes Cluster Feat. Neo4J, Kafka, Confluent, Zookeeper, Mongo, & PostGres

In the screenshot on the next page, I'm sending a simple JSON message to the ML microservice (which I can intercept to manipulate the request/response pairs), which triggers a number cypher queries and sets a flag in MongoDB that the product is ready to be listed to the channel.

Fig. 151: Man-in-the-Middle Interception With Burp Suite PortSwagger

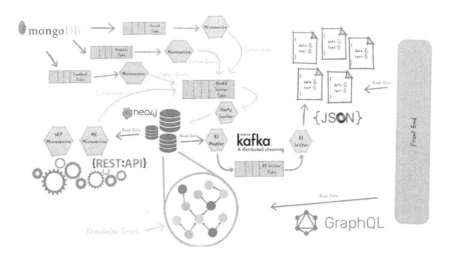

Fig. 152: Example Enterprise AI Architecture — GraphDB/QL, Nanoservices, Streaming & NoSQL

Now depending on whether the product successfully matches a valid women's fashion category on the channel specified, i.e. eBay vs. Amazon, the status will change from received to ready to list.

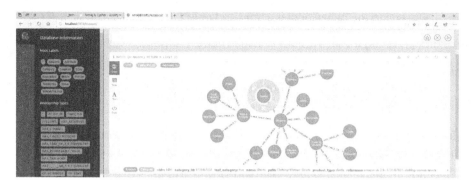

Fig. 153: Knowledge Graphs Utilizing Neo4J

Once the channel listing service identifies a cube of 10,000 products on that are ready to list to a channel, it publishes them to the appropriate marketplace every 15 minutes.

Fig. 154: Containerized MongoDB With Compass & Robo 3T

So as a cognitive engineer, where do I focus my efforts to prove the system is performant, resilient, and can scale?

1. Observing the behavior of the front end or API.

2. Interpreting the interactions between node/endpoints within the ecosystem (upstream and downstream) i.e. Kafka producers and consumers.

3. Modelling the sentiment/context of the business processes (cause and effect modelling) i.e. how long does it take images to list on the channel?

Traditional performance testing focuses on observing the behavior of the endpoint (UI/API). So if the response time for a REST call took longer than a few hundred milliseconds, then the microservice was worth investigating.

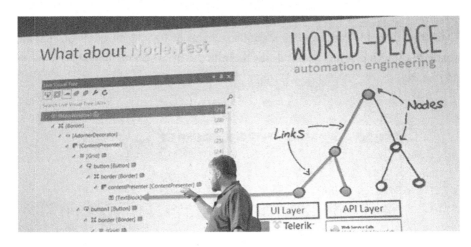

Fig. 155: STARWest – Think You Can Just "Test" That API? Think Again

However, that is no longer the case, due to system dynamics (epistemic and systemic entropy). This leads to so many unknowns. For example, in our example above the REST call, it triggers a number cypher queries and sets a flag in MongoDB (which minus the overhead, establishing and closing the MongoDB connection is lighting fast).

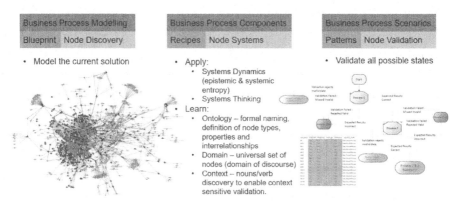

Fig. 156: The Digital Ecology — British Computer Society, 2015

In our example, our understanding is that this REST call triggers (or causes) a number of cascading events (i.e. Kafka producers and consumers, cypher queries, GraphDB, schema registry calls, drools, and TensorFlow).

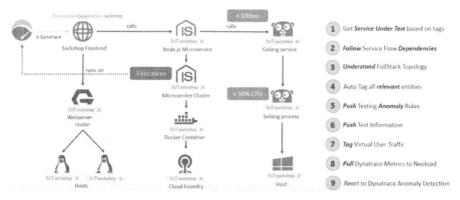

Fig. 157: Dynamic Headers (NeoLoad) & Multi-Dimensional Transactional Data (DynaTrace)

So how can we easily discover other compute-related events (i.e. unknown/unknowns)? The reverse discovery based on dynamic requests is one approach that intelligent APMs take to understand the full stack topology when auto-tags discover nodes (i.e. traffic and ambient noise).

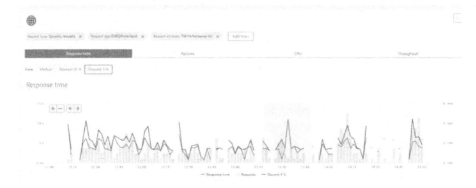

Fig. 158: Hyper-Baselining Based on Request Tags in DynaTrace

In the example above, we can overlay the dynamic requests with a specific request attribute to filter down to the individual transaction level and then break down the service flow of that request and how long each service call took (i.e. root cause analysis).

Fig. 159: Pinpoint Failure Analysis & Diagnostics Engine From DynaTrace

Multi-dimensional transactional correlation allows us to establish the baseline blueprint/schematic of the flow of events (i.e. cause and effect modelling) along with associated time series data for every request/response over time.

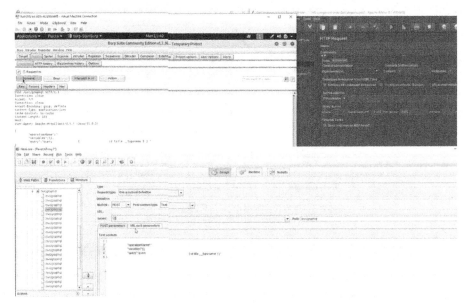

Fig. 160: Man-in-the-Middle Proxy on Kali & Burpsuite With NeoLoad IDE

Alternately, you could also use a proxy like Portswagger to intercept (man in the middle) messages between endpoints using a Raspberry PI Zero with Kali installed. Then you can use a performance engineering technique to create a digital twin by reverse engineering the BAU/DX sessions (either through captured R/R pairs or DX sessions).

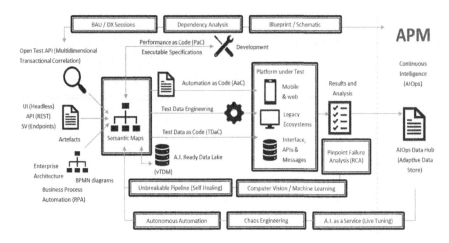

Fig. 161: Digital Experience Analytics (DXI) Platform With Intelligent Operations (AIOps)

Finally, the slide above is taken from a recent keynote on Intelligent Operations (AIOps).[173] It demonstrates how you can shift right and create a digital twin by pulling the BAU/digital experiences (DX) sessions from APM to generate semantic maps (user journeys, digital interactions, and transactions) through open testing API available through the digital experience analytics (DXI) platform (AIOps).

In summary, when testing complex ecosystems of ecosystems (such as AI as a Service or Contact Tracing for COVID-19), the need for next-generation digital experience analytics (DXI) platforms is absolutely essential.

---

173 Intelligent Operations Keynote https://youtu.be/_1kyNIOFY6s

Chapter 18:
The Paradox of Machine Learning: Building an ML Testing Solution From Scratch

Yarin Podoler

Yarin Podoler is a Principal Solution Architect at Perforce Software. He studied software is a passionate entrepreneur. Yarin fell in love with computers and programming when he was 13 years of age. Two years later, he started a BSc in computer science at the Open University in Israel. He served in a confidential technological unit in the IDF for 4.5 years and gained significant experience in various types of technologies. Yarin worked in the high-tech industry in different roles and a few years ago founded TestCraft, which was acquired in early 2020. In addition to his love for technology, Yarin enjoys sports and used to play in the Israel U17 National soccer team when he was younger, and later on as an elite road cyclist. Today, Yarin lives in Tel Aviv, Israel, with his amazing wife and two children.

WHAT IS THE PARADOX OF MACHINE LEARNING?

We live in such a marvelous time. Technology is all around us, and it is straightforward to leverage it for our advantage. One type of technology that is continuously changing our lives is ML. It is already here, big time! And it is surrounding us wherever we go.

One can find such technologies in many different verticals:

- In **consumer** goods — A doll can "listen" and respond intelligently.

- In **healthcare** systems — ML systems can leverage image recognition to detect early signs of cancer.

- In **manufacturing** — Companies today can predict when parts are going to fail and when they need immediate service.

- In **automotive** — Autonomous driving is the holy grail, and it seems like it is going to change the industry entirely.

There are many more examples of machine learning systems in our lives — enough to be a complete book of its own.

In general, there are three different types of machine learning algorithms: **supervised learning, unsupervised learning**, and **reinforcement learning**. Unsupervised learning helps the computer ("the machine") find patterns in the data and group different inputs together. Reinforcement learning is fascinating and uses a rewards mechanism to help the "machine" learn.

In my opinion, supervised learning is the most straightforward one. Instead of telling a computer what to do, like any other standard computer program, we show it different types of options while guiding it on what the result should be. In response, the algorithm "tweaks its brain" to adapt to those specific examples.

Let's imagine we are building a traffic sign recognition system, the first thing that we will need to start with is picking a proper algorithm to use. The list of algorithms that can be used for this purpose is quite long: Nearest Neighbor, Naive Bayes, Decision Trees, Linear Regression, Support Vector Machines, and Neural Networks. Each of these algorithms has sub-categories to choose from as well. In the scope of this chapter, I will not dive into how to select the right algorithm for the task.

Following the algorithm selection stage, one should progress to the training part. The developers of the algorithm will feed it with images of different traffic signs, and in addition, they will teach it what the result should be for each case.

You can think about the following analogy of a little boy pointing out to an object and asking his father, "What is that?" and the father answers, "This is a dog."

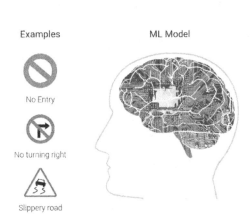

Fig. 162: Training a Model With Different Traffic Signs
(Source: TestCraft)

That's it! Assuming developers did everything correctly, they've got a trained model. Obviously, this is a very high-level abstract description, but it can be useful to explain the idea.

Now the developers of the model can show this trained model a new image of a traffic sign, and it should output which one it is. This is a traditional classification problem — developers are training a machine learning algorithm to help us classify the input into a predefined list of buckets.

If we try to generalize the process, we might say that to create a ML algorithm, we would need to do three steps:

1. Select the required algorithm.
2. Train the model.
3. Be happy.

So, what is the catch? That sounds pretty easy! Why not train our own ML algorithm if it is so simple? Obviously, you can do it!

But one thing that you need to remember and focus on is the **DATA**!

Developers need to have and use data, and preferably, a lot of useful and relevant data. Going back to the previous example, in order to train the model to recognize all the available traffic signs, developers would need to feed the algorithm with a lot of different images.

Fig. 163: 150 Traffic Signs (Source: Google)

How many images? It is complicated.

Assuming we need to have few hundred images per classifier, let's start with 500 (usually we will need more than that). So, if to put this into simple math, this model will require 500 images X 150 signs = 75,000 images of all signs, from different angles, lighting, and positions.

That is a problem!

For a developer who digs a bit deeper into machine learning technologies, he will find out that choosing an algorithm can be achieved quite easily through investigation and learning what's available online. The tricky and more complicated part, however, is capturing the 75,000 images — this is **HARD**!

So, how can one implement a machine learning algorithm inside their project or company without having any data? Below I will try to explain how to do it.

FROM MY OWN PERSONAL EXPERIENCE AT TESTCRAFT

In the following section, I will make a short detour from machine learning algorithms and data and explain how one can combine both into a successful solution. I will give a bit of background about myself, including my experience in the past few years, which I think is very relevant for this topic.

A few years back, I was part of a team that transitioned from the standard software development model of waterfall into the new and very fresh Agile methodology. One of the core principles of Agile is the "short-cycle:"

"Deliver working software frequently, from a couple of weeks to a couple of months, with a preference to the shorter timescale."[174]

We were all in, and started implementing short development cycles and frequent daily releases. We used the latest CI/CD tools. From the moment a developer announced the feature as done, it was deployed to production in less than an hour.

But we were facing a problem, a huge one which we did not see coming.

Let's assume that we're looking at an app of about 1,000,000 lines of code, and a developer adds a new feature that consists of an additional 1,000 lines of code.

---

174 *Agile Manifesto https://agilemanifesto.org/principles.html*

Basically, we're looking at an additional ~0.1% from the entire codebase. But in order to validate that nothing got broken, the team needs to go over the entire 100% of the application.

This means that the time that should be invested during the testing phase is way bigger than within the actual development, and that obviously translates into the need for automation. Automation should cover a large portion of the application to meet the desire for such short cycles.

The existing tests were not sufficient. So, we started to invest more time in writing all kinds of tests: unit tests, integration, E2E, and many more. Fairly quickly, the team got to a point where it invested around 40% of the time in writing test automation. That was very inefficient.

After a while, the team started tackling a second problem, and that was around tests that began to break. In reality, nothing was actually broken in the app, but the tests were fragile. As the team added more tests to their suite, even a low percentage of flakiness could paralyze the entire development process. About 75% of the time was wasted on supporting the short cycle approach, and it felt like chasing our own tail.

A few months later, I took the opportunity and started my own company, TestCraft — a SaaS codeless test automation platform, which was acquired a few years later. I started it because I believed there was a real need in the market, based on what I personally experienced.

Today, the product is focused on solving those two problems:

1. **Fast and easy creation** of test automation without the need to code.

2. **Reducing maintenance** by using ML to automatically heal test scenarios.

It was apparent that we needed to solve the maintainability problem somehow. Machine learning was an obvious candidate as part of the solution, but we faced the paradox of ML. We had no data when we founded TestCraft, so how could we have leveraged ML to our advantage?

Later in this chapter, I am going to share some real-life examples from my experience at TestCraft that will explain what was done to gather data for our ML algorithms per each case.

PROBLEM 1. ACTION SUGGESTION MECHANISM

Fast and easy test automation creation was one of the problems and objectives TestCraft was set to solve.

One of the methods in which a user can add a test step is to model it against a real live web application. To make it happen, one needs to make a sequence of two actions:

1. Select an element.
2. Run a specific action on the selected element.

A few examples to clarify the above:

- The user selects a **button** and chooses to **click** on it.
- The user selects a **date-picker** and **specifies** a **future date**.
- The user selects a **drop-down menu** and **chooses** a **specific option**.

From the basic examples above, you can understand that different elements have different sets of actions.

In TestCraft, after a user specifies an element, an overlay with different actions pops up based on the type of component selected.

Fig. 164: Action Suggestion for a Text Field in TestCraft (Source: TestCraft)

Fig. 165: Action Suggestion for a Button in TestCraft (Source: Test Craft)

We needed an algorithm that could understand what type of element the user selected. It's very important to understand that we had to deal with a lot of different element types and countless HTML implementations, thus making it a very complex problem.

We decided to go with a **supervised ML algorithm** for this classification problem. The solution we needed was a kind of black box with an HTML snippet input and an output with the type of element.

For this problem, we used a DIY (Do-It-Yourself) approach to gather the data and get it off the ground. DIY means to sit in front of a computer for hours and to scrape the data on your own.

We created a list of a few hundred websites: S&P 500 companies, small ones, local shops, banks, insurance companies, supermarkets, and more. Next, we went one by one and got out all the relevant information for different element types and placed them into one huge Excel file. In addition, when we started approaching customers (an arduous task on its own), we added their website to the list and optimized the algorithm accordingly.

This approach may sound very dull and conventional, but it is potent and cheap. If you are considering writing your own ML algorithm, and need data to make it work — keep that in mind. There is no replacement for DIY at the beginning. As an algorithm developer, you will learn so much about the process, about how you can optimize it, and about what it's missing.

PROBLEM 2. ADAPTING TO CHANGES AND TEST RESILIENCY

Reducing maintainability was the second problem TestCraft was set to solve.

One of the most problematic tasks in writing an end to end test, while working in an Agile methodology, is making sure that the test will be valid after 10 or 20 cycles of development. If you are not familiar with end to end testing, here is a very abstract view of how a test is programmed.

A single end to end test consists of multiple steps. Each step usually involves some kind of UI element and some user action or a validation. Most of the breakage in those kinds of tests is due to changes in the UI. Those changes cause a false identification of the element. This false identification is often because the test tries to identify a specific element in a way that is no longer relevant.

To explain that in a simpler way, consider this testing example. Let's assume that a person is in a library and wants to borrow a specific book to read. There are several ways to approach the librarian and ask them how to find the book:

- "Excuse me, can you please help me find the book, 'Continuous Testing for DevOps Professionals: A Practical Guide from Industry Experts' by Eran Kinsbruner?"
- "Sorry, can you please help me find a purple book with an infinity sign on it?"
- "Can you please help me find a book that has 366 pages about testing?"

All of those questions should lead you to the same book, but you might get a different answer for each. It is obvious that for the first question, you will get the best answer. The librarian will probably direct you to the specific place where the book is located or will let you know that all copies are checked out due to high demand. ●

For the second question, you might get a different answer. The librarian probably doesn't know how all the books are looking and will tell you that they don't have this book — though she might have it in the back.

As for the third question, you might get a different book because there is probably more than one book about testing that has 366 pages.

This is precisely the same challenge as identifying an element. To do so, one needs to specify a locator, and using it, the element will be identified. If the locator is fragile or wrongly determined, one might get a faulty element or none at all.

On a more technical front, let's look at the following:

We started by sampling the data, gathered 100,000 test steps, and analyzed the percentage of change from one test to the other for each attribute of HTML elements. Here are a few interesting examples:

1. The position of an element from one test to the next in our sample changed 1 in 5 times.

2. The ID attribute which is considered very robust changed 1 in 6 consecutive tests, and only appeared 40% of the time.

3. Aria-label attribute is very robust and changed 1 in 20 tests but was on 1 of 10 elements.

Attribute	Appearances	Changes
size	100%	3%
position	100%	21%
text	50%	17%
id	39%	15%
name	34%	14%
aria-label	10%	5%
placeholder	7%	4%

Fig. 166: Examples of Different Attributes and Frequency of Changes (Souce: TestCraft)

What we've learned was that there isn't a one size that fits all when identifying soft-ware elements, and that it varies on a case-by-case basis and per application. What it meant for us was that to reduce maintainability, we needed to have deep familiari-ty with each and every component per application. This doesn't sound reasonable.

We decided to leverage ML to help us tackle that challenge and go with the ap-proach of "get the help from your users."

We initially designed the TestCraft solution to query the user with a lot of questions regarding elements identification. If we were not 100% sure that the element was the correct element, we would ask the user to redefine it visually.

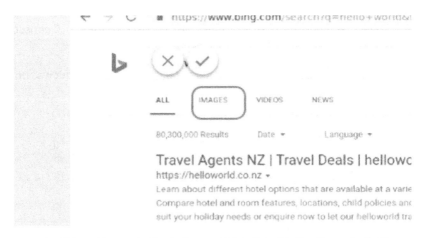

Fig. 167: Visual Element Identification Recovery With the Help of the User (Source: TestCraft)

After few months and a growing number of users who used the platform, we were able to extract all the data from all the elements and put in place the first TestCraft element identification model.

This method is still in place, and every time the number of inputs needed by the user is reduced, the model is bothering him less and less while giving more value over time. This approach is where the magic happens.

It may take more time to develop and design, but this gives the developers a gen-uinely scalable approach for gathering data as they go. When building your own

ML solution, always think about how you can leverage your users to help you with improving your dataset.

PROBLEM 3. WHAT ABOUT FALSE POSITIVES OR NEGATIVES?

After we went over the resiliency and identification problems, it was time to take it one step forward.

There is an essential factor about ML that one needs to be familiar with — like everything in life, errors happen. Nothing is perfect.

Assuming that nothing is perfect, how do we know that our ML algorithm is doing a good job? Or, if we have two different ML models, how can we know which one works better? Apparently, there is a good indicator for that, called **The Confusion Matrix**.

What Is the Confusion Matrix?

It is a pretty simple concept, and it is much easier to explain with a 2x2 matrix (hence the name).

Let's use the ML element identification problem as an example. The columns of the matrix will be the real-life outcome, meaning whether or not the element is in the application when we try to identify it. The rows represent the ML prediction, either "element found" or "not found."

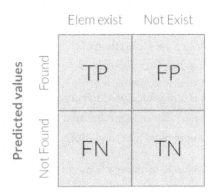

Fig. 168: Confusion Matrix (Source: Google)

We have four different sections above:

1. True-Positive (TP) — The element was identified correctly by the ML algorithm.

2. True-Negative (TN) — The element was not identified correctly by the ML algorithm.

3. False-Negative (FN) — No element was identified, meaning it should have been found.

4. False-Positive (FP) — A wrong element was identified.

Accuracy of an ML algorithm is defined as follows:

$$Accuracy = \frac{TP + TN}{TP + TN + FP + FN}$$

Let's compare two different algorithms. In case the accuracy of the ML algorithm is higher than the other, that usually means it is better. Also, the actual number of the accuracy level is essential, but we won't get into it here.

Back to our original algorithm. We have an ML model, and we want to improve it and increase its accuracy. How can this be done?

After a very long time of thinking it through, we got to our third approach of gathering data — outsourcing.

It is straightforward to outsource these days. You can do it in-house, as we did, or by an external service that allows you to do so, such as Fiverr, Upwork, Amazon Mechanical Turk, and more.

We were looking at ways to reduce both false negatives and false positives.

We built a side application, one that gives a user the ability to see two different images of screenshots with highlighted elements on both of them. The user would need to select "Yes" in case both refer to the same item, or "No" in case they do not.

Since we extracted data from our existing ML algorithm of such elements, the probability of a mistake was quite high, and there were ones that we weren't sure about the output of the algorithm.

The whole data extraction process took us some time, and we were able to provide about 30,000 elements and screenshots as an input for our human classification process.

After the human "Yes"/"No" classification was done by our own workers as a side task, we had a great dataset of examples that the original algorithm was unsure about, and we could feed more certain cases to improve the model. This increased our accuracy level dramatically.

I believe that outsourcing is an excellent way of gathering data when you can simplify the process. In our case, we needed to write a complete side application to do so. If you can do that, and you do it right, you can scale your data gathering immensely.

SUMMARY

Machine learning is both our future and probably the present as well. It can be extremely powerful and help solve complicated problems in ways we didn't think were possible a few years back.

You can use it for your advantages, but you need to consider the specifics of what will make the model great and of value.

As highlighted in this chapter, the secret is data, data, data! You'll need a lot of it and with high quality. The recommend practice with ML algorithms is around gathering the data and organizing it in a way that it can support your objectives.

I'll leave you with these final words: I encourage all of you to try it out. Read about it, learn about it. You'll find that it is super fun! And don't forget to smile. ●

MATURING CODE QUALITY AND DEVOPS
TEAM PRODUCTIVITY USING AI AND ML

Chapter 19:
Automated Code Reviews
With AI and ML

PERFORCE

Chuck Gehman

Chuck Gehman, Technical Marketing Engineer, Perforce Software, Chuck (@charlesgehman) is a Technical Marketing Engineer at Perforce Software. He has worked as a CTO, architect, developer, and product leader in startups and large enterprises. Chuck has been a member of the IEEE for 20 years, and he's an AWS Certified Solution Architect and Certified Developer. When he has spare time, he enjoys volunteering for technology education initiatives, attending Meetups, and writing.

It wasn't that long ago that code review was a synchronous, face-to-face experience that took people away from their work for a long meeting that more than a few participants did not want to attend. In many organizations, the process and outcomes of code review were not well defined, and as a result the process could be a missed opportunity to improve the team and organization.

In organizations with solid continuous improvement cultures, code reviews often focused on finding or fixing issues and were often done by teams around a table or by two developers sitting together. Now, of course, most code review workflows are automated and asynchronous. They happen after builds and tests are run, because we don't want to waste colleagues' time reviewing code that "might" be defective.

Much of the software development process has become automated. CI/CD and DevOps have become industry standard best practices. Build runners get better with each passing day. Docker and Kubernetes have been a veritable revolution. Expectations for automation and integration have been raised to the point where build, test, and deployment tooling ranks as a high priority in every aspect of our workflows.

AUTOMATED CODE REVIEW TODAY

I define asynchronous code reviews as those that happen in a code hosting and collaboration environment online. Prior to conducting the code review, automated steps happen in a CI pipeline:

- Linting or static code analysis
- Running a build
- Performing unit tests

The developer commits their code, and there is a pull or merge request. Next, a build runner orchestrates the tasks described above, and if the build and subsequent tests pass, a code review is created.

Let's address the good and bad about this kind of review. Remember that this could be happening very often with a team that is serious about the idea of "shift left" and expects each developer to commit four or five times a day. Fortunately, with containers and Kubernetes, automation can handle this volume of CI workload.

With code management and collaboration tools, you can automatically spread the workload of reviews out among members of your team, too. These reviews can be interactive albeit asynchronous, with back and forth between the author and the reviewers, until everyone is satisfied with the changes and the review is approved. The comments made in the reviews by all parties are kept "forever," and can be very useful down the road, such as in Agile iteration retrospectives or even in planning subsequent iterations or releases.

In addition to detecting defects, another key technical rationale for performing code reviews is the need to enforce coding and security standards. Today it is often better done via linting (perhaps pre-commit) and/or static code analysis (post-commit), again occurring automatically, before we waste the time of other team members. Integration between build runners and code management interfaces (e.g., source control or version control systems) alerts colleagues when code is ready for them to examine.

WHAT BENEFIT IS THERE IN CODE REVIEWS CONDUCTED BY HUMANS?

With all the automated testing, and the fact that the developer's changes did not break the build, let's talk about why we should conduct a time-consuming code review process that impacts the productivity of at least several people, and sometimes an entire team. It's because there are significant qualitative benefits that are not delivered by automation today.

The qualitative benefits of human code reviews for teams include:

- **Transparency** — The entire team gets a better picture of what everyone is working on, their "style," and even their level of productivity. In the big picture, code reviews also provide a sense, in "real time" of how projects are progressing beyond what is visible in tools like Jira. You can see what kind of problems the team is struggling with, and also who and what is succeeding.

- **Underscoring and Promoting Shared Values** — In an organization that values innovation, creativity, and high quality, one of the best things that can happen is that people are so proud of their work, they look forward to showing it to their colleagues. This becomes almost a viral phenomenon. Sometimes it becomes a competition, but it's better when it is legitimately driven by pride of ownership in the entire product.

- **Becoming More Cohesive** — It's at least anecdotally understood that many developers are introverts, and it is unquestionable that everyone spends a lot of time working heads down. This often makes it hard to ask for help, especially if your team is made up of "elite developers"— although Slack has made interactivity easier for even the most introverted among us. This makes code reviews one of the few venues available for the developer to explain what they are doing, and why— and for colleagues to praise it, and/or offer recommendations and guidance. This is why it is critically important to keep all reviews upbeat and positive, and most importantly, constructive and professional.

- **Builds Self-Esteem for New Developers** — This is corollary to the prior point: one of the few chances to show evidence of knowledge and skills, among both peers and leaders, is the code review. Having said this, even the most senior person can benefit from code reviews. It's important to remember that most people who are successful in software development got that way because they like to learn. Code reviews can be a great way for everyone to learn more about coding.

WHAT'S WRONG WITH HUMANS DOING CODE REVIEWS?

As much of an improvement as today's automation brings, human reviewers can be a significant impediment to process improvement. Sometimes, busy colleagues look at changes quickly so the developer (and they themselves) can move on to the next work item or go back to what they were doing. Unless they see something that obviously doesn't make sense, it is not uncommon to receive an approval without comment or with a cursory LGTM (looks good to me.)

Humans bring a pretty high degree of subjectivity. Academic researchers in a paper from McGill University, El Zanaty, et al., found that only 13% of pull requests are rejected due to technical reasons. Another study by Bosu, et al., found that module-based expertise shares a link with code review usefulness (as expressed by authors of the code changes). Meneely, et al. examined the association between the number of commits of developers and security problems in the Red Hat Enterprise Linux 4 kernel. Bosu and Carver found that code changes written by inexperienced authors tend to receive little review participation. These are all organizational problems that AI/ML could conceivably address.

There is also a range of issues that can plague asynchronous human workflows, but one of the biggest issues with this type of review is when reviewers "forget where they are," and address a colleague by making unprofessional or derogatory comments about other's work. There are numerous "social media-like" behaviors that can be manifested: using sarcasm, expressing opinions without facts, piling on with comments (which comes off as nitpicking or even bullying), using offensive emojis instead of words, and making judgements such as "Why didn't you do this, instead of that?". These are cultural problems which should be addressed for the sake of team health and productivity.

Face-to-face reviews are those that are conducted with two (or more) people interacting in real time, looking at each other. This can be sitting together in a conference room (or pulling a chair up to the author's cube), or if the developer and reviewer are in separate facilities (or the developer is working remote), using video, such as Skype or Slack. This type of review is great, because you can have an actual conversation. Such conversations can lead to insights that might not result from matter-of-fact Q&A in the web UI. These sessions can also foster relationships with between team members that are more likely than online reviews to deliver the qualitative benefits we discussed earlier. We may be a long way away from AI being able to duplicate the extremely beneficial aspects that this can bring.

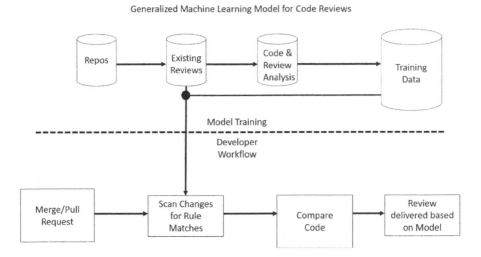

Fig. 169: Code Review Process Using Machine Learning (Source: Perforce)

WHAT IS THE STATE OF AI AND ML FOR CODE REVIEWS TODAY?

We are clearly a long way away from having a conversation with a bot in place of a face-to-face code review. However, there are many initiatives today focused on the problems and costs of code review that are either heading in the direction of AI and ML or already strongly applying AI/ML techniques to provide actionable insights, metrics, and functionality that are not possible without such algorithms.

Let's start with **Code Climate**, who described themselves as "an Engineering Intelligence platform allowing you to quickly and accurately diagnose where work gets stuck, who needs help, and where the greatest opportunities lie for continuous improvement."[175]

---

175 Code Climate Solution http://www.codeclimate.com/

Metrics like lines of code or tickets closed don't tell the real story of work that is completed, and work that is actually shipped. CodeClimate's Velocity product is a non-subjective way of looking at developer productivity and identifying where code is getting "stuck" in the workflow.

In a blog post, Code Climate points out that the **Accelerate** authors (Nicole Forsgren, et al.) found "elite" performers (making up just 7% of the industry) reach a cycle time of less than one hour. This means that those team's median cycle time is 80 times higher than that of the best performing organizations.

Velocity measures cycle time as the time between first commit and deploy of a changeset. They say that optimizing the amount of time between the two events will improve the team's efficiency potentially by as much as 20%. They key to better productivity is to measure and improve this metric, according to Code Climate. This makes a lot of sense.

Velocity breaks down the stage(s) of the process where productivity is blocked and gives you the ability to compare each of the stages to one another, providing the data to drill down and analyze why this is happening.

- **Time to Open** — The time between an engineer's first commit and when they open a pull request in their version control system. The Velocity data shows that this metric has the highest correlation with cycle time.

- **Time to Review** — The time between when a pull request is opened and when it receives its first review. Delays at this stage incentivize multi-tasking, so Code Climate says you'll want to minimize the time a merge of pull request is left waiting for review.

- **Time to Approve** — The time between when a pull request receives its first review and when it is approved, also known as the Code Review process. Clearly, as we discussed earlier, this is an area that needs analysis. You don't want LGTM reviews, but you also don't want people avoiding reviews or spending too long on them.

- **Time to Deploy** — Any additional time following the merge or pull request approval, before the change reaches production. This seems like it might be hard to measure in some environments, but it is absolutely worth doing.

This is fascinating stuff, and it's easy to see how this could significantly improve productivity by changing behaviors. The Velocity analysis, and the way it is presented, provides a great teaching opportunity and could be a great way to help instill organizational values as we discussed earlier. It's completely objective data, which should lead to relatively painless changing of behavior in a team.

WHAT IS THE DIFFERENCE BETWEEN STATIC CODE ANALYSIS TOOLS AND AI-DRIVEN CODE REVIEW?

DeepCode says that its AI platform can build its own recommendations based on large amounts of code.[176] As a result, it finds things humans might miss. The company says the platform can understand the intent of the code by autonomously consuming millions of repositories and noting the changes developers are making.

In true machine learning terms, they describe what happens next as training their AI engine with those changes so it can provide unique suggestions to every single line of code analyzed. The company claims to have far more rules than any competitor, with more than 250,000 rules and growing.

Amazon CodeGuru is a new product in review on AWS (at the time this book is being written), that takes a different approach to analyzing code.[177] Although it is listed as a code review tool, you would find it in the category of AWS machine learning tools. With a focus on performance, Amazon says it helps you find the most expensive lines of code that hurt application performance.

CodeGuru is based on millions of code reviews and thousands of applications profiled on open source and internal projects at Amazon. It currently only works with Java, but finds issues in code like resource leaks, potential concurrency race conditions, and wasted CPU cycles. According to Amazon, tens of thousands of their own developers have contributed to CodeGuru's training based on decades of experience in code review and application profiling.

Consisting of two "modules," Profiler and Reviewer, CodeGuru is trained using rule mining and supervised machine learning models with a combination of logistic regression and neural networks. During training to detect deviation from best practices,

176 DeepCode.ai http://www.deepcode.ai/
177 Amazon CodeGuru https://aws.amazon.com/codeguru/

it mines Amazon code bases for pull requests that include AWS API calls. It looks at code changes and cross-references them against documentation data, which it also mines in parallel. You can decide whether to accept each recommendation CodeGuru offers — the more feedback you give it, the better its recommendations get.

By focusing on performance, Profiler identifies your most "expensive" lines of code and recommends ways to fix them to reduce CPU utilization, cut compute costs, and improve application performance. The way it finds such issues is by looking at excessive recreation of expensive objects, expensive deserialization, usage of inefficient libraries, and excessive logging. It runs continuously while in production, unlike the other products we've talked about that either test dormant code or analyze data after the fact.

CodeGuru can be integrated with a CI/CD pipeline, both in the code review stage and the application performance monitoring stage. Reviewer is used for static code analysis backed with trained machine learning models, and the Profiler is used to monitor application performance when the code is deployed and executed on the target computer. CodeGuru only works with Java today, but other language support is planned by Amazon.

SUMMARY

Machine learning and AI are in the early adopter phase. It is very recent that use of such tools in software development has been available to many teams. We are still at an early phase of innovation as well. But the companies mentioned here, in addition to others, are very promising.

Part of the lack of adoption of AI/ML tools for code review today is relative immaturity of the tools. New, incompatible tools bring traceability issues. Requirements in one tool, with stories for building in another tool, brings consistency and traceability problems between tools. CI/CD pipeline execution is completely separate with no data integration today. When the day comes when these tools are truly integrated, then it will be possible to truly utilize AI/ML development tools for code review and much more.

Now is definitely the time to look closely at these tools, as well as others not mentioned here. But don't give up on asynchronous face-to-face code reviews just yet — whether it's live, code-management interfaces, or via Slack or Zoom.

REFERENCES

- January 2018 FullStory blog — ex-Google employee talks about "not just for catching bugs," but about culture[178]

- October 2007 — Guido Van Rossum discusses Mondrian at Google[179]

- History of Gerrit[180]

- January 2018 — Unlearning toxic behaviors in code reviews[181]

- March 2018 — Code Review Best Practices Palantir Blog[182]

- An Empirical Study of Design Discussions in Code Review[183]

- Information Needs in Contemporary Code Review[184]

178 FullStory Blog https://blog.fullstory.com/what-we-learned-from-google-code-reviews-arent-just-for-catching-bugs/
179 Guido's Van Rossum Talk https://www.youtube.com/watch?v=sMqI3Di4Kgc
180 History of Gerrit https://www.gerritcodereview.com/about.html
181 Code Reviews Blogs, Medium
     https://medium.freecodecamp.org/unlearning-toxic-behaviors-in-a-code-review-culture-b7c295452a3c
182 Code Reviews Best Practices, Medium https://medium.com/palantir/code-review-best-practices-19e02780015f
183 Study of Design Discussion in Code Review http://rebels.ece.mcgill.ca/papers/esem2018_elzanaty.pdf
184 Information Needs in Contemporary Code Reviews https://fpalomba.github.io/pdf/Conferencs/C36.pdf

Chapter 20:
Moving to Modern DevOps
With Fuzzing and ML

Justin Reock

Justin Reock has over 20 years' experience working in various software roles and is an outspoken free software evangelist, delivering enterprise solutions and community education on databases, integration work, architecture, and technical leadership. He is currently the Chief Architect at OpenLogic by Perforce.

PART 1: THE LAST MILE:
SOFTWARE FUZZING AND THE LIMITS OF HUMAN COGNITION

It is often observed that "doctors are the worst patients."

This observation seems to stem from a basic notion of trust between doctor and patient. When a patient understands that they know less than a doctor, they are apt to listen to the doctor for advice about their health. This is a good approach for a patient and makes the job of a doctor much easier.

Doctors as patients, on the other hand, are tricky. They come in with preconceived notions. They've already diagnosed themselves. Their professional hubris in some cases may interfere with their ability to listen to their treating physician at best, or outright reject advice at worst.

Following this logic thread (I promise I'm going somewhere with this) I think it is fair to say that coders are often the worst testers. Although there is a very good argument that professional and domain knowledge of a use case can lead to a more relevant test corpus, coders will tend to focus on areas of the system that they have assumed to be problematic and may outrightly miss areas of the system that they assume in the converse to be non-problematic.

This limitation is fairly recognized and is arguably one of the primary arguments for the formation of separate quality assurance and testing teams. But we've seen those processes become slow and cumbersome or even downright incompatible with the methodologies we have chosen to achieve rapid software development.

The tactical goal of software testing, or at least generating a set of input test data, called a test corpus, could be described as trying to take a piece of software down as many possible logical paths as it can create. Ideally then, a "fully tested" piece of software will have been made to exist in as many "states" that it can ever possibly exist in, reached by providing as many possible kinds of input to the program as can possibly be generated!

No big deal, right?

Automated testing is king, and so we live in a world where coders are increasingly being asked to write their own test cases. These are good practices for efficiency, but they can create massive blind spots in our test corpus.

Adding to the complexity of automated testing is the current modern landscape of open source software and library dependencies. We are very often building applications that are comprised of little or no bespoke code. I've spoken at length about the incredible gains we make to human innovation when we develop this way, but all of this power comes with the responsibility of ensuring that our particular data structures, input, localized languages, etc, all work well with the software we are consuming and using in our applications.

Should we be expected to write our own test cases and validations for software that has been widely accepted in other communities? Can we accept that the quality and security standards adopted by other organizations will be good enough for ours? Maybe. But wouldn't it be nice to have a little more assurance than that?

And therein we discover our question: "How can we account for as many scenarios, or 'states' of our application as possible when we design our test corpus without taking on the impossible task of accounting for every state by hand?"

Human cognition simply has limitations. We can't consider every possible path, every possible input provided to our application from every conceivable endpoint. It's hard enough to do that with code that we've written but how much of our code is really "our" code anymore? Even if we've written say a web application entirely from scratch down to the very HTTP transactions themselves, we still have the unknowns of what browser the user might use on the legitimate end, and what scripts or hacking tools might be used against our application on the nefarious end. And what about the OS and metal that are converting all our code into actionable work over which we have no control at all in most cases?

It was this problem that led to the notion of "software fuzzing" as a viable means of quality and security assurance. If we can't conceive of every possible input scenario, why not throw a massive amount of random and unexpected input at the program instead? The use of fuzzing has uncovered countless areas of vulnerability or malfunction that would not have been otherwise conceived, particularly in the realm of memory access, buffer overruns, etc.

When realized at the scale necessary for a testing mechanism to become effective against modern sophisticated applications, software fuzzing removes the bias of the tester, allowing possible inputs to be applied to the application that would not have been conceived otherwise. Bearing in mind our original goal of inducing as many program states as possible, these inputs cascade into the action of inducing program states that would not have been induced by a human-generated test corpus.

That's because software fuzzing is, more or less, "throwing random data" at an app. But, in order for fuzzing to truly be effective in this new and complex software landscape, we have to develop much more sophisticated means of fuzzing.

The most basic fuzz of a piece of software follows a workflow like:

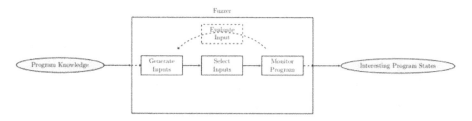

Figure 1: Fuzzing Process

Fig. 170: Fuzzing Process (Source: https://arxiv.org/pdf/1906.11133.pdf)

As our applications grow more circuitous in their ability to generate states, as the input vectors bloom and change protocols, so must our monitoring, our definition of an "interesting state" and of course our test corpus. These changes lead to new questions: Where do we focus our testing surface? What do we change if we find we didn't hit a wide enough testing surface? And, ultimately, can we use machine learning to automate that tweaking?

Fuzzing Defined

Fuzzing itself is just as much about software observability as it is randomness. The successful correlation of particular types of "unexpected input" to "interesting states" is the real goal of fuzzing, and it is often a difficult goal. The vast majority of unexpected input that is thrown at an application will do nothing at all to the program state. So, recognizing when that input does impact state, trapping that input, and deciding if the state is representative of a bug or vulnerability is the art form.

> ### "Test Corpus"
>
> **"Test Corpus" Definition:** Before your Baader-Meinhof sensors go off, let's revisit that term "test corpus" quickly! The original definition of "corpus" from Oxford is: "A collection of written texts, especially the entire works of a particular author or a body of writing on a particular subject." So you could see then where it's not too much of a stretch to think about those written texts as generated input. The computer science definition matches even more closely, with: "A collection of written or spoken material in machine-readable form, assembled for the purpose of studying linguistic structures, frequencies, etc." It derives one to one from the Latin "corpus" which simply means "body," so the test corpus should be thought of as a digital assembly of material that represents the entire body of testing inputs.

Looking at an extremely simplified example (one we can hopefully catch without the need for fuzzing!) imagine the following function:

```
(a,b) => {
    return (a / b);
}
```

Imagine for a moment that it wasn't immediately evident that providing an input of b=0 would yield in a divide by zero fatal condition. Given that, especially with long-running backend services, causing a fatal condition can cause service interruption and can therefore be considered an attack vector, it is safe to assume that we have created a potential vulnerability with this code. Imagine for a moment though that it wasn't immediately evident that providing an input of b=0 would yield in a divide by zero fatal condition. In this example, code fuzzing would be a viable means of discovering a vulnerability.

Let's design a quick fuzzer where random integer inputs are selected for the values a and b, constrained to the values [0 – 10]. Running a few cycles with this fuzzer, we would yield one very "interesting" state after a random amount of non-interesting states:

```
1:   [a=7,b=2] => 7 / 2 => A non-interesting state
2:   [a=3,b=5] => 3 / 5 => A non-interesting state
3:   [a=10,b=2] => 10 / 2 => 5 => A non-interesting state
4:   [a=0,b=10] => 0 / 10 => 0 => A non-interesting state

....

??: [a=9,b=0] => 9 / 0 => An interesting state! Fatal divide by 0
condition
```

While it is arguably impractical to have created a fuzzer to detect this bug/vulnerability in the code, we can quickly imagine where using a process like this at scale with a more complicated application could prove helpful, were we able to generate enough relevant inputs to create enough interesting states.

Think of other conditions that are common attack vectors which are difficult to find by simply tracing through code, like improper variable assignments, buffer overruns, uncaught code injection vectors, unauthorized privilege escalation, etc. **If you instead begin to imagine these runtime errors as "interesting states," you can start drawing lines backwards from those states to the inputs that could potentially cause them.**

Conversely, as we begin to imagine those states, the reality sinks in of just how many random values would have to be generated to reach those states. We might start to consider the complexity of trapping and identifying those states, and even further separating those states into categories that could potentially be used to cause harm vs. those that are benign.

Even with our very simple example, we might burn through 100 possible a/b combinations before stumbling across our b=0 trigger. And that's after we gave the fuzzer several very important hints: we told the fuzzer to stick to whole integers, and we told the fuzzer to range between 0 and 10. If we had given the fuzzer limitless (or what we might call 'naïve') possibilities to choose its input from, it may never have bothered to try b=0, which, if you think about it, is quite a needle in a haystack given the spectrum of possible UTF-8 (and beyond) input that true randomness would call for.

So, in most cases, the first example of fuzzing, the most basic type, or what we'd called "naïve" fuzzing is almost never practical. This is exactly what it sounds like — ideally unbounded and un-typed random data provided to inputs in the hopes of generating valuable and interesting program states.

I mentioned that the practice of fuzzing has come a long way in the last couple of decades. Really, that means that separate disciplines of fuzzing have arisen to try and address some of these specific issues that are endemic to naïve fuzzing:

- **Mutation-Based Fuzzing** – In which our test corpus is based on modifications to existing valid test cases, or rather any corpus of test cases that has been known to generate "interesting states." We might take our normal unit test cases and randomly change some part of that data. That would be considered a mutation of the corpus, as long as the pre-defined cases were picked because they generate known "interesting states." We might also run a naïve fuzzer until we accumulate a useful amount of "interesting inputs." We could then mutate these interesting inputs to create a new test corpus.

  As far as the mutation itself, it is generally unbounded. The fuzzer will decide what part of the data it should mutate and how much of that data should be mutated — really the length of that data to be mutated. Where it chooses to mutate could be determined randomly. There might be some specific mutation that is sought, really the choices are fairly endless. Further, the fuzzer may randomly generate some new value to then use in place, or mutate according to a gated set of rules. Theoretically, the mutations to the data itself can be completely naïve, and so mutation based fuzzers are really meant to be just a step up from naïve fuzzers in that they are still very random and don't have a sense of expected data types. They will just munge the normal input that would be passed by a legitimate test case.

- **Generation-Based Fuzzing** – A generation-based fuzzer Improves on some of the problems with mutation-based fuzzing by generating a test corpus based on the same input rules that are used to frame the normal test cases. An interesting thing to note about generation-based fuzzing is that, because the input types are defined, they are bounded and finite. The corpus may still be very, very large, but it is bounded. That means that it is possible to measure how much of the allowable or possible input test data has been generated.

- **Evolutionary Fuzzing** – Evolutionary fuzzers apply a bit of learning to the test corpus generated in a mutation-based way. Whereas mutation-based fuzzers make some educated decisions about where and how to modify the data, evolutionary fuzzers will make these decisions based on the "performance" of previous mutations to the input. If that performance were gauged, say, on the number of new "interesting states" that were generated by a particular mutation, that mutation might be repeated and combined with another bit of interesting, or just random data.

The combination of having to keep track of the performance of historic attempts at fuzzing, as well as combine and transform inputs in a way that makes sense for learning, makes evolutionary fuzzing considerably more resource-intensive than generation and mutation-based fuzzing. But it also bears the most promise in terms of true practicality when realized at scale.

Modern distributed patterns and advances in data analytics and the underlying substrates that facilitate those systems have made it possible to consider methods of evolutionary fuzzing that would not have been computationally practical even just a few years ago.

When we look at the available methods of fuzzing, we start to see where it's the evolutionary and generation-based fuzzers that bear the most potential for applying machine learning successfully. If we could replace the human process of validating inputs to states with machine learning, we could achieve intelligent fuzzing at completely automated scale. We then truly would limit our ability to thoroughly examine every potential state of an application only to our available compute resources, eliminating the software bottleneck.

Of course, evolutionary and generation-based fuzzing are much different approaches which each may generate vastly different test corpus. This opens the potential for new strategies across the board. For instance, the fact that we can actually measure the total possible testing surface covered by a generational test corpus means that we have an easy yardstick for measuring the training performance of our neural network. How quickly and efficiently can a trained model that, say, predicts the likelihood of a generation-based bit of input to create an interesting state or not be used to also perform rapid fuzzing on new versions of the same software? How great would it be to run a full surface test in a very short period of time on new versions as a normal part of CI/CD?

And what about the implications for evolutionary fuzzing? As we'll dissect further, one of the weaknesses of evolutionary fuzzing is the sheer amount, truly infinite amount, of possible test corpus that can be created. But we also know how powerful learning algorithms can be, and an evolutionary algorithm is already a powerful tool on its own. By building on known-interesting cases input and even combining known-interesting input with other good input, we can add some dynamic intelligence to the way our fuzzer navigates the probabilistic test bed. By training a neural network on what kind of combinations, and of course what kind of initial mutations yield "better" or "worse" results, or further break that down into taxonomy of what kind of primitive mutations (e.g. text replacement, encoding changes, type changes, etc.) tend to yield results for different categories of applications, the possibilities are quite exciting.

The remainder of this narrative then will focus on the possibilities of applying machine learning techniques specifically to the area of evolutionary fuzzing and generational fuzzing. In the next part, we'll explore some of the current problems and limitations with applying these techniques and where machine learning is already showing great promise in increasing efficient decision-making in the area of corpus generation and mutation.

PART 2: PRACTICAL FUZZING AND WHERE IT FAILS

On the surface, it seems like we have a theoretically infallible solution for discovering all possible states of a program, and from there it isn't a difficult stretch to consider that we could then narrow those states down to states that impact quality or security. In other words, the design of fuzzing suggests a "no stone unturned" approach to security. On the surface, that assessment is correct.

Of course, if it was that easy, we'd just run all of our software through fuzzers until our test corpus exhausts all possible states and there'd be no such thing as bugs or vulnerabilities anymore! It isn't that easy, and we already understand why. Exhausting all possible states means providing the necessary input to cascade into all of those possible states. This may be possible (or at least measurable) with generational input fuzzing, but generational fuzzing can leave massive blind spots. We know that evolutionary fuzzing is akin to mutation-based fuzzing, which means that both leave us with a corpus of theoretically infinite size.

So, as we've already alluded to, we have created one of the best kinds of problems to have in the world of computing. We have created a problem for which we currently lack the necessary computational resources to fully solve for. And until we have that kind of resource, we have to get smarter and more efficient about the way that our fuzzing algorithms work. None of this, by the way, should trivialize the impressive state of fuzzing today. We have made gains in this area, discovering better ways to trace for interesting states, record our interesting states and inputs, and even apply modern distributed substrate architectures to the problem.

The popular "LibFuzzer" engine, for instance, provides a sophisticated evolutionary fuzzing engine that also combines elements of generation-based fuzzing. As part of the open-source LLVM project, developers can use this engine to fuzz parts or all of their applications natively, as part of their build process.

LibFuzzer will take a corpus of seed data which should be comprised of arbitrary, valid or invalid, input data that roughly matches the taxonomy of input data that would be used in a program. For instance, if you were writing a library to unarchive ZIP files, you might provide a bunch of .zip files, some of which are complete and some of which are corrupted in some way. You would not provide, say, a Word Document file, or even another kind of archive file. That is the part of LibFuzzer that operates in a generation-based way.

But LibFuzzer will take that a step further and start creating mutations in the data and will invoke its evolutionary-based algorithms to keep track of which mutations led to newly discovered interesting states. The interesting input will just be retained as part of LibFuzzer's corpus for the application and will be used again later by LibFuzzer to generate new entries to the corpus.

This is impressive code, but LibFuzzer's own developers are the first to point out that LibFuzzer is best tailored to applications with a relatively low amount of short-

> Q. So, what exactly this Fuzzer is good for?
>
> This Fuzzer might be a good choice for testing libraries that have relatively small inputs, each input takes < 10ms to run, and the library code is not expected to crash on invalid inputs. Examples: regular expression matchers, text or binary format parsers, compression, network, crypto.

lived input. From their own FAQ:

Fig. 171: What Is a Fuzzer Good For?
(Source: http://llvm.org/docs/LibFuzzer.
html#developing-libfuzzer)

That's because, although the engine itself is lightning-fast and capable of generating interesting input in an evolutionary way, it doesn't really know much about the program beyond that. That still leaves us with an infinite number of possibilities in our test corpus, and a limitation on

Reduce the Test Corpus

Arguably, all of these things are really just serving one purpose — to wrangle that infinite canvas of possible inputs that can be conceived by generation-based and evolutionary fuzzing engines into as small a test corpus as possible, but one which will still explore every possible program state offered by the application logic.

how far we can explore that surface given modern day constraints on computation resources.

So, random exploration can't get us all the way there yet, and we still have a lot of work to do to make this space realizable for modern, sophisticated applications. For microservices and small libraries, LibFuzzer has proven itself to be a valuable and timesaving tool that improves code quality, but we know that does not describe many applications that perform important work today.

We'd be remiss in not mentioning the opposite way of thinking as well. If we don't have enough monkeys on keyboards, so to speak, what about the area of static analysis? Modern static analysis, as an area of study, offers a number of approaches that will apply more deductive and logic-based techniques to derive interesting states. Mechanisms such as symbolic execution and data-flow analysis can be applied to our code to map, discover, and trace interesting states. But even these mechanisms require an as of yet not-realizable amount of computational power to exercise their full potential.

Symbolic execution requires an exponential amount of computational resource relative to its logic branches, and even seemingly simple applications can split off an overwhelming number of branches by executing modern tasks such as fulfilling an HTTP request or running a Javascript function inside of a web browser.

What does this all mean? We still have an incredibly difficult time seeing the forest from the trees when it comes to analyzing our code, whether through static techniques like symbolic execution or by trying to discover all of our interesting states by fuzzing our inputs. A huge amount of our input coverage still remains unexplored even when we pair these techniques together. Compounding the problem is a mushrooming test corpus. Even if we could generate all of that input, all we are doing is amplifying the need for computational resource as each of these new vectors for discovering interesting input will generate the need to execute that input, and mutations of that input, and so on.

What makes the approach of fuzzing unique also makes it difficult to achieve at a functionally ideal state. Theoretically, a fuzzer of some sort could be used to determine how unknown, black-box, or even alien technology works if we were able to provide input to that technology — electric impulses, sonic signals, emotional output and gesturing even — and if we were able recognize interesting states as interesting states. But those are big tasks with a lot of implication in terms of the amount of effort involved.

We've laid out a lot of the limitations of modern fuzzing already, and we still have only explored the first few stages of fuzzing — gathering program knowledge and generating inputs. The process of reducing those inputs intelligently, monitoring program state, and detecting and recognizing interesting states all come with their own set of specific challenges. Arguably, all of these things are really just serving one purpose — to wrangle that infinite canvas of possible inputs that can be conceived by generation-based and evolutionary fuzzing engines into as small a test corpus as possible, but one which will still explore every possible program state offered by the application logic.

Thinking through some of those challenges, we begin to see potential applications for things like deep learning in the realm of evolutionary and generational fuzzing, and we will look at those more closely in the final section, but for now let's consider some other specific limitations and challenges to modern fuzzing techniques:

Need for Domain Knowledge

One of the critical parts of the fuzzing workflow is the identification and reporting of an interesting state. That involves a number of analytical gymnastics, including:

- *Recognizing that the state itself is in fact different than other states which have previously been encountered.*

- *Knowing when we are spinning our wheels by generating a lot of varied input that's really just making the program "do the same thing" as it has been doing or other inputs.*

- *If it is a newly discovered logic branch, recognizing that the state is meaningful.*

- *Determining how to interpret that state and provide taxonomy, i.e. was this a crash, a non-fatal condition, etc.*

- *Deciding how to report that state based on its taxonomy, i.e. should a heap dump be provided.*

One can't really hope to accomplish this with any kind of accuracy with presuming at least some domain knowledge specific to application. Without a predictive model, it is fair to assume that this domain knowledge needs to be applied to the fuzzer in some way by a human. Knowledge of the program will drive the valid test corpus that we feed to our generational models, or the seed data that we feed to our evolutionary models.

That reality introduces an impedance to realizing the Platonic ideal of fuzzing at scale, i.e. where we could begin to drop applications anonymously into a fuzzing engine of some sort, and that engine were capable of determining interesting inputs and recognizing interesting states on its own. Because we must have a human with domain knowledge design parts of the test corpus, we:

- *Slow down the process, making it difficult to add to a blind pipeline.*

- *Introduce human bias into the analysis, creating potentially large gaps in our test coverage.*

What and How Do We Mutate?

Beyond using our domain knowledge to understand how to generate a more focused test corpus based on what it does to our program states, we should also look at the mutations themselves. While mutation-based models are, strictly speaking, random in the way that they munge their test input, we know that there are we have to apply some domain knowledge or other education to the calculus if we hope to reduce the size of our test corpus.

As humans, even as creative humans, we run into many of the same cognitive limitations with the ways we invent to mutate our data as we do with trying to predict program state in the first place. After all, it's natural to think that the opposite of one form of input might create an opposite state, i.e. providing a negative integer where a positive integer would be expected. What if that sign switch only matters when seven other inputs are in a particular state? Would we have been able to determine that using only deductive reasoning? Maybe, but, with what amount of effort?

Completely randomizing our mutations just re-introduces the problem of understanding our test coverage — the more randomness we introduce, the closer to an infinite test corpus we reach. It's difficult, then, to know exactly how to mutate our data to derive new and unexplored program states from our domain knowledge and valid or invalid reference corpus.

Understanding and Applying What We Are Seeing

Assuming we've solved as best as we can for these other considerations, what about the very act of understanding that we've hit a state that we haven't seen before, and that the state actually translates to something which could become a bug or a vulnerability?

And how do we weigh the results that we measure from the program when we do recognize an interesting state? Recall that our evolutionary models rely on an ability to determine which kind of input is interesting, and just **how** interesting that input is. That way, we can report back to the fuzzing engine that we should retain the traits of that input and use it again in our corpus, combined with other input or on its own.

If we want to be able to reduce and better manage our input, we should be able to properly categorize and prioritize the kinds of input that generate interesting states. We should be able to recognize and rank those interesting states in terms of how likely they are to provide us information that could lead to patching bugs or addressing vulnerabilities, and we should be able to provide that feedback to future iterations of this and other test corpus, to increase our overall program knowledge so that future tests can be better. This is not only ideal, but absolutely required in order to build evolutionary fuzzers. Recall, for example, how LibFuzzer retains interesting inputs that it discovers. It includes new entries into the corpus that are shown to create new interesting states.

The practicality of discovering the state cannot be ignored, either. Software vulnerabilities are complex and may rely on the interactivity of multiple states and inputs to be repeatable and demonstrable as a vulnerability. It's easy to say that we can just "do that analysis by hand," but realize that every time we decide on that course, we limit our ability to achieve our ideal: valuable fuzzing that is touch-free and can be repeated at scale.

We are solving a lot of these challenges today, with and without the application of machine learning. One of the largest modern projects is the ClusterFuzz project from Google.

ClusterFuzz

ClusterFuzz is a scalable fuzzing infrastructure that finds security and stability issues in software. Google uses ClusterFuzz to fuzz the Chrome Browser and as the fuzzing backend for OSS-Fuzz.

Fig. 172: Cluster Fuzz Definition (Source: https://google.github.io/clusterfuzz/)

Google is in a unique position to take advantage of its vast compute resources and interested developer community and create widespread and distributed fuzzing efforts, and it has done exactly that in the form of the ClusterFuzz engine, and, by extension, the OSS-Fuzz project.

If we can measure the effectiveness of a fuzzer by the amount of surface that it can explore, then we can say that these projects are absolutely leading the way in that space. Over a hundred million test cases are executed a day across hundreds of projects that are integrated with this infrastructure. If we want to get more tactical and just measure raw bugs or vulnerabilities, then more than 16,000 bugs have been found in the Chrome browser alone using ClusterFuzz, and roughly the same have been discovered across about 250 open source projects.[185,186]

---

185 As of May 2020, GitHub Repository https://google.github.io/clusterfuzz/
186 See "Trophies" and OSS Fuzz, OSS Fuzz GitHub Repository https://github.com/google/oss-fuzz

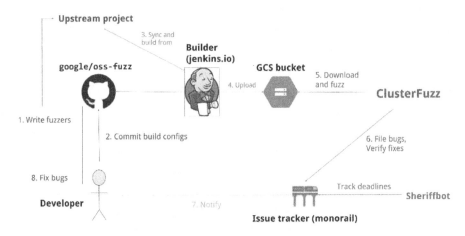

Fig. 173: OSS-Fuzz Workflow

(Source: https://github.com/google/oss-fuzz/blob/master/docs/images/process.png)

ClusterFuzz provides new ways of thinking at scale for a number of challenges with fuzzing that have been discussed, but even ClusterFuzz has serious limitations. First of all, the language itself matters, and as of now ClusterFuzz is limited to the fuzzing engines that it is based on: LibFuzzer and one that has not yet been mentioned in this book, the "American Fuzzy lop" or AFL engine. These two libraries are limited to fuzzing applications written in C/C++, Rust, and Go. While this covers a significant portion of the landscape, wouldn't it be better if our fuzzing engines could be trained to recognize deeper patterns that may exist behind the languages themselves?

Language constraints take us away from the ideal of achieving that ideal no-touch fuzzer, where can we improve on that situation?

Distributed computing lets us do what we already know to do at a grander scale, but, how about achieving new things? What about automating the generation of relevant input without having a great deal of program knowledge? What about recognizing new and undiscovered program states without having a need for human evaluation of the states and the related corpus?

In this final section, we will explore how machine learning techniques can bring us closer to the goal of completely automated fuzzing that realizes all possible program states.

PART 3: ML AND FUZZING

Hopefully by now you've gained some insight into the modern practice of software fuzzing and it is becoming clear just how far this testing practice has progressed. No doubt, projects like ClusterFuzz are proving to be valuable and capable of filling in the gaps for human cognition when it comes to discovering bugs and vulnerabilities in our software.

Most importantly, I hope we can recognize just how much work still needs to be done in this space to get to the ideal, touch-free fuzzer that we've theorized. The field of machine learning is offering up very interesting solutions to some of the common problems of fuzzing that we've discussed and in fact we've already mentioned how learning might be applied to some of the by-hand tasks that are necessary to improve our generation-based and evolutionary fuzzers.

For instance, deep learning might be applied to our generated input sets to help us reduce the amount of data that is part of our test corpus. "*Test scheduling*" is the process of assigning a priority to an element in the corpus, or more properly, a bit of test input, based on how likely those inputs are to generate an interesting state. It is not a stretch to think, for instance, that a deep convolutional network could be used to learn about what some of those inputs might be, given that we are able to measure the outcome.

Progress is already being made in areas such as this across several interesting projects.

One such study is led by Microsoft researcher Patrice Godefroid.[187] Godefroid has worked in extreme software quality for over twenty-five years across a range of disciplines including software fuzzing. His main project is an intelligent fuzzer called SAGE.[188] SAGE is a highly sophisticated fuzzing approach which combines symbolic execution with generation-based fuzzing. As we discussed earlier in this chapter, symbolic execution is a powerful but computationally demanding technique. The SAGE fuzzer optimizes the number of generation-based inputs that are created per completion of a single symbolic execution. To quote the article mentioned above, "This way, a single symbolic execution can generate thousands of

187 Microsoft Research by Patrice Godefroid https://patricegodefroid.github.io/
188 Sage Fuzzer Project https://dl.acm.org/doi/pdf/10.1145/2090147.2094081

new tests." Godefroid's approach, which has been termed "Whitebox fuzzing," has been proven to greatly optimize the input corpus, leading to a significantly smaller number of throw-away tests.

This approach takes advantage of the best parts of symbolic execution to derive input that is likely to create an interesting state in the code, and then amplifies that advantage by creating an exponential number of new entries in the corpus every time a single symbolic execution is completed.

While an interesting study on its own, the SAGE engine is not a learning solution in the modern sense, in that we aren't using a deep network or some other neural network to achieve further automation and scale. In 2017, Godefroid began writing about a technique he called "Learn & Fuzz,"[189] in which a recurrent neural network is used to help generate useful input for, in the case of this study, the PDF parser used in the Edge browser. One can see where input fuzzing against this parser could provide vulnerability data which would limit the capability of a PDF to carry malicious executable code which might exploit a vulnerable parser.

Recurrent neural networks contain hidden layers and are continuous time-based structures that typically consist of single neurons chained together, like so:

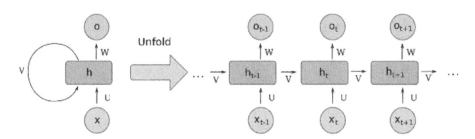

Fig. 174: Recurrent Neural Network Unfold Process
(Source: https://en.wikipedia.org/wiki/Recurrent_neural_network#/media/File:Recurrent_neural_network_unfold.svg)

The goal of the learning, in this study, is to create a trained model that will be able to assist in generating objectively valid input for a PDF. By objectively valid, in this case, we mean input that will not trigger a predefined or already accounted for bit of error handling logic, since those program states are expected and therefore non-interesting. RNNs are good at handling input of a variable length, and since the

---

189 Learn and Fuzz: Machine Learning for Input Fuzzing https://patricegodefroid.github.io/public_psfiles/ase2017.pdf

PDF format is just a contiguous structure of an unknown number of elements, the input and layer structure of an RNN suggests that it may be helpful with this type of learning problem.

If we could filter PDF input entries from our corpus that will trigger known error states in a parser, we can significantly reduce the size of the corpus which actually needs to be fuzzed. The full extent of the training details and algorithm are well-documented in the link above, but essentially a large corpus of valid PDF files was used to create one massive set of PDF parser inputs which were then split into smaller subsections of inputs.

Three different strategies competed on taking these bits of input and learning now to generate new, completely artificial bits of valid PDF input for the purpose of creating a input corpus for fuzzing. Once the model was sufficiently trained, a new algorithm called SampleFuzz was derived to use the model to decide whether a sample of generated input should be considered "worthy" of fuzzing based on a configurable probability threshold of generating valid PDF input:

Algorithm 1 $\texttt{SampleFuzz}(\mathcal{D}(\text{x}, \theta), t_{\texttt{fuzz}}, p_t)$

$\texttt{seq} := \text{"obj "}$
while $\neg$ $\texttt{seq.endswith}(\text{"endobj"})$ **do**
$\quad$ c,p(c) := $\texttt{sample}(\mathcal{D}(\texttt{seq}, \theta))$ (* Sample c from the learnt distribution *)
$\quad p_{\texttt{fuzz}} := \texttt{random}(0, 1)$ (* random variable to decide whether to fuzz *)
$\quad$ **if** $p_{\texttt{fuzz}} > t_{\texttt{fuzz}} \wedge p(c) > p_t$ **then**
$\quad\quad$ c := $\text{argmin}_{c'}\{p(c') \sim \mathcal{D}(\texttt{seq}, \theta)\}$ (* replace c by c' (with lowest likelihood) *)
$\quad$ **end if**
$\quad \texttt{seq} := \texttt{seq} + \text{c}$
$\quad$ **if** $\texttt{len(seq)} > \texttt{MAXLEN}$ **then**
$\quad\quad \texttt{seq} := \text{"obj "}$ (* Reset the sequence *)
$\quad$ **end if**
end while
return $\texttt{seq}$

Fig. 175: Learn and Fuzz: Machine Learning for Input Fuzzing, Section III – C
(Source: https://patricegodefroid.github.io/public_psfiles/ase2017.pdf)

Two of the three training sets "won" the learning exercise, called "Sample" and "SampleSpace" and were used to derive the algorithms that generate a competing test corpus for each:

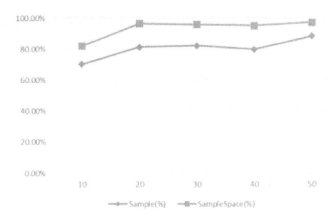

Fig. 5. Pass rate for Sample and SampleSpace from 10 to 50 epochs.

Fig. 176: Learn and Fuzz: Machine Learning for Input Fuzzing, Section III – C
(Source: https://patricegodefroid.github.io/public_psfiles/ase2017.pdf)

In this case, it was important to continue to compete more than one model since it was rating both the amount of coverage represented by the generation-based test corpus, and how much of that input is considered "passable" input, i.e. input that won't trigger known error states in the PDF parser. In other words, the ideal model would generate a test corpus that covered as much as possible of the generation-based test corpus with "valid" or passing data. That said, the objective is still to fuzz, and so coverage is really the most important metric. Coverage implies the number of cases in our corpus which represent unique instructions to the PDF parser, which is as we've learned is our yardstick for generation-based fuzzing.

The results demonstrate that applying trained models to the generation of an input corpus can improve the efficiency of that corpus, with one created using the SampleFuzz algorithm achieving the largest coverage with a perfectly adequate pass rate for cases:

Algorithm	Coverage	Pass Rate
SampleSpace+Random	563,930	36.97%
baseline+Random	564,195	44.05%
Sample-10K	565,590	78.92%
Sample+Random	566,964	41.81%
SampleFuzz	567,634	68.24%

Fig. 8. Results of fuzzing experiments with 30,000 PDF files each.

Fig. 177: Learn and Fuzz: ML for Input Fuzzing, Section IV – C
(Source: https://patricegodefroid.github.io/public_psfiles/ase2017.pdf)

While promising, it should be noted that this study is of mostly academic value. It shows that there is measurable promise in the notion of applying machine learning techniques to various mechanisms present in fuzzing engines for the purpose of making them more efficient. The authors themselves, however, denote an incredibly revealing and important kernel of truth which highlights the realities of automated, intelligent fuzzing:

"In addition to coverage and pass rate, a third metric of interest is of course the number of bugs found. During the experiments previously reported in this section, no bugs were found. Note that the Edge PDF parser had been thoroughly fuzzed for months with other fuzzers including SAGE [11]) before we performed this study, and that all the bugs found during this prior fuzzing had been fixed in the version of the PDF parser we used for this study."[190]

The authors note that a later study using similar techniques with a wider test corpus based on the Sample and Random algorithm did in fact turn up a valuable bug. And given that a lot of fuzzing techniques had already been employed which found a lot of bugs which were fixed, we can only wonder whether those bugs have been found faster using these ML-augmented engines. It's likely, and exciting to think about the possibilities, but the authors also take care to mention and underscore another important takeaway from this study. A repeatable phenomenon arises from the statistical data which suggests that the learning mechanisms present in the study may in fact be working against or causing "tension" with the goals of the fuzzer.

190 Learn and Fuzz: ML for Input Fuzzing, Section IV-H https://patricegodefroid.github.io/public_psfiles/ase2017.pdf

Notice in the study that the algorithm with the highest pass rate, Sample-10K, fell more than 2,000 cases behind the SampleFuzz algorithm. Given that the original goal of the neural network was

"Better learning does not imply better fuzzing."

to try and determine the probability that a randomly generated element of a test corpus would be "passable" input to the PDF parser, it is fair to say that the pass rate in the experiment is a measure of how well-trained the particular learning model is.

We observe the "tension" that the authors speak of here — the model that represents the "best" learning model did not generate the best input corpus for our fuzzing engine. The authors suggest that this is due to conflicting goals of learning and fuzzing — learning tries to find ordered patterns in data, where fuzzing tries to introduce as much unexpected activity as possible. As the authors themselves put it, "Better learning does not imply better fuzzing."[191]

So, SampleFuzz shows promise, but cold realities still emerge:

- Even highly sophisticated fuzzing engines that utilize ML will still create a highly significant number of interesting states which do not translate into bugs.
- Fuzzing and machine learning have largely been developed according to different schools of thought and with different goals, and there is evidence that those goals **may introduce tension that needs to be overcome**.

Hopefully, these criticisms are taken as highly constructive, the purpose of which is to point out the work that must still be done to achieve the goal of intelligent fuzzing at scale using machine learning. These impasses lend important focus to much-needed areas of improvement, even if they highlight that there is still in fact a great deal of work to be done. No matter how much more work and research must be done, this study demonstrates with clarity that machine learning can be employed to improve and minimize our input test corpus for fuzzing, which of course carries implications for evolutionary fuzzing as well.

The Godefroid approach is one example of a number of methods being explored to try and assist in the stage of fuzzing in which we generate our inputs, but in this

191 Learn & Fuzz: Machine Learning for Input Fuzzing, Section VI
https://patricegodefroid.github.io/public_psfiles/ase2017.pdf

part, we have also contemplated other areas of improved efficiency. For instance, we know that further down in the fuzzing process it is important to be able to recognize and categorize the interesting states of the program that we trigger with our input corpus. We need to know if generated states are unprecedented states and we need to know if they are the kinds of states that might lead to finding a bug or a vulnerability.

The biggest reason for the current slow progress appears to be a lack of labeled training sets. While unsupervised learning is possible when generating inputs, it is probably impossible to train a neural network on how to recognize an interesting state without that network being fed labeled data to determine the underlying patterns that make a state interesting. Right now, the best results using machine learning to perform things like taxonomy and categorization are achieved using supervised training based on labeled data sets. A widely distributed example is image categorization, which is now ubiquitous in the modern AI landscape. It is no accident that this new functionality largely appeared overnight – the publication of the ImageNet labeled image database gave AI developers the labeled training data necessary to complete their long-awaited AI taxonomy problems. So, you can think of the problem of applying ML to input selection as the problem of image categorization prior to the publication if ImageNet, we lack a large body of labeled training data to show a neural network what an interesting state looks like.

It isn't surprising then that these are largely human driven processes at the moment, and considerably less work is being done in the area of using machine learning to automatically recognize and categorize interesting states vs. unimportant ones. Work is being done, albeit slowly, with perhaps the most prominent work at the moment taking place in a project called "ExploitMeter."[192]

In the absence of a great deal of labeled data, ExploitMeter takes a triangulation approach to the problem of training a model to categorize whether an interesting state represents something that could be used to find a software vulnerability. ExploitMeter applies this logic to a decently sized sample set of common open source applications such as VLC and 7z to try and determine how likely it is, and to what degree, that the program is exploitable in some way.

---

192 *Exploit Meter: Combining Fuzzing with Machine Learning for Automated Evaluation of Software Exploitability*
   http://www.cs.binghamton.edu/~ghyan/papers/pac17.pdf

The framework looks at three key indicators:

- Static analysis methods are used to extract details suggestive of software that might be prone to certain threats, i.e. the possibility of generating a stack overflow.

- Fuzzers are used to generate crashes or other interesting states, we then regress the data against what we know from the static analysis to determine whether that state aligns with presumptions from the static analysis.

- Those key points can be used to derive an "exploitability" metric, the real goal of ExploitMeter, and that metric can be used as a label to provide feedback to a learning network as to whether various states encountered match the assumptions of the static analysis.

Some immediate gaps are apparent, i.e. we have implicit bias already in that we are only training against the areas for which we have performed static analysis and likewise made assumptions about how the code will perform, but, don't forget that this is more or less a human task that we already employ by-hand as part of our security research. We already make assumptions about our code based on the results of our static code analysis, and in some cases, we turn around and fuzz the same code to validate the findings of our static analysis.

In the design of ExploitMeter we see a goal of reducing the human input needed to adequately perform the steps of determining how likely an interesting state is to be an exploitable or vulnerable state, or part of some other workflow that might lead to a vulnerable state. ExploitMeter itself, as evidenced by digesting the above paper in its entirety, is appreciably marvelous in its design. It represents the closest widespread study of using traditional deep learning to begin to automate the process of determining whether an interesting state is in fact an exploitable state. Nevertheless, ExploitMeter's score itself is demonstrative of its own respectable self-awareness - not wanting to be more than advertised it doesn't point to specific vulnerabilities. It only tries to predict the likelihood and degree of that software's exploitability, represented by the results of the following sample run:

TABLE III
HIGH EXPLOITABILITY SCORES IN A SAMPLE RUN (E: EXPLOITABLE,
PE: PROBABLY_EXPLOITABLE, PNE:
PROBABLY_NOT_EXPLOITABLE, U: UNKNOWN)

Test order	Application	Score	E	PE	PNE	U
5	vlc	0.811	1	0	0	0
13	mediainfo	0.937	1	1	2	0
18	qpdfview	0.647	0	1	1	0
19	xpdf.real	0.824	1	0	1	0
22	evince	0.930	1	1	0	1
25	odt2txt	0.806	1	0	0	1
31	objcopy	0.986	2	1	1	3
35	xine	0.994	3	0	2	1
36	jpegtran	0.999	4	1	0	1
39	abiword	1.000	5	3	1	3
40	size	0.995	2	2	1	3
46	catdoc	0.828	1	0	1	2
49	pdfseparate	0.825	1	0	1	0
66	pdftk	0.824	1	0	1	0
67	avplay	0.841	1	0	2	0
74	pdftohtml	0.965	2	0	1	1
76	qpdf	0.961	2	0	0	0
82	ar	0.972	1	2	1	3
91	mpv	0.994	2	2	1	3
100	mencoder	0.989	2	1	3	1

Fig. 178: ExploitMeter Research Table (Source: http://www.cs.binghamton.edu/~ghyan/papers/pac17.pdf)

Again, there is a seeming mountain of work that we have yet to overcome, but the early results are very promising. The score itself in the case of ExploitMeter is arguably less important than the calculus by which we derive that score and demonstrates that with more methods for obtaining labeled data sets, we can hope to achieve more complicated predictions and even start to determine the kinds of vulnerabilities implied by various interesting states encountered via fuzzing. It is clear that deep learning can lower the amount of regression needed in our fuzzing by eventually helping to categorize various forms of interesting states that we encounter.

We will no doubt continue to discover new ways to apply machine learning techniques to the entire lifecycle of a fuzzing engine, but for now we'll look at one last area of improvement, selecting where and how to mutate our inputs.

A prominent study also involving Godefroid, along with two other researchers, Konstantin Bottinger and Rishabh Singh, does just this. The study involves reward models and treats fuzzing as a reinforcement learning exercise for the purpose of making decisions about how and where to mutate. It takes a game theory approach and rewards decisions that drive the learning closer to achieving the goal of generating input that triggers a unique interesting state.[193]

If you take a small intellectual leap, you can begin to compare the movements a fuzzer takes to the movements a player might take in a strategic game for which many outcomes are possible, such as Go. Each mutation to input could be represented as a "move" in the game, and that move either brings the player closer to or further away from the objective of winning the game. Conceivably there are a finite (if still incredibly large) number of program branches that can be explored by the logic — as we've discussed this is the hypothesis behind both static analysis and fuzzing as a whole — and so if we apply reinforcement techniques we should be able to train a network to make good decisions, just as how Deep Blue was taught to win at Chess, or DeepMind won at Go.

In the words of the study's authors:

> Intuitively, choosing the next fuzzing action given an input to mutate can be viewed as choosing a next move in a game like Chess or Go: while an optimal strategy might exist, it is unknown to us and we are bound to play the game (many times) in the search for it. By reducing fuzzing to reinforcement learning, we can then try to apply the same neural-network-based learning techniques that have beaten world-champion human experts in Backgammon [3], [4], Atari games [5], and the game of Go [6].[194]

Some of the largest machine learning problems are being solved with reinforcement learning. While its feedback-driven approach and need for elements such as backpropagation make it a complex utility, frameworks such as Google's TensorFlow project are making it easy for AI novices to grasp and make use of the logic in their applications.

---

193 *Deep Reinforcement Fuzzing https://arxiv.org/pdf/1801.04589.pdf*
194 *Deep Reinforcement Fuzzing, Section 1 https://arxiv.org/pdf/1801.04589.pdf*

In this case, a fuzzer will generate an input, fuzz that input, and reward the input based on the resulting state of the system. By rewarding and retaining the fuzzing actions that move us closer to the goal of discovering a bug or vulnerability in the software, we learn from past actions and try to build a network that generates the kind of input for our corpus that would provide the biggest reward.

When the fuzzer makes a decision about a mutation, that decision is evaluated using a Markov decision process. The result of a Markov decision manifests usefully as a chain of decisions in which each have a reward associated with any single decision. Whether any single decision moves the decision process into the next state of the overall decision is determined by single decisions chosen in the past. Markov decision models are used across the board in heuristic based applications ranging from economics to robotics.

Applying Markov decisions to input mutation allows us to do a number of important things, but more than anything we now have a benchmark for defining and formalizing the study of input mutation as reinforcement learning which paves the way for further research.

This study alone has given us several profound leaps, delivering perhaps surprisingly positive outcomes with improvements across key layers of the input mutation process when compared to a baseline, non-learning augmented algorithm:

	Improvement
Reward functions	
Code coverage r_1	7.75%
Execution time r_2	7%
Combined r_3	11.3%
State width $w = \|x'\|$	
r_2 with $w = 32$ Bytes	7%
r_2 with $w = 80$ Bytes	3.1%
Generalization to new inputs	
r_2 for new input x	4.7%

TABLE I

THE IMPROVEMENTS COMPARED TO THE BASELINE (AS DEFINED IN VI-C1) IN THE MOST RECENT 500 ACCUMULATED REWARDS AFTER TRAINING THE MODELS FOR 1000 GENERATIONS.

Fig. 179: Deep Reinforcement Fuzzing (Source: https://arxiv.org/pdf/1801.04589.pdf)

While not exhaustive, we've now seen the exciting potential of using known machine learning techniques to improve the ability for our fuzzers to optimize their inputs and expand their test coverage.

CLOSING THE LOOP, FULLY AUTOMATED FUZZING

In our digitally transformed future, software quality and quality of life will overlap almost completely. As computing becomes more ambient and fades into the background of our lives, the average participant will not need to know the steps that allowed us to achieve "perfect" software – software that cannot be hacked and that doesn't malfunction. Undoubtedly, intelligent software fuzzing will be a participant in this achievement, and projects such as ExploitMeter demonstrate the role of machine learning in this reality.

The "perfect" testing framework for the "perfect" piece of software will require little or no program knowledge, will be capable of generating valuable input, and will be capable of creating a large test coverage to exercise every possible state, bug, and vulnerability of an application. It will then categorize that bug or vulnerability — and who's to say what step after that might look like? Self-healing code? Self-generating code? Maybe someday, but as we've learned, we aren't even close to that stage.

Deep fuzzing at the kind of scale necessary to realize this future will require advancements across the board. Improvements to computational resources, further neural network development, prolific data labelling and raw experimentation are all needed to build an engine with the feasibility to eliminate human bottlenecks from automated testing processes. Despite these challenges, the future is deep fuzzing, and the future is bulletproof.

REFERENCES

- **ExploitMeter: Combining Fuzzing with Machine Learning for Automated Evaluation of Software Exploitability**
  http://www.cs.binghamton.edu/~ghyan/papers/pac17.pdf
  Guanhua Yan   Zhan Shu
  Junchen Lu   Yunus Kucuk
  Department of Computer Science Binghamton University
  State University of New York
  {ghyan, jlu56, zshu1, ykucuk1}@binghamton.edu

- **A Review of Machine Learning Applications in Fuzzing**
  https://arxiv.org/pdf/1906.11133.pdf
  Gary J. Saavedra   Philip W. Kegelmeyer
  Kathryn N. Rodhouse
  Sandia National Laboratories
  Albuquerque, NM, USA
  {gjsaave,knrodho,dmdunla,wpk}@sandia.gov

- **Deep Reinforcement Fuzzing**
  https://arxiv.org/pdf/1801.04589.pdf
  Konstantin Bottinger   Rishabh Singh
  Patrice Godefroid
  1 Fraunhofer AISEC, 85748
  Garching, Germany
  konstantin.boettinger@aisec.fraunhofer.de
  2Microsoft Research, 98052 Redmond, USA
  {pg,risin}@microsoft.com

- **Learn&Fuzz: Machine Learning for Input Fuzzing**
  https://patricegodefroid.github.io/public_psfiles/ase2017.pdf
  Patrice Godefroid Microsoft Research, USA
  pg@microsoft.com
  Hila Peleg Technion,
  Israel hilap@cs.technion.ac.il
  Rishabh Singh Microsoft Research, USA
  risin@microsoft.com

Chapter 21:
Guidelines to Maintaining AI & ML Test Scenarios

One of the main reasons for leveraging AI and ML for test automation creation is the flakiness of test cases, and the maintenance of the scripts over time, which are required upon constant changes to product and platforms under test. To maintain test code written using Selenium and/or Appium frameworks requires code changes, reporting visibility, and continuous code reviews. Maintaining test scenarios that were created using AI and ML tools (recorded, auto-generated, etc.) are different.

Record and playback tools often promise self-healing scripts with near-zero maintainability, but is this true?

To address the maintenance of ML-driven test automation, here are few considerations and "parameters" to keep in mind.

MAINTENANCE CADENCE AND WINDOWS

ML-driven testing can help keep your objects maintained by learning the entire DOM or object tree. It can choose between the objects based on probability and weights and find the "right" element in each execution. However, it is not sufficient enough to provide a test script free of flakiness.

Test engineers ought to enforce test audits for ML-driven scripts upon every two to three software iterations and execute their automation scripts in debug-mode to ensure they are fully ready and stable. In case there are specific UI and user flow changes to the product, obviously these scripts must be corrected within the software iteration itself.

During the maintenance points in the test script lifecycle, there can be different actions that need to be performed by practitioners, depending on the type of the test and ML use cases.

VISUAL AI TEST MAINTENANCE

For visual testing, the maintenance is slightly easier than that of a functional test. A visual AI testing cycle is based on a **pre-approved baseline** of images that are being **compared** upon execution across multiple platforms and screens.[195] During the execution, the solution will typically flag an inconsistent "**expected**" visual that is different than the "**actual**," asking the user to either override the existing baseline visual or decline and ignore the inconsistency as a false negative issue.

Specifically for Applitools' visual AI testing, they have also built a baseline of visuals into a version control system, which allows for comparisons between baselines. It makes the overall maintenance across different product versions easier.

Fig. 180: Applitools UI Version Control and Baseline Comparison (Source: Applitools Blog)

This type of visual maintenance is quite important — especially for mobile, web, and responsive web apps — which by definition run on a large set of UI configurations.

As with any testing type maintained through code across product versions and via version control, visual testing also requires the same level of maintenance, regardless of the AI engine, to ensure noise-free reporting and better focus on real UI defects.

---

195 Applitools Baseline Version Control https://applitools.com/blog/applitools-introduces-the-worlds-first-ui-version-control

FUNCTIONAL UI TEST MAINTENANCE (CODELESS)

Maintaining ML-driven functional test automation is a bit more complicated than visual testing. Functional test automation relies heavily on user flows, element locators, existing coverage, test history, test management and duplication, scoping within the CI, and more.

Like any test code that is maintained through version control and undergoes audits and "certification" to ensure it is solid and reliable enough, the same should apply to codeless test automation.

Codeless automation complements code-based automation. Therefore, there needs to be a sync between the two teams that are responsible for both testing types. This sync needs to include what is covered by what testing type. And when a test code in a specific area(s) is changed or requires modification, this needs to trigger a similar action on the codeless front.

There are also ML tools that provide live production data, which shows the most-used flows that can also trigger a maintenance requirement for uncovered areas, faulty areas, and more.

One advantage of codeless automation tools is their ability to self-heal element locators that are affected due to product changes. In that regard, codeless tools should quite easily be able to switch to a different element locator on the web or mobile app — based on ML in runtime and statistical probability — in order to be visible, actionable, and reliable.

All of the impacted codeless and code-based test scripts need to be reflected in the CI or other schedulers/triggers to ensure that the next test cycle already covers the

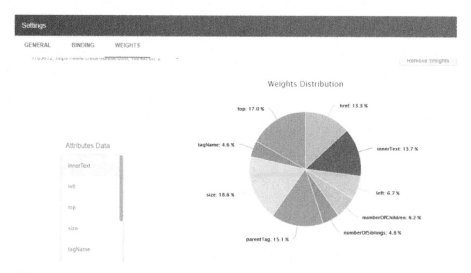

right scenarios, platforms, and elements per application.

Fig. 181: Element Locator Settings and Classification (Source: Perfecto Codeless)

SUPPORTING MAINTENANCE CAPABILITIES

In addition to visual testing, element locator strategy, and user flows, teams that leverage codeless automation (for visual, functional, and non functional testing) today have the ability to add more robustness and credibility into their test assets using a few capabilities: **tagging** mechanisms and **platform coverage** analytics.

By using tagging to classify specific **testing types** (functional, security, build accep-tance, etc.), **testing functional areas** (login, purchase checkout, etc.), and **stages in the cycle** (regressions, smoke, sanity, CI, performance, etc.), teams can better slice and dice test data in the abovementioned maintenance windows. This allows them to better control audits, focus on the right areas, and move forward much faster. Tags can add a new layer of visibility to codeless in the same way practitioners have

Time		Tags	Lab
Start	🏷 Build null		
Feb 27, 20:	🏷 Erank	🏷 4	PERFECTO
Feb 25, 20:	🏷 Responsive Build Validation	🏷 4	PERFECTO
Feb 25, 20:	🏷 Software Version: 1.6	🏷 4	PERFECTO

been tagging through Junit annotations in code-based testing.

Fig. 182: Tagging Functional Testing for Test Data Management (Source: Perfecto)

In addition to tagging, analytics and ML algorithms running on production data allow app developers to get insights on the **most-used platforms** (web, mobile) and buggy platforms that result in lower transactions times.

By using such data, teams can better maintain their labs and control their coverage configurations for better user-focused testing. There are also non-ML analytics solutions that are available and can also serve as an input to maintain your testing labs,

Device Category	Sessions	Goal Completions	contribution to total: Goal Completions
	6,432,646 % of Total: 100.00% (6,432,646)	17,593 % of Total 100.00% (17,593)	
1. 📊 desktop	3,061,943	56.02%	
2. 📊 tablet	1,949,762	32.83%	
3. 📊 mobile	1,420,941	11.16%	

like Google Analytics (Fig. 183 below) and HotJar solutions.[196]

Fig. 183: Platform Coverage Analytics Dashboard (Source: Google)

Like in the abovementioned examples of test data, and functional codeless test maintenance, practitioners ought to build into their SDLC processes time for debugging and validating the ML use cases. This includes the differential use cases, declarative use cases, and others. Automated code reviews, version changes and build changes require similar attention over time to accommodate any impact on the outputs and better serve the purpose of these tools.

Chapter 22: Maximizing Code Observability Within DevOps using AI and ML

Roy Nuriel, Sr. Director of Product Management, Logz.io

Roy Nuriel is a Senior Director of Product Management at Logz.io. He has over 15 years of experience in product management, specializing in DevOpsSaaS products in several startups as well as large companies. Over the course of his career, his roles have spanned across engineering, product delivery, and product management. Roy spearheaded complex projects as an innovation leader, growing ideas into market-leading solutions.

Charlie Klein, Product Marketer, Logz.io

Charline Klein is a Product Marketer focused on helping modern DevOps teams deliver performant, reliable, and secure services. He currently works at Logz.io, which helps these teams gain observability into their production environments.[197] Previously, he worked at Synopsys, which helps software engineers build more secure applications.

INTRODUCTION TO OBSERVABILITY

Modern DevOps teams gain observability into their production environments so they can understand what is happening in their system, and why it's happening. To better understand the inner workings of a system, these teams orchestrate their tech stacks to expose telemetry data — consisting of logs, metrics, and traces.

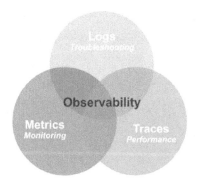

Metrics are lightweight data points that are great for monitoring the saturation of a system's infrastructure, such as CPU and memory. More advanced observability operations may analyze custom metrics, which are generated by applications to measure business KPIs like the average value of a shopping cart for unfinished purchases.

---

197 Logz.io http://logz.io/

Logs are records of events that happened in a system. A log is unstructured text that's typically parsed (or enriched) with metadata before it is analyzed. It can include IP addresses, geolocation, and other helpful information. Logs are very helpful when engineers need to troubleshoot production issues.

Traces are most helpful for monitoring performance and identifying bottlenecks in distributed systems. The interconnectedness of microservices can make it exceptionally difficult to track latency. By mapping out service requests, traces make it easy to monitor and visualize how distributed systems are performing.

An "observable" system exposes this telemetry data so it can be collected by an analytics solution for engineers to monitor and explore. There are a variety of ways to orchestrate a system to expose and ship telemetry data, depending on the data type and analytics solution.

Organizations that either moved to continuous delivery or are in the process of increasing their deployment frequency usually start to shift the operation responsibility closer to the engineering organizations. DevOps teams take full ownership both on the deployment phase as well as on monitoring the production environment — and as part of that being at the front line to address production issues.

Continuous delivery extends the definition of quality — teams need to take full accountability of the software quality both pre-production as well as post-production. In order for them to have that visibility, they need the right tools to monitor the applications and more so find the root cause of the issues.

Microservices architecture and cloud infrastructure allow developers to increase their velocity, develop independently, and simplify the deployment process. On the other hand, it makes it more complex to monitor as those environments are dynamic by nature and constantly changing.

Business-critical applications, such as SaaS (Software as a Service) solutions, have to ensure that the service is up and running, identify issues as early as possible, and once an issue occurred those issues need to be addressed quickly, as they are linked directly to business loss.

Monitoring solutions have been available for many years. Companies like Splunk, IBM, CA, and many more have been providing great tools for IT, helping them monitor and manage their applications in production.

While DevOps teams need to find good monitoring solutions, they tend to prefer open source tools as those are the ones that are more accessible for them. They allow them to leverage the large eco-system of the community.

For the last few years, there has been an increasing number of open source tools providing multiple observability solutions across all three pillars. The most popular projects (as of writing this book) are:

- *Log Analytics — ElasticSearch, Logstash, and Kibana — Also known as the ELK stack.*
- *Infrastructure Monitoring — Prometheus is the leading time-series database for metrics. The main driver for Prometheus' high adoption is the seamlessly-integrated solution it has for Kubernetes. Grafana is the most popular user interface (UI).*
- *Application Performance Monitoring (APM)/Tracing — There is an increasing trend in Jeager adoption.*

THE ROLE OF MACHINE LEARNING IN OBSERVABILITY

Modern cloud environments consist of many interconnected and interdependent components such as VMs, databases, orchestrators, and containers — each of which generates varying types of telemetry data.

No human is equipped to process this amount of data. Some systems produce terabytes of telemetry data per day, which requires advanced analytics to find actionable insights in this data. This is where machine learning can have an important impact.

Applying ML to Logs, Metrics, and Tracing Analytics

Logs

It is easy for logged events that clearly indicate a serious oncoming production incident to go completely unnoticed because they are surrounded by a sea of log data. "Trying to find a needle in a haystack" is the perfect saying for trying to find critical logs generated by production.

With the help of ML, log analytics solutions can find the needle by learning which logs are important to engineers based on what's being discussed on online forums like StackOverflow and GitHub. These forums are filled with problems being discussed by engineers. ML can use this information to predict which logs are worthy of attention.

Logz.io's Cognitive Insights scrapes log messages discussed on those forums and cross references those discussions with incoming logs. When a log from an environment is matched with a log being discussed on these forums, it's flagged so engineers know to take a look.

For example, if an environment produces 50 SQL Syntax error logs out 1,000,000 logs in an hour, this could result in a big problem, but it would be very difficult to catch unless a team was actively monitoring for it. However, Cognitive Insights cross referenced the SQL Syntax errors logs with StackOverflow forums like this one:

> MySQL error: You have an error in your SQL syntax; check the manual that corresponds to your MySQL server version for the right syntax to use near

Since other engineers were discussing this log as a problem on StackOverflow, Cognitive Insights predicted that could likely be a problem in this case as well.

In addition to anomaly detection, ML can also help engineers make sense of large amounts of log data. The scale and variety of log data makes it difficult to quickly see the most common logs generated by a system. But by clustering logs with similar messages together, it's easier to understand the most common types of log data.

The logs below follow a basic pattern:

```
Account 358 was created , waiting for kibana indexes to be created
 Account 1265 was created , waiting for kibana indexes to be created
 Account 871 was created , waiting for kibana indexes to be created
 Account 1291 was created , waiting for kibana indexes to be created
 Account 309 was created , waiting for kibana indexes to be created
```

While these logs may not seem like a problem, if there are millions of these logs clogging up searches and slowing down troubleshooting, they can quickly become a nuisance.

There is no need to view all of these logs. ML capabilities can identify the pattern in these logs, so you know they exist without needing to scroll through all of them. Here is the corresponding pattern for the logs above:

```
Account Number was created, waiting for kibana indexes to be created
```

In the following case, Logz.io uses ML to identify repeated patterns in log messages, and cluster similar logs into small, manageable groups so engineers can quickly make sense of their log data.[198] Notice the fields are "Time" and "Message." Scrolling through all of this unstructured log data to find specific information is not the best use of time.

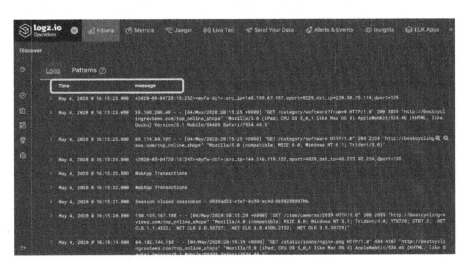

Fig. 184: Sample Logs Filtered By Time and Message (Source: Logz.io)

In this case, Logz.io's Log Patterns uses ML to identify repeated patterns in log messages, and cluster similar logs into small, manageable groups so engineers can quickly make sense of their log data. Notice the fields include "Time," "Count," "Ratio," and "Pattern."

198 Logz.io Cloud Observability Platform Home Page https://logz.io/

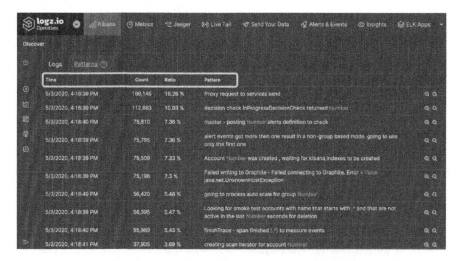

Fig. 185: Sample Logs Filtered By Time and Message (Source: Logz.io)

Now, it's easy to understand all of the log data that was generated by this environment, rather than scrolling through them.

Metrics

ML can also be applied to metrics to identify anomalies that could be indicative of a production issue. Unlike logs, metrics don't represent events in an environment, so analyzing individual data points won't be helpful. Rather, analyzing the trends in metrics is a much more useful exercise.

Basic ML capabilities will identity spikes or dips in metrics that do not normally take place. This means analyzing specific metrics over time to understand its common behavior and triggering an alert when the metric deviates from that behavior. This could indicate a random spike in CPU usage or sharp dip in traffic.

More advanced algorithms can use multivariate analysis to understand how all metrics in a system trend together. By building these models one can understand when there is an unknown problem where the metrics don't trend together.

One of the biggest challenges for any monitoring solution is what will trigger an alert, especially for complex and dynamic environments. In most cases it is hard to understand what alerts are needed and what should be the measurements to trigger them. Machine learning can be used in few aspects:

1. Identify anomalies based on historical data and propose the users a set of alerts and conditions.

2. One alert is triggered — Identify all the anomalies and help find the root cause of the problem as well understand what the potential impact on additional systems or components in the system will be.

3. Dynamic alerts — Automatically identify anomalies in the system and trigger alerts with all the relevant information.

There are several levels of complexity and the more the model is trained the more value it gives, and it enables the next model:

1. Anomalies on a single metric.

2. Anomalies across several metrics.

3. Learn dependencies between components and wisely identify anomalies between those components.

Traces

To find areas of improvement in application latency, it can be helpful to gather and organize information from traces. Examples could include the top 100 most common error types or the 100 slowest spans. This can make it easier to focus on areas of improvement.

In addition to identifying problems in the applications, ML can be used for finding problems in the tracing itself. In large distributed applications, it can be difficult to identify traces that are incomplete or not showing helpful information. ML can be applied to identify time gaps within specific traces, which are indicative of coverage problems and prompt a check on the tracing instrumentation. Additionally, surfacing traces where all of the spans are the same length could indicate a timeout or some other performance problem.

Another example would be to find what causes latency across multiple traces in order to prioritize areas for potential improvements in the system. Estimate what would be an impact of a change/performance improvement on specific flows as well across the system.

Machine Learning Is Changing the Observability Landscape

Machine learning models can be applied also across the three pillars of observability. Finding correlation between anomalies across the pillars — such as an increase of memory on specific containers together with increased logs with the same pattern — can help identify the issues and in some cases automatically remediate it and overall reduce the Minimum Time To Know (MTTK) and Minimum Time To FIX (MTTF) significantly.

Observability is one of the domains that machine learning is changing and will continue to change in the future. The ability to process mass amounts of data and provide smart insights in real time will allow machines to identify, alert, and in some cases even remediate issues in ways humans were not able to do. It is clear that we still have more to come.

Chapter 23:
Using Machine Learning to Improve Static Analysis Results

Andrew Bedford

Andrew Bedford is a software developer at Perforce who works on Klocwork, a static analysis tool. He has a PhD in computer science and specializes in language-based security and formal methods.

Claude Bolduc

Claude Bolduc is a static code analysis enthusiast since completing their PhD in formal methods at Laval University, Canada. Since then, Claude has worked for different companies on topics like static analysis and automatic code generation for embedded systems. Claude is now leading the software analysis team for the Klocwork product at Perforce Software.

Konstantin Popov

Konstantin Popov is an engineer and scientist who spent almost a decade working on the static code analysis tool Klocwork. He holds a PhD from University of Alberta specializing in numerical methods and has worked for several years as a postdoctoral fellow at University of Ottawa.

INTRODUCTION

Static analysis tools have become an essential component of any development process. Without executing the source code, static analysis tools are able to analyze the code to detect security vulnerabilities, potential runtime errors (e.g., memory leaks, concurrency violations, use of uninitialized data) and other defects. They can also be used to enforce coding standards and best practices (e.g., CERT, OWASP, MISRA C/C++, AUTOSAR).

Static analysis tools can generate many findings, which can be overwhelming to a user. Especially since some of the findings might be false positives (i.e., the analyzer found a potential defect, but it was not a real defect) due to the undecidable nature of static analysis.

In this chapter, we present some of the experiments that we did to help users handle static analysis findings. While we used the static analysis tool Klocwork, these experiments could have been done with any static analysis tool.

Klocwork is a commercial static analysis tool, a SAST tool, that does deep semantical analysis of source code written in C/C++, Java, and C#. It is used for analyzing safety-critical and non-safety-critical software, and works well for analyzing embedded systems. It is also certified for use in IEC 61508, ISO 26262, IEC 62304, and EN 50128 projects.

EXPERIMENTS

This section describes some experiments that we did with the Klocwork static code analysis tool. However, they can be easily adapted to other static analysis tools.

GROUPING DEFECTS

As the name implies, grouping defects consists of grouping together defects that are similar in nature. By doing so, users can review similar defects one after the other, which reduces context-switching cognitive efforts.

Defects can be grouped together by defining and calculating a similarity measure. This measure could be based on information such as the defect message and elements of interest (e.g. variables, functions, files) found within the defect. However, there are two possible problems with this approach:

1. The similarity measure is likely static and non-configurable by the user.

2. It may not guarantee a real relationship with every defect in the group.

A more promising approach is to use unsupervised machine learning clustering algorithms in order to automatically group defects together. For our experiment, we used the "K-Means" clustering algorithm. The "K" in K-Means corresponds to the number of clusters that need to be identified by the algorithm. It is an iterative algorithm that computes the center of clusters (see Fig. 186 for example).

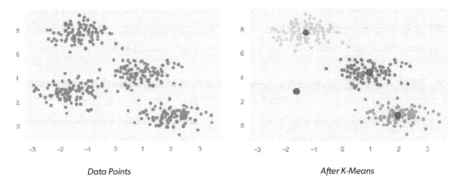

Fig. 186: K-Means Clustering Example Produced Using SciKit

Performance of such algorithms typically depends on the choice of features. In order to pick those features, let us consider a sample C++ code with a defect in it (see Fig 187).

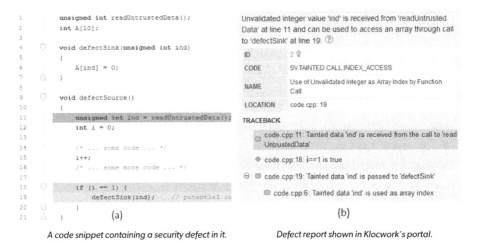

A code snippet containing a security defect in it. | Defect report shown in Klocwork's portal.

Fig. 187: A Typical Static Analysis Defect Report From Klocwork

In this example, a call to `readUntrustedData()` is performed at line 11 and its result is stored in variable `ind`. This call presumably reads a value from an untrusted source, such as a network socket or any other untrusted data source.

Later, at line 19, this variable is passed to function `defectSink()`, where it is used as an index to access array A. Since no validation is being done on index `ind`, this could lead to out-of-bounds read/write operations, which represents a security risk.

Klocwork correctly detects this defect and reports the following information (see Fig.2 (b)):

- Defect code SV.TAINTED.CALL.INDEX_ACCESS and message "Unvalidated integer value 'ind'..."
- Defect traceback identifying:
    - Defect source (line 11)
    - Defect sink (line 6)
    - Path events indicating the control flow (lines 18, 19)

Intuitively, two defects appear to be similar to each other if they have the same source, the same sink, or the control flow for these defects take common paths. In other words, the more common aspects that the two defects have, the more similar the defects will appear to be to the user, and the faster they will be to review. For this reason, we decided to use details from the defect reports as features.

For example, whether a defect involves variable `ind`, functions `readUntrustedData()` or `defectSink()`, the defect code SV.TAINTED.CALL.INDEX_ACCESS, the file names, etc. More formally, all such details found in all the available defect reports determine an N-dimensional defect feature space.

Every unique detail (defect kind, trace message line, etc.) determines one dimension in the feature space. If a defect report has that detail present in it, then its corresponding coordinate in that dimension is assigned to 1. Otherwise, the coordinate is assigned to 0.

For any reasonably sized analyzed project, the feature space dimension will be on the order of thousands to tens or hundreds of thousands, with each defect only having a few dozen nonzero coordinates in it. This feature space composition is not dissimilar to some email spam filtering systems.

Based upon the K-means clustering of defects that were reported by Klocwork through its analyzing open source project Far File Manager, we were able to identify 17 distinct defect clusters.[199] Each of which could be further subdivided into more subclusters based on the desired AI analysis granularity.

---

199 *Far Manager Official Site https://www.farmanager.com/*

An example of two randomly selected defects that were clustered together by the machine learning algorithm is shown in Fig. 188. While the two defects in this example were reported in different files, and for different variables, intuitively they look similar and related. The reason for this is that they have the same source and function `Alloc()`, which is highlighted by the gray background in Fig. 188.

This similarity can be used for presentation convenience or reporting purposes.

Defect #146, assigned to cluster 1.

Code	NPD.FUNC.MUST
Title	Result of function that may return NULL will be dereferenced
Message	Pointer 'buffer.str' returned from call to function 'cat' at line 83 may be NULL and will be dereferenced at line 85.

Trace	Trace message	Line
	Pointer 'buffer.str' returned from call to function 'cat' at line 83 may be NULL and will be dereferenced at line 85.	83
	'this->str' is assigned the return value from function 'vcat'	131
	'str' is assigned the return value from function 'Alloc'.	147
	'this->str' is assigned the return value from function 'realloc'.	74
	'this->str' is returned by 'Alloc'.	75
	'str' is returned by 'vcat'.	147
	'this->str' is returned by 'cat'.	133
	buffer.c_str(): returns 'buffer.str'	85
	'buffer.str' is dereferenced by passing argument 1 to function 'fputsSocket'.	85
	'str' is passed to function 'fputsSocket'.	38
	'str' is explicitly dereferenced.	42

File	D:\Sources\Far\plugins\ftp\ConnectSock.cpp

Defect #698, also assigned to cluster 1.		
Code	NPD.FUNC.MUST	
Title	Result of function that may return NULL will be dereferenced	
Message	Pointer 'this->str' returned from call to function 'Alloc' at line 264 may be NULL and will be dereferenced at line 265.	
Trace	*Trace message*	*Line*
	'this->str' is assigned the return value from function 'Alloc'.	264
	'this->str' is assigned the return value from function 'realloc'.	74
	'this->str' is returned by 'Alloc'.	75
	'this->str' is dereferenced by passing argument 1 to function 'StrCpy'.	265
File	D:\Sources\Far\plugins\ftp\FStdLib\FARStdlib\fstd_String.cpp	

Fig. 188: Example of Two Arbitrarily Chosen Defects Belonging to the Same Cluster

Overall, we were pleased with the results of this experiment. Most defects within the same cluster were reasonably similar to each other and different from those in different clusters. It is a promising approach that can noticeably lessen the work required to investigate a typical set of defect reports from a static code analysis product.

RANKING DEFECTS

Another way to improve static analysis results and make them easier to review is by ranking defects by likelihood of being real defects (i.e. true positives).

There are different strategies for finding defects in static code analysis tools, the most popular being to find defects using only syntactic information. Another strategy is to find defects using dataflow and control flow analyses (multiple variants exist).

In the case of defects found using only syntactic information, the results are usually very reliable, with a very high percentage of true positives and a low percentage of false positives. This is because most of the analyses based only on syntactic information have decidable algorithms and should almost always have accurate detection. However, the syntactic analyses are usually shallow and cannot identify complex defects.

On the other hand, defects found according to dataflow and control flow analyses require semantical analyses of the code and are often undecidable. Because of that, analyses use heuristics to find potential defects and abstractions to control the speed and accuracy of the analysis. As a result, these defects are more likely to be false positives because of their undecidable nature.

In our experiments for ranking, we concentrated only on defects found according to dataflow and control flow analyses, since they are the main contributor to false positives. These potential defects are found by a static analysis tool by a procedure that might involve approximations.

An approximation example would be multiplying a variable that is known to be within the range [0, 1000] by 2. It would be accurate to say that the result of this multiplication will be in the set of even numbers between 0 and 2000. However, it would be an approximation to say that it could be any number between 0 and 2000. Our hypothesis was that the fewer approximations that are made while finding a defect, the more likely the defect is to be real.

We tested this hypothesis on multiple open source projects, including Apache HTTPD.[200] Our results indicated that this new ranking method sorts better than Klocwork's previous ranking method. The overall ratio of real defects in this project was 74% for the checks enabled (dataflow and control flow analyses). You can see in the figure that the first 70 defects (out of the 430 found) given by the ranking algorithm (named "new ranking" in the figure) were real defects.

200 The Apache HTTP Server project https://httpd.apache.org/

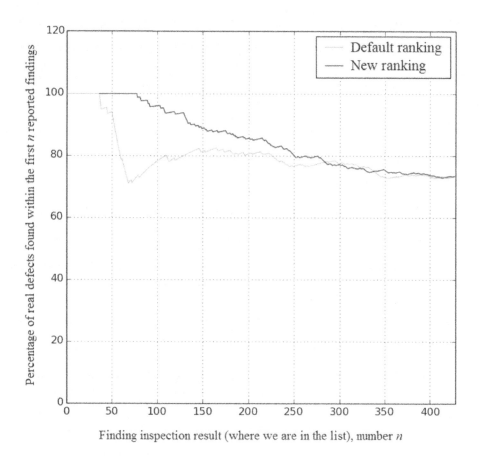

Fig. 189: Percentage of Real Defects Found Within the First N Reported Findings
(For the Apache HTTPD Open Source Project)

This new ranking method also has a beneficial side effect: Straightforward defects are ranked higher than more complex defects. Meaning: If two defects are linked together (e.g. they have the same sink), and the reviewer is going through the list in a sequential manner, then there is a chance that the more complex potential defect would be fixed by just looking at the more straightforward defect.

AI-ASSISTED DEFECT RANKING

While the approach described above is useful in prioritizing defect reports based on the number and quality of approximations made during analysis, it relies on internal knowledge about analysis details. For this reason, it is difficult to generalize for use with other tools. One can offer a more general approach that would prioritize defects that are likely true positive reports based on them being "similar" to defects reported in the past and confirmed to be real problems by a user.

Similarly, if a defect report "looks like" a problem that has been reported previously by a human observer, this defect can be considered as a likely false positive. As a result, the defect report can be deprioritized by the ranking system.

Therefore, we are considering a machine learning-based approach that establishes similarity and assigns defect reports to a particular group, "True Positive Reports" (TP) and "False Positive Reports" (FP). These two groups are based on the results of a human reviewer assignment of the defects reported in the past.

The family of machine learning algorithms that build their statistical models based on sets of labeled examples is called "supervised machine learning algorithms." Researchers have access to a large variety of these algorithms, many of which are constantly being improved.

In our experiments, we used several supervised machine learning algorithms. The one algorithm family that seems particularly useful for our purposes and was also found to produce the most encouraging results is the algorithm based on the Support Vector Machine (SVM) model.

The SVM model works with the labelled examples mapped into an N-dimensional feature space and attempts to separate them by a hypersurface. This results in examples that have different labels being located on different sides of the hypersurface (see Fig. 190). The model is solved for a hypersurface of a predefined shape by minimizing the total distance from examples to the hypersurface.

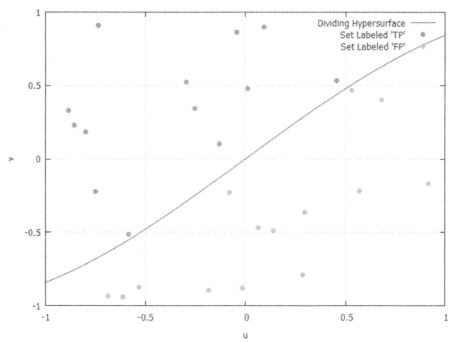

Fig. 190: Hypersurface Dividing Labeled Examples in an N-Dimensional (u-v) Space

In our experiments, we started by mapping defect reports to a high-dimensional feature space based on the report details. This process is similar to the procedure described above in the K-means clustering section.

We then used the one dataset with a relatively large number of labeled examples of defect reports assessed by human reviewers: Our own Klocwork codebase historical defect reports. This dataset contained more than 2000 defect reports that have all been mapped to ~7000-dimensional feature space. The dataset has been divided into training and testing subsets in the 70/30 proportion.

To build and test the model, we used an open source SVM model implementation called "libSVM."[201] This is a C/C++ library with comprehensive documentation and interface and is available under "modified BSD license."

The library supports a number of predefined hypersurface shapes (kernels), including linear, polynomial, radial basis function, sigmoid, or a data points predefined

---

201 LIBSVM: A Library for Support Vector Machines https://www.csie.ntu.edu.tw/~cjlin/libsvm/

kernel function. We found that the simple linear kernel function resulted in the best quality predictions. It was very convenient for us that the library offers input in the form of sparse vectors that fit our data structure well.

Our experiments were dependent on the details of defect-to-feature mapping and random training/testing subsets subdivision. We applied the SVM algorithm to the testing subset, and the "FP" and "TP" categories. The resulting mapping was accurate with probability in the range of 79%-85%.

This satisfactory result indicates that supervised learning — when used for defect postprocessing with available historical defect reports review data — can be a useful tool for prioritizing reports. Especially those that are more likely to be associated with a real problem in the code.

CONCLUSION

The experiments presented in this chapter show that machine learning can improve the results of static analysis tools when used for postprocessing analysis results reports. In addition, the techniques used in these experiments can be applied to many static analysis tools. Our experiments also showed that clustering and ranking can be used separately or together to reduce the effort required by users to review defects.

The last experiment introduced a future research area for the team: combining our static ranking algorithm with history-aware machine learning classifiers. For more details on our experiments and related works by others in the field, please refer to our Embedded World 2019 Conference paper.[202]

---

202 C. Bolduc, K. Popov. Approaches for Improving Handling of Static Analysis Findings. In: Proceedings of the Embedded World 2019 Conference; 26-28 Feb. 2019; Nuremburg, Germany, pp. 592-599. Alternatively, available online as a whitepaper at https://www.perforce.com/resources/kw/approaches-how-improve-handling-static-analysis-findings

Chapter 24:
How Does AIOps Benefit DevOps Pipeline and Software Quality?

While the majority of this book covers topics focused on the left side of the DevOps pipeline — like functional, unit, API, and other processes related to automation that benefit AI and ML — this chapter is all about the right side of the DevOps process.

As this book is being developed, there is already an advanced approach by IT leaders toward a more efficient operation that aims to address inefficiencies and bottlenecks standing in the way of automated production and operation environment management.

Things like noise reduction for false production alerts through clustering and pattern-matching algorithms, identifying root causes of incidents in production and pre-production through smart correlation of the issues with user journeys, detection of abnormal conditions and product behavior, business impact analysis traced to issues, defect trends that may result in production outages, and generic triaging of problems are among the key objectives behind ops managers looking into AI and ML as possible solutions.

When armed with advanced abilities that make an AIOps portfolio valuable, IT managers can make an impact on the entire software delivery cycle, production quality, and more. Abilities as mentioned above can translate specifically into anomalies detection, automated pattern discovery and predictions, software topological analysis for greater accuracy in issues classification as well as impacted dependent areas and resolution, and statistical data analysis that can result in clustering of issues, correlations of issues, and better decision making within the entire product life cycle.

All of the above is an introduction to and breakdown of the modern term called AIOps. IBM defines this term accordingly: "AIOps, (for artificial intelligence for IT operations) is the application of artificial intelligence (AI) to enhance IT operations. Specifically, AIOps uses big data, analytics, and machine learning capabilities to do the following:

- Collect and aggregate the huge and ever-increasing volumes of operations data generated by multiple IT infrastructure components, applications, and performance-monitoring tools.

- Intelligently sift 'signals' out of the 'noise' to identify significant events and patterns related to system performance and availability issues.

- Diagnose root causes and report them to IT for rapid response and remediation — or, in some cases, automatically resolve these issues without human intervention."[203]

An AIOps complete solution does not only cover smart **APM** (application performance monitoring) solutions, but also leverages **ITIM** (IT Infrastructure Monitoring) and **ITSM** (IT Service Monitoring) to build a comprehensive layer of production and operational insights analysis that can run on big data and against advanced modern software architecture (micro-services, cloud, etc.).

With the power of AI-based operations, teams can better focus on determining the service heath of their applications, and gain control and visibility over their production data. With that, DevOps teams can expedite their MTTR (mean time to resolution) using automated incident management in real time and quickly.

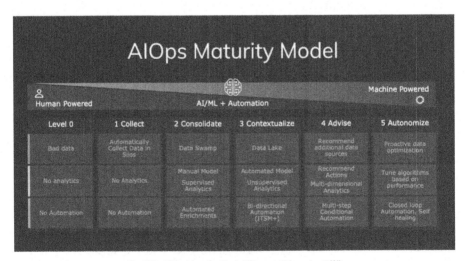

Fig. 191: AIOps Maturity Model (Source: ScienceLogic[204])

203 IBM Definition of AIOps https://www.ibm.com/cloud/learn/aiops
204 Science Logic Definition of AIOps and its Maturity Model https://sciencelogic.com/solutions/aiops

Looking into the above suggested maturity model for AIOps within a DevOps organization, we can learn what good looks like, and the necessary path and metrics needed to get there or position your own maturity in such a model.

The path starts from a fully human-oriented approach (level 0) where it is reactive to issues that are happening, trying to reduce noise and false negatives and only filter and cluster real issues, toward a more automated and smart approach. The path goes through collection and analysis of big production data in an automated fashion (**level 1**), through data consolidation and contextualization (**levels 2 and 3**) that fits into a smart model of IT service monitoring (ITSM) and an unsupervised model, and then to the higher maturity of automation of data (**levels 4 and 5**) through predictions, recommendations, and advisories to IT managers on how to proactively optimize their data usage and autonomous operations.

A different maturity model suggested by Gartner also looks at five levels toward autonomous IT Service Management. It goes from a state of manually and inefficiently detecting issues and trying to map them to patterns and clusters to reduce noise and increase MTTR.[205]

Such a model evolves through issues prevention using proactive alerting and determining what Gartner calls "**causality.**" The final stage in the proposed model looks at service management automation that can analyze tickets through chatbots, change risk analysis, and more.

All of the abovementioned benefits take the business from a state of being **reactive** to **proactive** to **predictive**.

What AIOps Consists Of and Landscape Examples

As mentioned earlier, to build an advanced AIOps model requires a combination of tools that can analyze big data and deliver a relevant and up-to-date analysis of issues. To succeed in this very complex task, an AIOps tool stack must be able to "run" on sets of data like the below (obviously there are more):

- Historical analysis of issues (e.g. service tickets).

- Current and older performance analysis.

- High-risk product anomalies that were detected.

- Outages and other service-related issues.

- Key user journey analysis.

- Pattern discovery and correlation.

- Market-specific KPIs and analytics (benchmarks).

- Product specific inputs.

The end goal should be continuous insight to IT managers/ops around their service quality, product quality, and other anomalies in the product that occur in real time and can prevent a high-severity outage in an autonomous manner.

To embed AIOps into a DevOps workflow requires an E2E process change. It starts with developers who can identify potential risks in their code and alert it to the DevOps engineer to "plug" it into the AI system as a potential and categorized risk, so when something similar occurs or is reported through a ticket, the time to address it will be either zero or as short as possible. The logging of an incident done by the DevOps engineer should then be translated into an automated test scenario that runs against a pre-production and of course production monitoring system (APM) so the loop is being closed throughout the entire SDLC continuously.

The AIOps landscape is evolving and will continue to evolve throughout the main categories that were mentioned above (APM, ITIM, ITSM). These players collectively are trying to help in the automation of detection and clustering of production issues and anomalies, predictability of issues and prevention of these issues, and for specific issues that do rich production — an automated RCA (root cause analysis) for faster MTTR.

If to mention a few players in the industry for each of these categories, I would start by looking into what the following vendors offer:

APM

- New Relic[206]

- Dynatrace[207]

- Cisco AppDynamics[208]

ITIM

- Logz.io[209] (also covered in Chapter 22)

- Elastic Search[210]

- Splunk[211]

- DataDog[212]

ITSM

- BMC Predictive IT Service Management Solution[213]

- ServiceNow[214]

Mapping or visualizing AIOps as a continuous process was very well defined and explained in an insightful post on Medium.[215]

206 NewRelic APM https://newrelic.com/
207 Dynatrace Monitoring https://www.dynatrace.com/
208 AppDynamics https://www.appdynamics.com/
209 Logz.io https://logz.io/
210 Elastic Search ITIM https://www.elastic.co/
211 Splunk Monitoring and ITIM solutions https://www.splunk.com/
212 DataDog Monitoring and Analysis https://www.datadoghq.com/
213 BMC Heilx ISTM https://www.bmc.com/it-solutions/bmc-helix-itsm.html
214 Service Now Solutions https://www.servicenow.com/
215 AIOps, The new member in the DevOps Family
    https://medium.com/faun/aiops-the-new-member-in-the-devops-family-d76bab14c98e

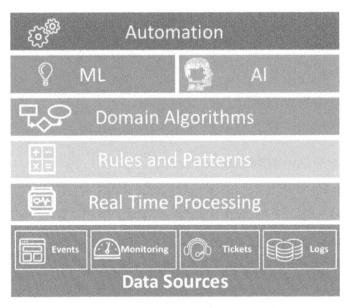

Fig. 192: AIOps Process Explained (Source: Medium)

The above architecture is being mapped into a complete DevOps workflow that again, was very well defined in the abovementioned Medium article.

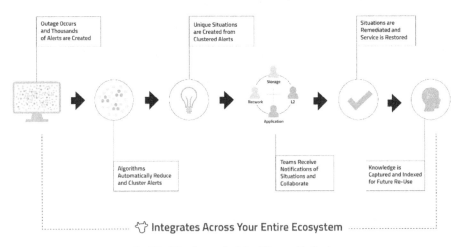

Fig. 193: AIOps Process Explained (Source: Medium)

BOTTOM LINE

To optimize a full DevOps pipeline takes a village. And that means entire teams play a role in it. It is often stated that maximum automation enables CI/CD, and this is correct. However, in the context of modern DevOps, with optimized software delivery, this also requires a smart assistant in the shape of AI and ML agents.

Such assistive technologies must also capture the software after its release and ensure that noise is eliminated. Real issues must be addressed quickly or prevented through predictive analysis, smart monitoring solutions, and autonomous software corrections across the various clusters that the algorithms defined.

The future of DevOps relies on E2E AI and ML from the early development phases, through code quality, defects resolution, deployment to production, and post-production issues remediation.

Chapter 25:
Expediting Release Cycles
With Test Impact Analysis
Using AI/ML

The Chapter was Co-Authored With Eran Sher, Co-Founder, SeaLights

Eran Sher has over 20 years of experience as an entrepreneur, building emerging and high-growth enterprise software companies. He is currently the co-founder and CEO of SeaLights, the Software Quality Governance Platform.

Prior to founding SeaLights, Eran co-founded Nolio, one of the first Application Release Automation platforms, which was acquired by CA Technologies. Following that, Eran lead the DevOps Business Unit as VP Strategy. Prior to Nolio, Eran held senior management positions at PortAuthority Technologies (acquired by Websense), Mercury Interactive (acquired by HP), and Conduct (acquired by Mercury Interactive).

Martin Fowler perfectly defined test impact analysis (TIA) as "a modern way of speeding up the test automation phase of a build. It works by analyzing the call-graph of the source code to work out which tests should be run after a change to production code."[216]

The benefits of adopting and maintaining TIA include both the cost savings of software development, as well as the risk reduction around escaped defects. When properly implemented, TIA can **focus the regression testing and the overall scoping** of a test cycle upon each and every code change.

As an example, for a standard mobile banking application that runs on iOS and Android devices, upon a change to the "check deposit" functionality, a TIA system can help scope the relevant test scenarios that can both test this functionality, as well as cover potentially-impacted areas within the app. Such an assessment will result in a triggered test cycle running on relevant devices to provide feedback as quickly as possible to the developer.

---

216 *The Rise of Test Impact Analysis https://martinfowler.com/articles/rise-test-impact-analysis.html*

HOW CAN TIA PRODUCE THE PROPER OUTPUTS UPON CODE CHANGES?

While there are various ways to implement and use TIA, the most efficient ones use either AI/ML models or simple tagging that helps classify the tests based on features, user journeys, testing types, and more.

There are other notable tools, such as Google Blaze, referred to in Fig 194, which creates a single navigation path within a source code repository like the Google search web page and helps plan the post build/code changes in each file. With such a tool, it is clear which code has been impacted and which tests could be relevant to execute upon relevant code changes. There are also code coverage solutions that can help in TIA.

As Martin Fowler explains in his article, Microsoft VSTest also built a nice TIA mapping mechanism that, while not ML based, does have an efficient way of providing a nice resolution to the test scoping upon code changes. In the Microsoft example, an automated mechanism dynamically collects dependencies between code and the tests while the tests are running to generate a map that attaches test cases with code files.

```
Testcasemethod1 <--> a.cs, b.cs. d.cs
Testcasemethod2 <--> a.cs, k.cs, z.cs
```

As described in the article, when a new code commit is done on a given class (e.g. a.cs), a test execution is triggered on all **Testcasemethod**(s) that include class *a.cs* as their dynamic dependency. This map is maintained and updated by the tool automatically.

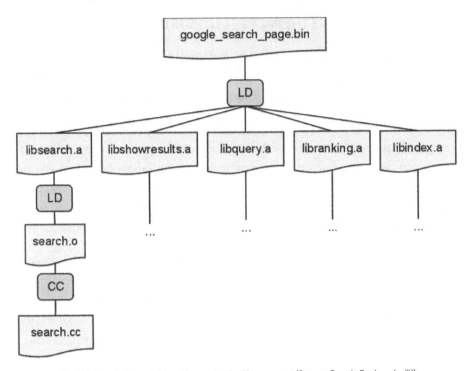

Fig. 194: Google Blaze Build and Dependencies Management (Source: Google Engineering[217])

Among the key challenges teams have with adopting TIA are the implementation and maintenance of such strategies. Modern software uses open source libraries, APIs, and other dependencies in addition to the developers' code. Continuously understanding code impact on quality requires sophisticated analysis of the code repositories early in the cycle and upon code changes.

As if that is not complicated enough, the entry points are the old code coverage or TIA, since there was no analysis made on the new build and there was no new test automation code developed. TIA must work retroactively as well as on current re-pos. If an uncovered area is detected between software iterations, regression tests must be executed in the nearest cycle.

217 *Google Engineering, Project Blaze*
  http://google-engtools.blogspot.com/2011/08/build-in-cloud-how-build-system-works.html

TEST IMPACT ANALYSIS USING TAGGING

While not 100% focused on AI and ML, tagging methods are extremely powerful in planning and scoping test cycles. Such tags have infinite classifications and categories that when given enough thought can dramatically impact the productivity of an entire DevOps team — that includes developers, testers, DevOps engineers, and executives.

Built into the **Selenium** test framework, there are already-supported annotations that can help classify and prioritize test scenarios.[218] Such annotations or tags can be fundamental in TIA.

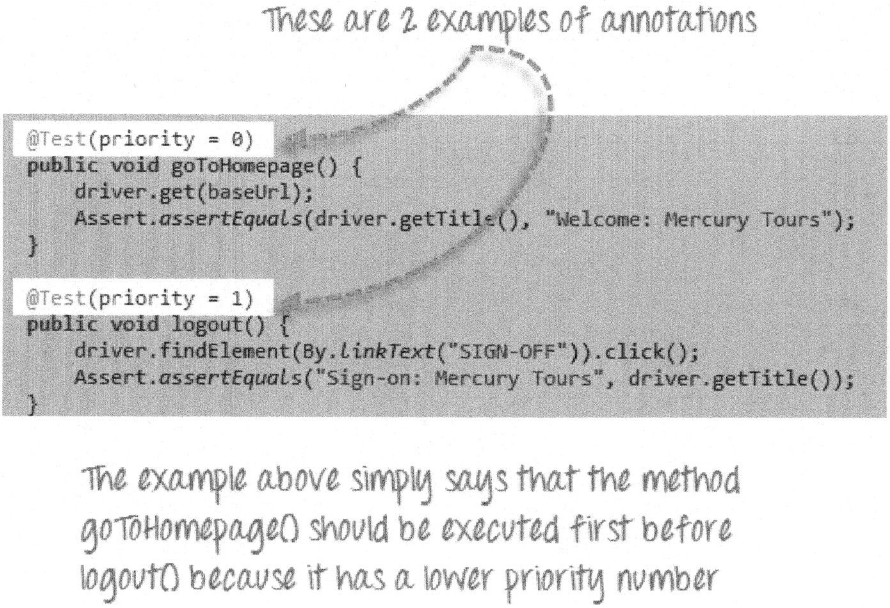

These are 2 examples of annotations

```
@Test(priority = 0)
public void goToHomepage() {
    driver.get(baseUrl);
    Assert.assertEquals(driver.getTitle(), "Welcome: Mercury Tours");
}

@Test(priority = 1)
public void logout() {
    driver.findElement(By.LinkText("SIGN-OFF")).click();
    Assert.assertEquals("Sign-on: Mercury Tours", driver.getTitle());
}
```

The example above simply says that the method goToHomepage() should be executed first before logout() because it has a lower priority number

Fig. 195: Using Annotations Within Selenium to Prioritize Test Execution (Source: Guru99)

In an old article I wrote on reporting test driven development (RTDD), I gave an overview on the benefits of reporting and tagging strategy as part of smarter test creation, maintenance, and execution.[219]

218 Selenium TestNG Annotations https://www.guru99.com/all-about-testng-and-selenium.html
219 Reporting Test Driven Development https://dzone.com/articles/introducing-reporting-test-driven-development-rtdd

Below are some high-level categories to consider when implementing a tagging strategy that can be used by the triggered event (e.g. code commit) to run these from CI or other scheduler tool. As can be seen in the visual, there's tagging that can relate to the type of test execution (unit vs. regression), tags that are for functional areas or features, and more specific tags around the test environment, CI/CD servers, etc.

Again, this is not driven by any ML or AI algorithms. These are part of the Perfecto reporting SDK and are built into a testNG/Maven project to run as part of Selenium/Appium scripts.

Suggested Tagging for Advanced Digital Quality Visibility

Execution Level Tags Categories		Single Test Report Tags		Logical Test Steps Tags	
Categories	Examples	Categories	Examples	Categories	Examples
Test type (Regression, Unit, Nightly, Smoke)	"Regression", "Unit", "Nightly", "Smoke"	Test Scenario Identifiers	"Banking Check Deposit", "Geico Login"	Functional Areas	"Login", "Search"
CI	Build number, Job, Branch	Environmental Identifiers	"Testing 2G conditions", "Testing on iOS Devices", "Testing Device Orientation", "Testing Location Changes", "Persona"	Functional Actions	"Launch App", "Press Back", "Click on Menu", "Navigate to page"
CI Server Names	"Alexander"				
Team Names	"iOS Team", "Android Team", "UI Team"				
Platforms	"iOS", "Android", "Chrome", "IOT"				
Release/Sprint Versions	"9.x"				
Test Frameworks Associations	"Appium", "Espresso", "Selenium", "UFT"				
Test Code Languages	"Java", "C#", "Python"				

Fig. 196: Reporting and Tagging Strategies for Productive Test Scoping and Execution (Source: Dzone)

It is imperative to maintain tagging strategies across teams in order to have the latest and greatest impact on such a tool, and to avoid any escaped defects. Also, tagging is a way of eliminating flakiness from the entire test suite. Marking a test case with a flaky keyword can classify it and others in the category for re-factoring and exclude them automatically from the next cycle. On the other hand, classifying a test with a tag of "regression defect" or something similar can automatically increase its priority. It ensures it is included until there are further changes in any cycle, since such tests were effective in detecting critical defects in the past.

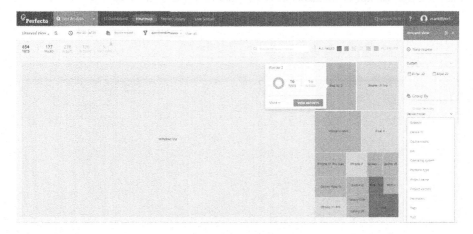

Fig. 197: Example of Using Perfecto's Reporting SDK With Tagging to Filter Test Executions[220]

This section did not cover and AI and ML, but it still can be a semi-automated productivity solution for TIA and other data-driven decisions by DevOps leaders. The next section will show a fully AI/ML solution for TIA.

TEST IMPACT ANALYSIS USING ML & AI

In this category, there is a significant use of ML/AI models to determine which tests should run, when, and for how long. By knowing which tests to run, how much time such test cases will take to be executed, as well as how much time can be saved per software iteration, executives and DevOps managers can scope their ongoing roadmap with greater accuracy.

220 Perfecto Reporting SDK https://developers.perfectomobile.com/display/PD/Download+the+Reporting+SDK

There are already a few solutions out there that can provide an AI-based TIA, and in this chapter, I decided to feature SeaLights.[221]

The following is how SeaLights defines the impact of its TIA engine upon each code change when integrated into the workflow: "**Test Impact Analysis engine correlates every test in every test suite right down to the actual method code each one is testing. This engine then automatically analyzes each build for new and changed code. This results in correlating the test and build to identify only those tests needed to verify the code changes for that particular build.**"

Fig. 198: SeaLights Parallel Test Impact Analysis Model (Source: SeaLights Website)

SeaLights implements TIA by providing deep insights into the alignment between tests and the application code. The platform dynamically instruments the application at runtime using byte code instrumentation techniques and no changes to the application are required.

---

221 SeaLights Test Impact Analysis https://www.sealights.io/product/test-impact-analysis/

As the tests are executed against the application, SeaLights ML learns the paths and "footprints" that each test step takes across the application. This, aligned with the Build Scanner which identifies the code deltas for every build, allows SeaLights to identify which tests are impacted by any code change.

By identifying these impacted tests and applying additional policies to build out the dynamic test suite (e.g. new tests, recently failed tests, mandatory tests), SeaLights executes only the tests that need to be run for each build.

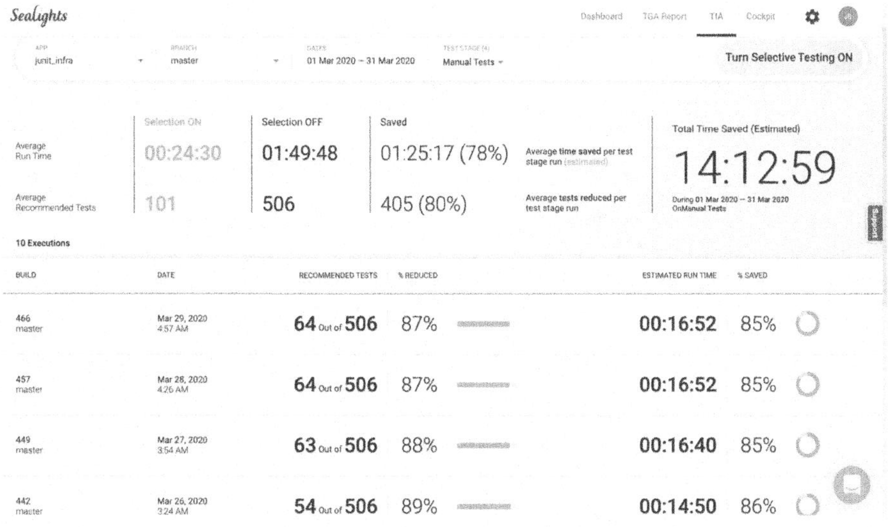

Fig. 199: SeaLights Parallel Test Impact Analysis Model (Source: SeaLights Website)

Test impact analysis is one of a comprehensive set of capabilities SeaLights offers to its customers.

What SeaLights offers, is a software quality governance platform that traces every software change for each build and identifies quality risks at every test stage as the changes pass through the pipeline. By capturing and analyzing millions of data points, SeaLights can help prioritize the mitigation of quality risks and identify where additional testing is required.

By applying risk scoring and organizational policies, SeaLights is able to provide quality governance by preventing untested or risky changes from reaching production.

Through the tool, clients can define a build (production, e.g.) as a reference build, which serves as a benchmark or comparison build for pre and future builds.

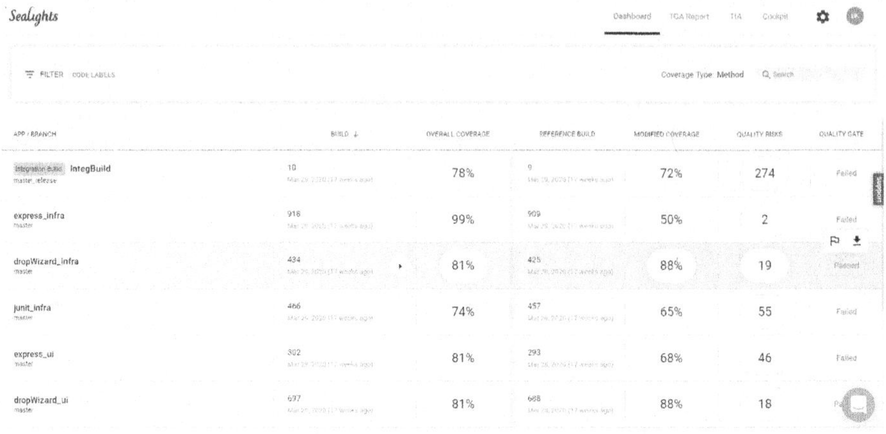

Fig. 200: SeaLights Quality Governance Platform (Source: SeaLights Demo)

Through SeaLights executive dashboard (above), developers and testers get the ability to drill down into the technical aspects of each build or test suite and evaluate the specific quality risks as presented in the below screenshot. The highlighted quality risks show the file and code commit that occurred but did not undergo any type of testing, such as functional, regression, end to end, or even manual tests.

Fig. 201: SeaLights Quality Governance Platform — Quality Dashboard (Source: SeaLights Demo)

Additionally, teams can drill even deeper into the gap analysis and understand the bigger test coverage risks in order to make data-driven decisions.

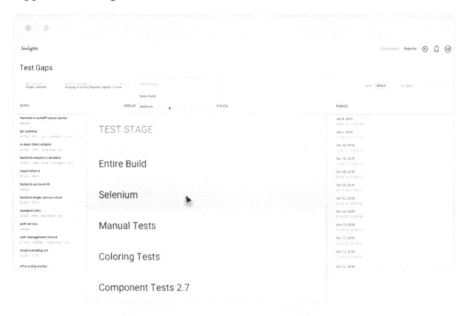

Fig. 202: SeaLights Quality Governance Platform — Test Gaps Dashboard (Source: SeaLights Demo)

Release managers and other executives within a DevOps team can use the above dashboard to understand what was covered and not covered by testing in the previous sprint. This dashboard also shows what can become a quality risk and scope missing tests into the upcoming release test cycles.

In addition to the above assessment, the SeaLights platform also provides a production agent or listener that can highlight used features and areas within the product that either were or were not tested in the previous build. With this feature, managers can identify which areas are more commonly used by customers and must be constantly tested per each build.

One more important feature that SeaLights provides is a quality gate mechanism that is based on organizational compliance requirements, code changes, advanced coverage methods, quality risks, and other rules. Upon embedding these gates in relevant builds, when there is a violation of a quality gate, the build will fail and trigger the root cause to the teams.

BOTTOM LINE

Test impact analysis is not a new method, but without AI and ML it often is not fully utilized because it requires tedious maintenance and implementation. With the rise of AI and ML, such a TIA strategy can be embedded into CI/CD and help boost overall team productivity and quality.

It is also important to mention that software quality varies based on the target application (mobile, web), the dependency on third-party code, open-source libraries, and more. Therefore, implementing code coverage and TIA using AI and ML will become the new normal in DevOps going forward.

222 Test Impact Analysis, Tricentis Accelerate 2018 https://www.youtube.com/watch?v=_p9u1EwFoq8
223 Microsoft Azure DevOps TIA
    https://docs.microsoft.com/en-us/azure/devops/pipelines/test/test-impact-analysis?view=azure-devops

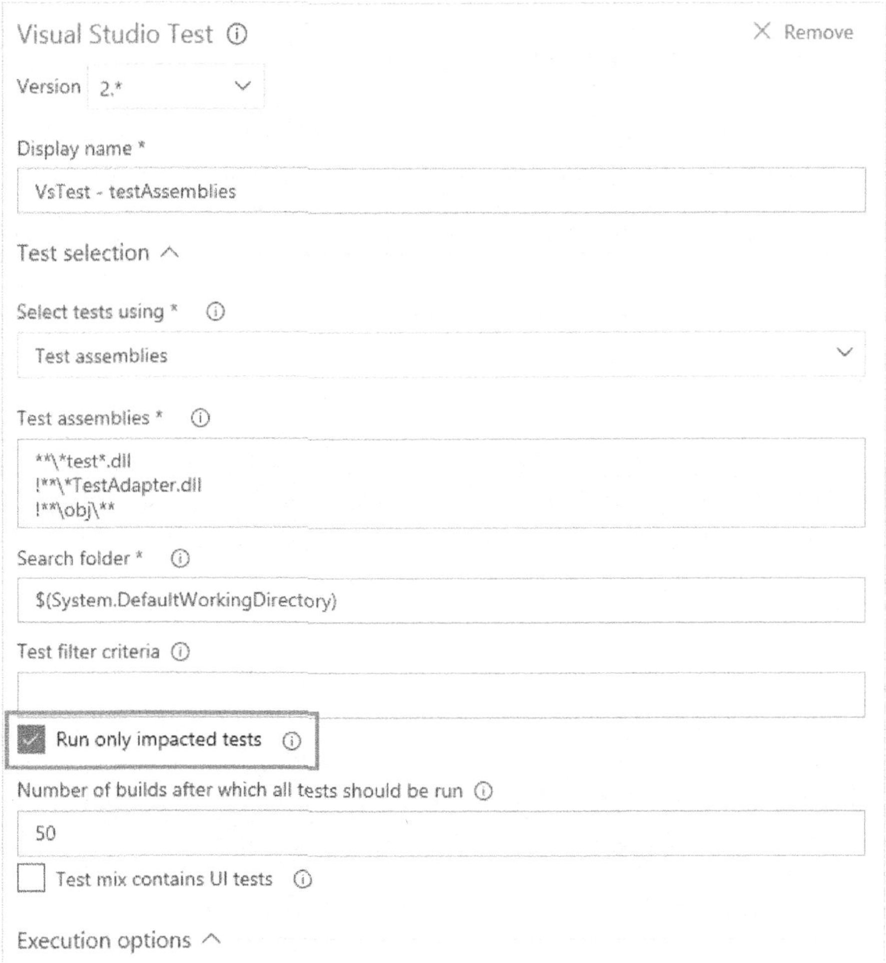

Fig. 203: Microsoft Azure DevOps, VSTest TIA (Source: Microsoft Documentation)

Here are a few more additional and useful references for TIA:

- *TIA session given at Accelerate 2018, Dr. Elmar Juergens*[222]

- *Microsoft Azure DevOps TIA (see Fig 203)*[223]

Chapter 26:
What's Next for AI/ML Testing Tools?

This book covered in-depth the main use cases of AI and ML in testing as well as development activities, targeting specific challenges, pains, inefficiencies, and more.

Some of the topics that were covered in the book are already available today and can be used either through commercial or open source solutions. Some use cases are still being considered and being developed as solid AI/ML solutions to these problems. In addition, there are even more advanced topics in software development and test automation that are not even being worked on. The future will tell when, how, and in which use cases we will first see these solutions introduced.

Specifically, around test automation, as it relates to AI and ML, this book provides solid coverage of the abilities that exists today. However, even these abilities are not 100% fully leveraging smart algorithms.

In some of today's cases, AI and ML are helping through the self-healing of scripts by adjusting element locators upon changes to the product. In other cases, AI and ML are being used for automated visual testing and root-cause analysis classification. These are all stand-alone solutions for specific challenges. The future of test automation, however, holds an even greater functionality that many developers and vendors are starting to consider as this book is being authored.

Fully autonomous testing may seem like an impossible thing to accomplish. However, based on the following visual that shows different levels of test automation, level 5 is where the market aims to be.

Simply pointing a mobile or web application to an AI/ML autonomous testing solution will process and model the app, then generate a full set of screens, user flows, and key business cases. Based on these artifacts, it will generate proper testing scenarios. Maintenance of such scripts will not be a huge obstacle for these tools, since the creation of the tests will be based on an end-to-end journey through the app or website. Whenever there is a new element, screen, or business flow that disrupts the already-learned app, the machine learning solution will regenerate the proper testing scenarios.

The future of testing will not be as simple and easy as I describe above, since there will need to be process-related matching between the testing artifacts and the CI/CD workflows. In addition, defect management and test management will also need to be addressed by next-generation tools in order to be adopted by existing DevOps teams who have built solid working processes over the years.

In addition, specific verticals as well as app-specific abilities (mobile vs. web) will need to be very well addressed and supported by the next wave of AI/ML that aims to be completely autonomous.

5 Levels of Test Automation

Fig. 204: Microsoft Azure DevOps, VSTest TIA (Source: Microsoft Documentation[224])

NEXT-GEN TEST AUTOMATION TOOLS: CHALLENGES AND ROADBLOCKS

Some of the expected challenges for the next wave of autonomous AI/ML tools are also relevant to existing AI/ML tools evolving in the market already.

The above challenges are not only the responsibility of the tool providers, but also a checklist for teams that will be evaluating such tools in the future. Teams should assess these tools to ensure they match their DevOps reality at the time of evaluation and for the future.

---

224 Appvance 5 Levels of Test Automation https://www.appvance.ai/5-levels-ai-testing-autonomy

- Autonomous test creation and maintenance for mobile and web.

- Test execution, orchestration, and scalability.

- Reporting and analysis of test results.

- DevOps process fit: integration with tools, complementing code-based solutions.

- Keeping up with evolving technologies.

Let's expand a bit on each of the above challenges.

Autonomous Test Creation and Maintenance for Mobile and Web

Autonomous testing tools must be platform agnostic and support advanced capabilities of the mobile and web platforms. This means that supporting gestures, sensors, events, alerts, and other platform specifics must be at the core of these tools. Test automation by nature is something that runs continuously in parallel across platforms, and it's triggered by code changes. Having hiccups in the testing flow will fail such tool adoptions.

All of the complexities mentioned above also relate to the maintenance and lifecycle of test cases. If the tools promise zero-touch creation and maintenance, they must stand behind the promise.

Test Execution, Orchestration, & Scalability

The creation phase is great, but in DevOps and Agile processes, execution at scale has equally the same importance. Execution speed and scalability contribute to fast feedback upon code changes, and to fast resolution of defects. The generated tests also need to run seamlessly across different platforms, including mobile and web. This by itself is a huge challenge, since these platforms are very much different across screens, form factors, OS versions, and more.

Consider running autonomous scripts on various Android, iOS, and desktop browsers that are different in many ways — Android custom vs. stock OS versions, screen sizes and resolution, supported capabilities per iOS/Android OS families, and more.

Reporting & Analysis of Test Results

At the end of each test execution, developers and test automation engineers must have a reliable, fully detailed set of test reports that can give them sufficient data to base their decision and analysis on. In addition, the executions as mentioned above are large in scale and continuous, and that means dealing with an ongoing large test report. Slicing and dicing abilities of test data as traditional test automation tools offer today (Perfecto, for example) must be also part of autonomous testing tools.

If teams have to spend hours analyzing test results that are generated by autonomous tools, the cost effectiveness of these tools will decrease in a significant way. The idea behind autonomous testing should be that since the tools "learn" all the business flows of the apps and create scripts accordingly, the tools can quickly spot anomalies and defects. It is nice in theory and must be proven in reality and across platforms. Generating too many false negatives will cause a loss of trust by both developers and testers — hence, this needs to be well designed and baked into the tools.

DevOps Process Fit

Autonomous tools must "play" nice with existing tools. Testing is done throughout the pipeline upon code changes, prior to build acceptance and version releases. Depending on the app, the vertical, and the practitioner, the DevOps process uses a wide range of tools — from performance and monitoring, through CI servers, deployment, environment virtualization, third-party tools, APIs, and many more. The expectation as well as challenge for autonomous testing is that their use will be seamless, and not cause a separate, whole new process.

Keeping Up With Evolving Technologies

Last, but definitely not least, is technology and innovation. Creating a set of working autonomous scenarios for product version X is nice and promising. However, both the product and its features evolve, and the market constantly shifts.

Any new feature that is introduced for desktop browsers or mobile platforms (OS, devices) must be supported quickly by autonomous tools, or else the work-around will be to revert back to automating via code-based tools. In today's reality, communities like Selenium and Appium are chasing each and every iOS and Android release and making many efforts to support test automation developers. The same approach should be taken by the autonomous testing vendors.

While I kept this summary focused on autonomous testing, and less on no-code development and non-functional activities like code reviews, security audits, and other software-related use cases, the market will clearly invest in parallel with the test creation domain, while also aiming to solve various development challenges.

BOTTOM LINE

The future of test automation is brighter than ever. Many practitioners, tool vendors, and analysts are placing their bets on AI and ML to finally boost test automation coverage, reliability, and success toward a true DevOps reality.

To deliver on this hype, pitfalls from previous years and the considerations listed in this book must be well thought out so that organizations will have a solid foundation to rely on for automating both development activities and testing.

It may take few iterations of autonomous tools to get closer to this vision. But when this happens, teams will achieve higher productivity than ever.

Made in the USA
Monee, IL
07 September 2020